VOICES OF FREEDOM

A Documentary History

Sixth Edition

EDITED BY

ERIC FONER

Volume 2

W.W. NORTON & COMPANY · NEW YORK · LONDON

W. W. Norton & Company has been independent since its founding in 1923, when William Warder Norton and Mary D. Herter Norton first published lectures delivered at the People's Institute, the adult education division of New York City's Cooper Union. The firm soon expanded its program beyond the Institute, publishing books by celebrated academics from America and abroad. By midcentury, the two major pillars of Norton's publishing program—trade books and college texts—were firmly established. In the 1950s, the Norton family transferred control of the company to its employees, and today—with a staff of four hundred and a comparable number of trade, college, and professional titles published each year—W. W. Norton & Company stands as the largest and oldest publishing house owned wholly by its employees.

Editor: Steve Forman
Production Manager: Sean Mintus
Composition: Westchester Publishing Services
Manufacturing: Maple Press
Book Design: Antonina Krass

Library of Congress Cataloging-in-Publication Data

Names: Foner, Eric, 1943- editor.
Title: Voices of freedom : a documentary history / edited by Eric Foner.
Description: Sixth edition. | New York : W.W. Norton & Company, [2020]
Identifiers: LCCN 2019021569 | ISBN 9780393696912 (pbk. : v. 1) |
   ISBN 9780393696929 (pbk. : v. 2)
Subjects: LCSH: United States—History—Sources. | United States—Politics
   and government—Sources.
Classification: LCC E173 .V645 2020 | DDC 973.—dc23 LC record available at
   https://lccn.loc.gov/2019021569

ISBN: 978-0-393-69692-9 (pbk.)

W. W. Norton & Company, Inc., 500 Fifth Avenue, New York, NY 10110
   www.wwnorton.com
W. W. Norton & Company Ltd., 15 Carlisle Street, London W1D 3BS
1 2 3 4 5 6 7 8 9 0

ERIC FONER is DeWitt Clinton Professor Emeritus of History at Columbia University, where he earned his B.A. and Ph.D. In his teaching and scholarship, he focuses on the Civil War and Reconstruction, slavery, and nineteenth-century America. Professor Foner's publications include *Free Soil, Free Labor, Free Men: The Ideology of the Republican Party Before the Civil War*; *Tom Paine and Revolutionary America*; *Politics and Ideology in the Age of the Civil War*; *Nothing but Freedom: Emancipation and Its Legacy*; *Reconstruction: American's Unfinished Revolution, 1863–1877*; *Freedom's Lawmakers: A Directory of Black Officeholders During Reconstruction*; *The Story of American Freedom*; *Who Owns History? Rethinking the Past in a Changing World*; and *Forever Free: The Story of Emancipation and Reconstruction*. His history of Reconstruction won the *Los Angeles Times* Book Award for History, the Bancroft Prize, and the Parkman Prize. He has served as president of the Organization of American Historians and the American Historical Association. In 2006 he received the Presidential Award for Outstanding Teaching from Columbia University. His most recent books are *The Fiery Trial: Abraham Lincoln and American Slavery*, winner of the Bancroft and Lincoln prizes and the Pulitzer Prize for History, *Gateway to Freedom: The Hidden History of the Underground Railroad*, winner of the New York Historical Society Book Prize, and *The Second Founding: How the Civil War and Reconstruction Remade the Constitution*.

Contents

17

Freedom's Boundaries, at Home and Abroad, 1890–1900

18

The Progressive Era, 1900–1916

19

Safe for Democracy: The United States and World War I, 1916–1920

20

From Business Culture to Great Depression: The Twenties, 1920–1932

21

The New Deal, 1932–1940

22

Fighting for the Four Freedoms
World War II, 1941–1945

23

The United States and the Cold War, 1945–1953

24

An Affluent Society, 1953–1960

25

The Sixties, 1960–1968

26

The Conservative Turn, 1969–1988

27

From Triumph to Tragedy, 1989–2004

28

A Divided Nation

Preface

Voices of Freedom is a documentary history of American freedom from the earliest days of European exploration and settlement of the Western Hemisphere to the present. I have prepared it as a companion volume to *Give Me Liberty!*, my survey textbook of the history of the United States centered on the theme of freedom. This sixth edition of *Voices of Freedom* is organized in chapters that correspond to those in the sixth edition of the textbook. But it can also stand independently as a documentary introduction to the history of American freedom. The two volumes include more than twenty documents not available in the fifth edition.

No idea is more fundamental to Americans' sense of themselves as individuals and as a nation than freedom, or liberty, with which it is almost always used interchangeably. The Declaration of Independence lists liberty among mankind's inalienable rights; the Constitution announces as its purpose to secure liberty's blessings. "Every man in the street, white, black, red or yellow," wrote the educator and statesman Ralph Bunche in 1940, "knows that this is 'the land of the free' ... 'the cradle of liberty.'"

The very universality of the idea of freedom, however, can be misleading. Freedom is not a fixed, timeless category with a single unchanging definition. Rather, the history of the United States is, in part, a story of debates, disagreements, and struggles over freedom. Crises like the American Revolution, the Civil War, and the Cold War have permanently transformed the idea of freedom. So too have demands by various groups of Americans for greater freedom as they understood it.

In choosing the documents for *Voices of Freedom*, I have attempted to convey the multifaceted history of this compelling and contested idea. The documents reflect how Americans at different points in our history have defined freedom as an overarching idea, or have understood some of its many dimensions, including political, religious, economic, and personal freedom. For each chapter, I have tried to select documents that highlight the specific discussions of freedom that occurred during that time period, and some of the divergent interpretations of freedom at each point in our history. I hope that students will gain an appreciation of how the idea of freedom has expanded over time, and how it has been extended into more and more areas of Americans' lives. But at the same time, the documents suggest how freedom for some Americans has, at various times in our history, rested on lack of freedom—for example, slavery, indentured servitude, the subordinate position of women—for others.

The documents that follow reflect the kinds of historical developments that have shaped and reshaped the idea of freedom, including war, economic change, territorial expansion, social protest movements, and international involvement. The selections try to convey a sense of the rich cast of characters who have contributed to the history of American freedom. They include presidential proclamations and letters by runaway slaves, famous court cases and obscure manifestos, ideas dominant in a particular era and those of radicals and dissenters. They range from advertisements in colonial newspapers seeking the return of runaway indentured servants and slaves to debates in the early twentieth century over the definition of economic freedom, the controversy over the proposed Equal Rights Amendment for women, and recent Supreme Court decisions dealing with the right of gay Americans to marry one another.

I have been particularly attentive to how battles at the boundaries of freedom—the efforts of racial minorities, women, and others to secure greater freedom—have deepened and transformed the concept and extended it into new realms. In addition, in this sixth edition I have included a number of new documents that illustrate how the very definition of American identity—answers to the question "Who is an American?"—have affected the evolution of the idea of freedom. These include Benjamin Franklin's argument in 1751 for restricting immigration to English men and women; J. Hector St. John de Crèvecoeur's observations at the time of the War of Independence on the emergence of the American, a "new man," from the diverse peoples of European descent in the new nation; Frederick Douglass's remarkable "Composite Nation" speech soon after the Civil War; Randolph Bourne's 1916 essay "Trans-National America"; and historian Oscar Handlin's critique of the law adopted in 1924 that severely restricted immigration from southern and eastern Europe.

All of the documents in this collection are "primary sources"—that is, they were written or spoken by men and women enmeshed in the events of the past, rather than by later historians. They therefore offer students the opportunity to encounter ideas about freedom in the actual words of participants in the drama of American history. Some of the documents are reproduced in their entirety. Most are excerpts from longer interviews, articles, or books. In editing the documents, I have tried to remain faithful to the original purpose of the author, while highlighting the portion of a text that deals directly with one or another aspect of freedom. In most cases, I have reproduced the wording of the original texts exactly. But I have modernized the spelling and punctuation of some early documents to make them more understandable to the modern reader. Each document is preceded by a brief introduction that places it in historical context and is followed by two questions that highlight key elements of the argument and may help to focus students' thinking about the issues raised by the author.

A number of these documents were suggested by students in a U.S. history class at Juniata College in Huntingdon, Pennsylvania, taught by Professor David Hsiung. I am very grateful to these students, who responded enthusiastically to an assignment by Professor Hsiung that asked them to locate documents that might be included in *Voices of Freedom* and to justify their choices with historical arguments. Some of the documents are included in the online exhibition "Preserving American Freedom" created by the Historical Society of Pennsylvania.

Taken together, the documents in these volumes suggest the ways in which American freedom has changed and expanded over time. But they also remind us that American history is not simply a narrative of continual progress toward greater and greater freedom. While freedom can be achieved, it may also be reduced or rescinded. It can never be taken for granted.

Eric Foner

VOICES OF FREEDOM

A Documentary History

Sixth Edition

Volume 2

CHAPTER 15

"What Is Freedom?": Reconstruction, 1865–1877

96. Petition of Black Residents of Nashville (1865)

Source: Newspaper clipping enclosed in Col. R. D. Mussey to Capt. C. P. Brown, January 23, 1865, Letters Received, ser. 925, Department of the Cumberland, U.S. Army Continental Commands, National Archives.

At the request of military governor Andrew Johnson, Lincoln exempted Tennessee from the Emancipation Proclamation of 1863 (although many slaves in the state gained their freedom by serving in the Union army). In January 1865, a state convention was held to complete the work of abolition. A group of free blacks of Nashville sent a petition to the delegates, asking for immediate action to end slavery and granting black men the right to vote (which free blacks had enjoyed in the state until 1835). The document emphasized their loyalty to the Union, their natural right to freedom, and their willingness to take on the responsibilities of citizenship. The document offers a revealing snapshot of black consciousness at the dawn of Reconstruction.

We the undersigned petitioners, American citizens of African descent, natives and residents of Tennessee, and devoted friends of the great National cause, do most respectfully ask a patient hearing of your honorable body in regard to matters deeply affecting the future condition of our unfortunate and long suffering race.

First of all, however, we would say that words are too weak to tell how profoundly grateful we are to the Federal Government for the good work of freedom which it is gradually carrying forward; and for the Emancipation Proclamation which has set free all the slaves in some of the rebellious States, as well as many of the slaves in Tennessee.

After two hundred years of bondage and suffering a returning sense of justice has awakened the great body of the American people to make amends for the unprovoked wrongs committed against us for over two hundred years.

Your petitioners would ask you to complete the work begun by the nation at large, and abolish the last vestige of slavery by the express words of your organic law.

Many masters in Tennessee whose slaves have left them, will certainly make every effort to bring them back to bondage after the reorganization of the State government, unless slavery be expressly abolished by the Constitution.

We hold that freedom is the natural right of all men, which they themselves have no more right to give or barter away, than they have to sell their honor, their wives, or their children.

We claim to be men belonging to the great human family, descended from one great God, who is the common Father of all, and who bestowed on all races and tribes the priceless right of freedom. Of this right, for no offence of ours, we have long been cruelly deprived, and the common voice of the wise and good of all countries, has remonstrated against our enslavement, as one of the greatest crimes in all history.

We claim freedom, as our natural right, and ask that in harmony and co-operation with the nation at large, you should cut up by the roots the system of slavery, which is not only a wrong to us, but the source of all the evil which at present afflicts the State. For slavery, corrupt itself, corrupted nearly all, also, around it, so that it has influenced nearly all the slave States to rebel against the Federal Government, in order to set up a government of pirates under which slavery might be perpetrated.

In the contest between the nation and slavery, our unfortunate people have sided, by instinct, with the former. We have little fortune to devote to the national cause, for a hard fate has hitherto forced us to live in poverty, but we do devote to its success, our hopes, our toils, our whole heart, our sacred honor, and our lives. We will work, pray, live, and, if need be, die for the Union, as cheerfully as ever a white patriot died for his country. The color of our skin does not lessn in the least degree, our love either for God or for the land of our birth.

We are proud to point your honorable body to the fact, that so far as our knowledge extends, not a negro traitor has made his appearance since the begining of this wicked rebellion. . . .

Devoted as we are to the principles of justice, of love to all men, and of equal rights on which our Government is based, and which make it the hope of the world. We know the burdens of citizenship, and are ready to bear them. We know the duties of the good citizen, and are ready to perform them cheerfully, and would ask to be put in a position in which we can discharge them more effectually. We do not ask for the privilege of citizenship, wishing to shun the obligations imposed by it.

Near 200,000 of our brethren are to-day performing military duty in the ranks of the Union army. Thousands of them have already died in battle, or perished by a cruel martyrdom for the sake of the Union, and we are ready and willing to sacrifice more. But what higher order of citizen is there than the soldier? or who has a greater trust confided to his hands? If we are called on to do military duty against the rebel armies in the field, why should we be denied the privilege of voting against rebel citizens at the ballot-box? The latter is as necessary to save the Government as the former....

This is not a Democratic Government if a numerous, law-abiding, industrious, and useful class of citizens, born and bred on the soil, are to be treated as aliens and enemies, as an inferior degraded class, who must have no voice in the Government which they support, protect and defend, with all their heart, soul, mind, and body, both in peace and war.

Questions

1. Why do the petitioners place so much emphasis on their loyalty to the Union cause during the war?

2. What understanding of American history and the nation's future do the petitioners convey?

97. Petition of Committee on Behalf of the Freedmen to Andrew Johnson (1865)

Source: Henry Bram et al. to the President of the United States, October 28, 1865, P-27, 1865, Letters Received, ser. 15, Washington Headquarters, Freedmen's Bureau Papers, National Archives.

By June 1865, some 40,000 freedpeople had been settled on "Sherman land" in South Carolina and Georgia, in accordance with Special Field Order 15. That summer, however, President Andrew Johnson, who had succeeded Lincoln, ordered nearly all land in federal hands returned to its former owners. In October, O. O. Howard, head of the Freedmen's Bureau, traveled to the Sea Islands to inform blacks of the new policy.

Howard was greeted with disbelief and protest. A committee drew up
petitions to Howard and President Johnson. Their petition to the president pointed out that the government had encouraged them to occupy
the land and affirmed that they were ready to purchase it if given the
opportunity. Johnson rejected the former slaves' plea. And, throughout
the South, because no land distribution took place, the vast majority
of rural freedpeople remained poor and without property during
Reconstruction.

EDISTO ISLAND S.C. Oct 28th, 1865.

To the President of these United States. We the freedmen of Edisto
Island South Carolina have learned From you through Major General
O O Howard commissioner of the Freedmans Bureau. with deep sorrow and Painful hearts of the possibility of government restoring
These lands to the former owners. We are well aware Of the many
perplexing and trying questions that burden Your mind, and do therefore pray to god (the preserver of all and who has through our Late and
beloved President (Lincoln) proclamation and the war made Us A free
people) that he may guide you in making Your decisions, and give you
that wisdom that Cometh from above to settle these great and Important Questions for the best interests of the country and the Colored
race: Here is where secession was born and Nurtured Here is were we
have toiled nearly all Our lives as slaves and were treated like dumb
Driven cattle, This is our home, we have made These lands what they
are. we were the only true and Loyal people that were found in poses-
sion of these Lands. we have been always ready to strike for Liberty and
humanity yea to fight if needs be To preserve this glorious union.
Shall not we who Are freedman and have been always true to this
Union have the same rights as are enjoyed by Others? Have we broken
any Law of these United States? Have we forfieted our rights of property
In Land?—If not then! are not our rights as A free people and good citizens of these United States To be considered before the rights of those
who were Found in rebellion against this good and just Government

(and now being conquered) come (as they Seem) with penitent hearts and beg forgiveness For past offences and also ask if their lands Cannot be restored to them are these rebellious Spirits to be reinstated in their *possessions* And we who have been abused and oppressed For many long years not to be allowed the Privilege of purchasing land But be subject To the will of these large Land owners? God forbid, Land monopoly is injurious to the advancement of the course of freedom, and if Government Does not make some provision by which we as Freedmen can obtain A Homestead, we have Not bettered our condition.

We have been encouraged by Government to take Up these lands in small tracts, receiving Certificates of the same—we have thus far Taken Sixteen thousand (16000) acres of Land here on This Island. We are ready to pay for this land When Government calls for it. and now after What has been done will the good and just government take from us all this right and make us Subject to the will of those who have cheated and Oppressed us for many years God Forbid!

We the freedmen of this Island and of the State of South Carolina— Do therefore petition to you as the President of these United States, that some provisions be made by which Every colored man can purchase land. and Hold it as his own. We wish to have A home if It be but A few acres. without some provision is Made our future is sad to look upon. yess our Situation is dangerous. we therefore look to you In this trying hour as A true friend of the poor and Neglected race. for protection and Equal Rights. with the privilege of purchasing A Homestead—A Homestead right here in the Heart of South Carolina.

We pray that God will direct your heart in Making such provision for us as freedmen which Will tend to united these states together stronger Than ever before—May God bless you in the Administration of your duties as the President Of these United States is the humble prayer Of us all.—

In behalf of the Freedmen
        Henry Bram
Committee   Ishmael Moultrie.
        yates. Sampson

Questions

1. How important is it for the petitioners to obtain land on Edisto Island, as opposed to elsewhere in the country?

2. What do they think is the relationship between owning land and freedom?

---

98. The Mississippi Black Code (1865)

Source: Walter L. Fleming, ed., Documentary History of Reconstruction *(Cleveland, 1906–07), vol. 1, pp. 281–90.*

During 1865, Andrew Johnson put into effect his own plan of Reconstruction, establishing procedures whereby new governments, elected by white voters only, would be created in the South. Among the first laws passed by the new governments were the Black Codes, which attempted to regulate the lives of the former slaves. These laws granted the freedpeople certain rights, such as legalized marriage, ownership of property, and limited access to the courts. But they denied them the right to testify in court in cases that only involved whites, serve on juries or in state militias, or to vote. And in response to planters' demands that the freedpeople be required to work on the plantations, the Black Codes declared that those who failed to sign yearly labor contracts could be arrested and hired out to white landowners. The Black Codes indicated how the white South would regulate black freedom if given a free hand by the federal government. But they so completely violated free labor principles that they discredited Johnson's Reconstruction policy among northern Republicans.

Vagrant Law

Sec. 2.... All freedmen, free negroes and mulattoes in this State, over the age of eighteen years, found on the second Monday in January,

1866, or thereafter, with no lawful employment or business, or found unlawfully assembling themselves together, either in the day or night time, and all white persons so assembling themselves with freedmen, free negroes or mulattoes, or usually associating with freedmen, free negroes or mulattoes, on terms of equality, or living in adultery or fornication with a freed woman, free negro or mulatto, shall be deemed vagrants, and on conviction thereof shall be fined in a sum not exceeding, in the case of a freedman, free negro, or mulatto, fifty dollars, and a white man two hundred dollars, and imprisoned at the discretion of the court, the free negro not exceeding ten days, and the white man not exceeding six months....

Sec. 7.... If any freedman, free negro, or mulatto shall fail or refuse to pay any tax levied according to the provisions of the sixth section of this act, it shall be *prima facie* evidence of vagrancy, and it shall be the duty of the sheriff to arrest such freedman, free negro, or mulatto or such person refusing or neglecting to pay such tax, and proceed at once to hire for the shortest time such delinquent tax-payer to any one who will pay the said tax, with accruing costs, giving preference to the employer, if there be one.

CIVIL RIGHTS OF FREEDMEN

Sec. 1.... That all freedmen, free negroes, and mulattoes may sue and be sued, implead and be impleaded, in all the courts of law and equity of this State, and may acquire personal property, and choses in action, by descent or purchase, and may dispose of the same in the same manner and to the same extent that white persons may: *Provided*, That the provisions of this section shall not be so construed as to allow any freedman, free negro, or mulatto to rent or lease any lands or tenements except in incorporated cities or towns....

Sec. 2.... All freedmen, free negroes, and mulattoes may intermarry with each other, in the same manner and under the same regulations that are provided by law for white persons: *Provided*, That the clerk of probate shall keep separate records of the same.

Sec. 3.... All freedmen, free negroes, or mulattoes who do now and have herebefore lived and cohabited together as husband and wife shall be taken and held in law as legally married, and the issue shall be taken and held as legitimate for all purposes; that it shall not be lawful for any freedman, free negro, or mulatto to intermarry with any white person; nor for any white person to intermarry with any freedman, free negro, or mulatto; and any person who shall so intermarry, shall be deemed guilty of felony, and on conviction thereof shall be confined in the State penitentiary for life; and those shall be deemed freedmen, free negroes, and mulattoes who are of pure negro blood, and those descended from a negro to the third generation, inclusive, though one ancestor in each generation may have been a white person.

Sec. 4.... In addition to cases in which freedmen, free negroes, and mulattoes are now by law competent witnesses, freedmen, free negroes, or mulattoes shall be competent in civil cases, when a party or parties to the suit, either plaintiff or plaintiffs, defendant or defendants; also in cases where freedmen, free negroes, and mulattoes is or are either plaintiff or plaintiffs, defendant or defendants, and a white person or white persons, is or are the opposing party or parties, plaintiff or plaintiffs, defendant or defendants. They shall also be competent witnesses in all criminal prosecutions where the crime charged is alleged to have been committed by a white person upon or against the person or property of a freedman, free negro, or mulatto: *Provided*, that in all cases said witnesses shall be examined in open court, on the stand; except, however, they may be examined before the grand jury, and shall in all cases be subject to the rules and tests of the common law as to competency and credibility.

Sec. 5.... Every freedman, free negro, and mulatto shall, on the second Monday of January, one thousand eight hundred and sixty-six and annually thereafter, have a lawful home or employment, and shall have written evidence thereof....

Sec. 6.... All contracts for labor made with freedmen, free negroes, and mulattoes for a longer period than one month shall be in writing, and in duplicate, attested and read to said freedman, free negro, or mulatto by a beat, city or county officer, or two disinterested white persons of the county in which the labor is to be performed, of which each party shall have one; and said contracts shall be taken and held as entire contracts, and if the laborer shall quit the service of the employer before the expiration of his term of service, without good cause, he shall forfeit his wages for that year up to the time of quitting.

Sec. 7. . . . Every civil officer shall, and every person may, arrest and carry back to his or her legal employer any freedman, free negro, or mulatto who shall have quit the service of his or her employer before the expiration of his or her term of service without good cause. . . . *Provided*, that said arrested party, after being so returned, may appeal to the justice of the peace or member of the board of police of the county, who, on notice to the alleged employer, shall try summarily whether said appellant is legally employed by the alleged employer, and has good cause to quit said employer; either party shall have the right of appeal to the county court, pending which the alleged deserter shall be remanded to the alleged employer or otherwise disposed of, as shall be right and just; and the decision of the county court shall be final.

CERTAIN OFFENSES OF FREEDMEN

Sec. 1. . . . That no freedman, free negro or mulatto, not in the military service of the United States government, and not licensed so to do by the board of police of his or her county, shall keep or carry firearms of any kind, or any ammunition, dirk or bowie knife, and on conviction thereof in the county court shall be punished by fine, not exceeding ten dollars, and pay the costs of such proceedings, and all such arms or ammunition shall be forfeited to the informer. . . .

Sec. 2. . . . Any freedman, free negro, or mulatto committing riots, routs, affrays, trespasses, malicious mischief, cruel treatment to animals, seditious speeches, insulting gestures, language, or acts, or assaults on any person, disturbance of the peace, exercising the function of a minister of the Gospel without a license from some regularly organized church, vending spirituous or intoxicating liquors, or committing any other misdemeanor, the punishment of which is not specifically provided for by law, shall, upon conviction thereof in the county court, be fined not less than ten dollars, and not more than one hundred dollars, and may be imprisoned at the discretion of the court, not exceeding thirty days.

Sec. 3. . . . If any white person shall sell, lend, or give to any freedman, free negro, or mulatto any fire-arms, dirk or bowie knife, or ammunition, or any spirituous or intoxicating liquors, such person or persons so offending, upon conviction thereof in the county court of his or her county, shall be fined not exceeding fifty dollars, and may be imprisoned, at the discretion of the court, not exceeding thirty days. . . .

Sec. 5. . . . If any freedman, free negro, or mulatto, convicted of any of the misdemeanors provided against in this act, shall fail or refuse for the space of five days, after conviction, to pay the fine and costs imposed, such person shall be hired out by the sheriff or other officer, at public outcry, to any white person who will pay said fine and all costs, and take said convict for the shortest time.

Questions

1. Why do you think the state of Mississippi required all black persons to sign yearly labor contracts but not white citizens?

2. What basic rights are granted to the former slaves and which are denied to them by the Black Code?

---

99. A Sharecropping Contract (1866)

Source: Records of the Assistant Commissioner for the State of Tennessee, Bureau of Refugees, Freedmen, and Abandoned Lands, National Archives.

Despite the widespread desire for land, few former slaves were able to acquire farms of their own in the post–Civil War South. Most ended up as sharecroppers, working on white-owned land for a share of the crop at the end of the growing season. Sharecropping was a kind of compromise between blacks' desire for independence from white control and planters' desire for a disciplined labor force. This contract, representative of thousands, originated in Shelby County, Tennessee. The laborers sign with an X, as they are illiterate. Typical of early postwar contracts, it gave the planter the right to supervise the labor of his employees. Later sharecropping contracts afforded former slaves greater autonomy. Families would rent parcels of land, work it under their own direction, and divide the crop with the owner at the end of the year. But as the price of cotton fell after the Civil War, workers found it difficult to profit from the sharecropping system.

THOMAS J. ROSS agrees to employ the Freedmen to plant and raise a crop on his Rosstown Plantation ... On the following Rules, Regulations and Remunerations.

The said Ross agrees to furnish the land to cultivate, and a sufficient number of mules & horses and feed them to make and house said crop and all necessary farming utensils to carry on the same and to give unto said Freedmen whose names appear below one half of all the cotton, corn and wheat that is raised on said place for the year 1866 after all the necessary expenses are deducted out that accrues on said crop. Outside of the Freedmen's labor in harvesting, carrying to market and selling the same and the said Freedmen whose names appear below covenant and agrees to and with said Thomas J. Ross that for and in consideration of one half of the crop before mentioned that they will plant, cultivate, and raise under the management control and Superintendence of said Ross, in good faith, a cotton, corn and oat crop under his management for the year 1866. And we the said Freedmen agrees to furnish ourselves & families in provisions, clothing, medicine and medical bills and all, and every kind of other expenses that we may incur on said plantation for the year 1866 free of charge to said Ross. Should the said Ross furnish us any of the above supplies or any other kind of expenses, during said year, are to settle and pay him out of the net proceeds of our part of the crop the retail price of the county at time of sale or any price we may agree upon. The said Ross shall keep a regular book account, against each and every one or the head of every family to be adjusted and settled at the end of the year.

We furthermore bind ourselves to and with said Ross that we will do good work and labor ten hours a day on an average, winter and summer. The time to run from the time we commence to the time we quit.... We further agree that we will lose all lost time, or pay at the rate of one dollar per day, rainy days excepted. In sickness and women lying in childbed are to lose the time and account for it to the other hands out of his or her part of the crop at the same rates that she or they may receive per annum.

We furthermore bind ourselves that we will obey the orders of said Ross in all things in carrying out and managing said crop for said year and be docked for disobedience. All is responsible for all farming utensils that is on hand or may be placed in care of said Freedmen for the year 1866 to said Ross and are also responsible to said Ross if we carelessly, maliciously maltreat any of his stock for said year to said Ross for damages to be assessed out of our wages for said year.

Samuel (X) Johnson, Thomas (X) Richard, Tinny (X) Fitch, Jessie (X) Simmons, Sophe (X) Pruden, Henry (X) Pruden, Frances (X) Pruden, Elijah (X) Smith

Questions

1. How does the contract limit the freedom of the laborers?

2. What kinds of benefits and risks for the freedpeople are associated with a sharecropping arrangement?

100. Elizabeth Cady Stanton, "Home Life" (ca. 1875)

Source: "Home Life," manuscript, ca. 1875, Elizabeth Cady Stanton Papers, Library of Congress.

Women activists saw Reconstruction as the moment for women to claim their own emancipation. With blacks guaranteed equality before the law by the Fourteenth Amendment and black men given the right to vote by the Fifteenth, women demanded that the boundaries of American democracy be expanded to include them as well. Other feminists debated how to achieve "liberty for married women." In 1875, Elizabeth Cady Stanton drafted an essay demanding that the idea of equality, which had "revolutionized" American politics, be extended into private life. Genuine liberty for women, she insisted, required an overhaul of divorce laws (which generally required evidence of adultery, desertion, or extreme abuse to terminate a marriage) and an end to the authority men exercised over their wives.

Women's demand for the right to vote found few sympathetic male listeners. Even fewer supported liberalized divorce laws. But Stanton's extension of the idea of "liberty for women" into the most intimate areas of private life identified a question that would become a central concern of later generations of feminists.

———

WE ARE IN the midst of a social revolution, greater than any political or religious revolution, that the world has ever seen, because it goes deep down to the very foundations of society.... A question of magnitude presses on our consideration, whether man and woman are equal, joint heirs to all the richness and joy of earth and Heaven, or whether they were eternally ordained, one to be sovereign, the other slave.... Here is a question with half the human family, and that the stronger half, on one side, who are in possession of the citadel, hold the key to the treasury and make the laws and public sentiment to suit their own purposes. Can all this be made to change base without prolonged discussion, upheavings, heartburnings, violence and war? Will man yield what he considers to be his legitimate authority over woman with less struggle than have Popes and Kings their supposed rights over their subjects, or slaveholders over their slaves? No, no. John Stuart Mill says the generality of the male sex cannot yet tolerate the idea of living with an equal at the fireside; and here is the secret of the opposition to woman's equality in the state and the church—men are not ready to recognize it in the home. This is the real danger apprehended in giving woman the ballot, for as long as man makes, interprets, and executes the laws for himself, he holds the power under any system. Hence when he expresses the fear that liberty for woman would upset the family relation, he acknowledges that her present condition of subjection is not of her own choosing, and that if she had the power the whole relation would be essentially changed. And this is just what is coming to pass, the kernel of the struggle we witness to day.

This is woman's transition period from slavery to freedom and all these social upheavings, before which the wisest and bravest stand appalled, are but necessary incidents in her progress to equality. Conservatism cries out we are going to destroy the family. Timid reformers answer, the political equality of woman will not change it. They are both wrong. It will entirely revolutionize it. When woman is man's equal the marriage relation cannot stand on the basis it is to day. But this change will not destroy it; as state constitutions and statute laws did not create conjugal and maternal love, they cannot annual them.... We shall have the family, that great conservator of national strength and morals, after the present idea of man's headship is repudiated and woman set free. To establish a republican form of government [and] the right of individual judgment in the family must of necessity involve discussion, dissension, division, but the purer, higher, holier marriage will be evolved by the very evils we now see and deplore. This same law of equality that has revolutionized the state and the church is now knocking at the door of our homes and sooner or later there too it must do its work. Let us one and all wisely bring ourselves into line with this great law for man will gain as much as woman by an equal companionship in the nearest and holiest relations of life.... So long as people marry from considerations of policy, from every possible motive but the true one, discord and division must be the result. So long as the State provides no education for youth on the questions and throws no safeguards around the formation of marriage ties, it is in honor bound to open wide the door of escape. From a woman's standpoint, I see that marriage as an indissoluble tie is slavery for woman, because law, religion and public sentiment all combine under this idea to hold her true to this relation, whatever it may be and there is no other human slavery that knows such depths of degradations as a wife chained to a man whom she neither loves nor respects, no other slavery so disastrous in its consequences on the race, or to individual respect, growth and development....

• • •

By the laws of several states in this republic made by Christian representatives of the people divorces are granted to day for... seventeen reasons.... By this kind of legislation in the several states we have practically decided two important points: 1st That marriage is a dissoluble tie that may be sundered by a decree of the courts. 2nd That it is a civil contract and not a sacrament of the church, and the one involves the other....

A legal contract for a section of land requires that the parties be of age, of sound mind, [and] that there be no flaw in the title.... But a legal marriage in many states in the Union may be contracted between a boy of fourteen and a girl of twelve without the consent of parents or guardians, without publication of banns.... Now what person of common sense, or conscience, can endorse laws as wise or prudent that sanction acts such as these. Let the state be logical: if marriage is a civil contract, it should be subject to the laws of all other contracts, carefully made, the parties of age, and all agreements faithfully observed....

Let us now glance at a few of the popular objections to liberal divorce laws. It is said that to make divorce respectable by law, gospel and public sentiment is to break up all family relations. Which is to say that human affections are the result and not the foundation of the canons of the church and statutes of the state. . . . To open the doors of escape to those who dwell in continual antagonism, to the unhappy wives of drunkards, libertines, knaves, lunatics and tyrants, need not necessarily embitter the relations of those who *are* contented and happy, but on the contrary the very fact of freedom strengthens and purifies the bond of union. When husbands and wives do not own each other as property, but are bound together only by affection, marriage will be a life long friendship and not a heavy yoke, from which both may sometimes long for deliverance. The freer the relations are between human beings, the happier. . . .

• • •

Home life to the best of us has its shadows and sorrows, and because of our ignorance this must needs be. . . . The day is breaking. It is something to know that life's ills are not showered upon us by the Good Father from a kind of Pandora's box, but are the results of causes that we have the power to control. By a knowledge and observance of law the road to health and happiness opens before [us]: a joy and peace that passeth all understanding shall yet be ours and Paradise regained on earth. When marriage results from a true union of intellect and spirit and when Mothers and Fathers give to their holy offices even that preparation of soul and body that the artist gives to the conception of his poem, statue or landscape, then will marriage, maternity and paternity acquire a new sacredness and dignity and a nobler type of manhood and womanhood will glorify the race!!

Questions

1. How does Stanton define the "social revolution" the United States underwent after the Civil War?

2. How does Stanton believe that individual freedom within the family can be established?

101. Frederick Douglass, "The Composite Nation" (1869)

Source: *Philip S. Foner and Daniel Rosenberg, eds.,* Racism, Dissent, and Asian Americans from 1850 to the Present *(Westport, Conn., 1993), pp. 217–30.*

Another group that did not share fully in the expansion of rights inspired by the Civil War and Reconstruction was Asian-Americans. Prejudice against Asians was deeply entrenched, especially on the West Coast, where most immigrants from Asia lived. When the Radical Republican Charles Sumner, senator from Massachusetts, moved to allow Asians to become naturalized citizens (a right that had been barred to them since 1790), senators from California and Oregon objected vociferously, and the proposal was defeated.

Another advocate of equal rights for Asian-Americans was Frederick Douglass. In his remarkable "Composite Nation" speech, delivered in Boston in 1869, Douglass condemned anti-Asian discrimination and called for giving them all the rights of other Americans, including the right to vote. Douglass's comprehensive vision of a country made up of people of all races and national origins and enjoying equal rights was too radical for the time, but it would win greater and greater acceptance during the twentieth century.

———

THERE WAS A time when even brave men might look fearfully at the destiny of the Republic. When our country was involved in a tangled network of contradictions; when vast and irreconcilable social forces fiercely disputed for ascendancy and control; when a heavy curse rested upon our very soil, defying alike the wisdom and the virtue of the people to remove it; when our professions were loudly mocked by our practice and our name was a reproach and a by word to a mocking earth; when our good ship of state, freighted with the best hopes of the oppressed of all nations, was furiously hurled against the hard and flinty rocks of derision, and every cord, bolt, beam and bend in her body quivered beneath the shock, there was some apology for doubt and despair. But that day has happily passed away. The storm has been weathered, and the portents are nearly all in our favor.

There are clouds, wind, smoke and dust and noise, over head and around, and there will always be; but no genuine thunder, with destructive bolt, menaces from any quarter of the sky.

The real trouble with us was never our system or form of Government, or the principles under lying it; but the peculiar composition of our people; the relations existing between them and the compromising spirit which controlled the ruling power of the country.

We have for a long time hesitated to adopt and may yet refuse to adopt, and carry out, the only principle which can solve that difficulty and give peace, strength and security to the Republic, *and that is* the principle of absolute *equality*.

We are a country of all extremes, ends and opposites; the most conspicuous example of composite nationality in the world. Our people defy all the ethnological and logical classifications. In races we range all the way from black to white, with intermediate shades which, as in the apocalyptic vision, no man can name a number.

In regard to creeds and faiths, the condition is no better, and no worse. Differences both as to race and to religion are evidently more likely to increase than to diminish.

We stand between the populous shores of two great oceans. Our land is capable of supporting one fifth of all the globe. Here, labor is abundant and here labor is better remunerated than any where else. All moral, social and geographical causes, conspire to bring to us the peoples of all other over populated countries.

Europe and Africa are already here, and the Indian was here before either. He stands to-day between the two extremes of black and white, too proud to claim fraternity with either, and yet too weak to with stand the power of either. Heretofore the policy of our government has been governed by race pride, rather than by wisdom. Until recently, neither the Indian nor the negro has been treated as a part of the body politic. No attempt has been made to inspire either with a sentiment of patriotism, but the hearts of both races have been diligently sown with the dangerous seeds of discontent and hatred.

The policy of keeping the Indians to themselves, has kept the tomahawk and scalping knife busy upon our borders, and has cost us largely in blood and treasure. Our treatment of the negro has slacked humanity, and filled the country with agitation and ill-feeling and brought the nation to the verge of ruin.

Before the relations of these two races are satisfactorily settled, and in spite of all opposition, a new race is making its appearance within our borders, and claiming attention. It is estimated that not less than one-hundred thousand Chinamen are now within the limits of the United States. Several years ago every vessel, large or small, of steam or sail, bound to our Pacific coast and hailing from the Flowery kingdom, added to the number and strength of this element of our population.

Men differ widely as to the magnitude of this potential Chinese immigration. The fact that by the late treaty with China, we bind ourselves to receive immigrants from that country only as the subjects of the Emperor, and by the construction, at least, are bound not to naturalize them, and the further fact that Chinamen themselves have a superstitious devotion to their country and an aversion to permanent location in any other, contracting even to have their bones carried back should they die abroad, and from the fact that many have returned to China, and the still more stubborn that resistance to their coming has increased rather than diminished, it is inferred that we shall never have a large Chinese population in America. This however is not my opinion.

It may be admitted that these reasons, and others, may check and moderate the tide of immigration; but it is absurd to think that they will do more than this. Counting their number now, by the thousands, the time is not remote when they will count them by the millions. The Emperor's hold upon the Chinaman may be strong, but the Chinaman's hold upon himself is stronger.

Treaties against naturalization, like all other treaties, are limited by circumstances. As to the superstitious attachment of the Chinese to China, that, like all other superstitions, will dissolve in the light and heat of truth and experience. The Chinaman may be a bigot, but it does not follow that he will continue to be one, tomorrow. He is a man, and will be very likely to act like a man. He will not be long in finding out that a country which is good enough to live in, is good enough to die in; and that a soil that was good enough to hold his body while alive, will be good enough to hold his bones when he is dead.

Those who doubt a large immigration, should remember that the past furnishes no criterion as a basis of calculation. We live under new and improved conditions of migration, and these conditions are constantly improving. America is no longer an obscure and inaccessible country. Our ships are in every sea, our commerce in every port, our language is heard all around the globe, steam and lightning have revolutionized the whole domain of human thought, changed all geographical relations, make a day of the present seem equal to a thousand years of the past, and the continent that Columbus only conjectured four centuries ago is now the center of the world.

• • •

I have said that the Chinese will come, and have given some reasons why we may expect them in very large numbers in no very distant future. Do you ask, if I favor such immigration, I answer *I would*. Would you have them naturalized, and have them invested with all the rights of American citizenship? *I would*. Would you allow them to vote? *I would*. Would you allow them to hold office? *I would*.

But are there not reasons against all this? Is there not such a law or principle as that of self preservation? Does not every race owe something to itself? Should it not attend to the dictates of common sense? Should not a superior race protect itself from contact with inferior ones? Are not the white people the owners of this continent? Have they not the right to say what kind of people shall be allowed to come here and settle? Is there not such a thing as being more generous than wise? In the effort to promote civilization may we not corrupt and destroy what we have? Is it best to take on board more passengers than the ship will carry?

To all this and more I have one among many answers, altogether satisfactory to me, though I cannot promise that it will be so to you.

I submit that this question of Chinese immigration should be settled upon higher principles than those of a cold and selfish expediency. There are such things in the world as human rights. They rest upon no conventional foundation, but are external, universal, and indestructible. Among these, is the right of locomotion; the right of migration; the right which belongs to no particular race, but belongs alike to all and to all alike. It is the right you assert by staying here, and your fathers asserted by coming here. It is this great right that I assert for the Chinese and the Japanese, and for all other varieties of men equally with yourselves, now and forever. I know of no rights of race superior to the rights of humanity, and when there is a supposed conflict between human and national rights, it is safe to go to the side of humanity. I have great respect for the blue eyes and light haired races of America. They are a mighty people. In any struggle for the good things of this world they need have no fear. They have no need to doubt that they will get their full share.

But I reject the arrogant and scornful theory by which they would limit migratory rights, or any other essential human rights to themselves, and which would make them the owners of this great continent to the exclusion of all other races of men.

I want a home here not only for the negro, the mulatto and the Latin races; but I want the Asiatic to find a home here in the United States, and feel at home here, both for his sake and for ours. Right wrongs no man. If respect is had to majorities, the fact that only one fifth of the population of the globe is white, the other four fifths are colored, ought to have some weight and influence in disposing of this and similar questions. It would be a sad reflection upon the laws of nature and upon the idea of justice, to say nothing of a common Creator, if four-fifths of mankind were deprived of the rights of migration to make room for the one fifth. If the white race may exclude all other races from this continent, it may rightfully do the same in respect to all other lands, islands, capes and continents, and thus have all the world to itself. Thus what would seem to belong to the whole, would become the property only of a part. So much for what is right, now let us see what is wise.

And here I hold that a liberal and brotherly welcome to all who are likely to come to the United States is the only wise policy which this nation can adopt.

• • •

I close these remarks as I began. If our action shall be in accordance with the principles of justice, liberty, and perfect human equality, no eloquence can adequately portray the greatness and grandeur of the future of the Republic.

We shall spread the network of our science and civilization over all who seek their shelter whether from Asia, Africa, or the Isles of the sea. We shall mold them all, each after his kind, into Americans; Indian and Celt, negro and Saxon, Latin and Teuton, Mongolian and Caucasian, Jew and Gentile, all shall here bow to the same law, speak the same language, support the same government, enjoy the same liberty, vibrate with the same national enthusiasm, and seek the same national ends.

Questions

1. What does Douglass mean by the term "composite nation"?

2. Why does he believe that people should be allowed to move freely from one country to another?

102. Robert B. Elliott on Civil Rights (1874)

Source: **Civil Rights. Speech of Hon. Robert B. Elliott, of South Carolina, in the House of Representatives, January 6, 1874** *(Washington, D.C., 1874), pp. 1–8.*

One of the South's most prominent black politicians during Reconstruction, Robert B. Elliott appears to have been born in England and arrived in Boston shortly before the Civil War. He came to South Carolina in 1867, where he established a law office and was elected as a delegate to the state's constitutional convention of 1868. During the 1870s, he served in the legislature and was twice elected to the U.S. House of Representatives.

In January 1874, Elliott delivered a celebrated speech in Congress in support of the bill that became the Civil Rights Act of 1875. The measure outlawed racial discrimination in transportation and places of public accommodation like theaters and hotels. Thanks to the Civil War and Reconstruction, Elliott proclaimed, "equality before the law" regardless of race had been written into the laws and Constitution and had become an essential element of American freedom. Reconstruction, he announced, had "settled forever the political status of my race."

Elliott proved to be wrong. By the turn of the century, many of the rights blacks had gained after the Civil War had been taken away. It would be left to future generations to breathe new life into Elliott's dream of "equal, impartial, and universal liberty."

———

SIR, IT IS scarcely twelve years since that gentleman [Alexander H. Stephens] shocked the civilized world by announcing the birth of a government which rested on human slavery as its corner-stone. The progress of events has swept away that *pseudo*-government which rested on greed, pride, and tyranny; and the race whom he then ruthlessly spurned and trampled on are here to meet him in debate, and to demand that the rights which are enjoyed by their former oppressors—who vainly sought to overthrow a Government which they could not prostitute to the base uses of slavery—shall be accorded to those who even in the darkness of slavery kept their allegiance true to freedom and the Union. Sir, the gentleman from Georgia has learned much since 1861; but he is still a laggard. Let him put away entirely the false and fatal theories which have so greatly marred an otherwise enviable record. Let him accept, in its fullness and beneficence, the great doctrine that American citizenship carries with it every civil and political right which manhood can confer. Let him lend his influence, with all his masterly ability, to complete the proud structure of legislation which makes this nation worthy of the great declaration which heralded its birth, and he will have done that which will most nearly redeem his reputation in the eyes of the world, and best vindicate the wisdom of that policy which has permitted him to regain his seat upon this floor....

• • •

Sir, equality before the law is now the broad, universal, glorious rule and mandate of the Republic. No State can violate that. Kentucky and Georgia may crowd their statute-books with retrograde and barbarous legislation; they may rejoice in the odious eminence of their consistent hostility to all the great steps of human progress which have marked our national history since slavery tore down the stars and stripes on Fort Sumter; but, if Congress shall do its duty, if Congress shall enforce the great guarantees which the Supreme Court has declared to be the one pervading purpose of all the recent amendments, then their unwise and unenlightened conduct will fall with the same weight upon the gentlemen from those States who now lend their influence to defeat this bill, as upon the poorest slave who once had no rights which the honorable gentlemen were bound to respect....

No language could convey a more complete assertion of the power of Congress over the subject embraced in the present bill than is expressed [in the Fourteenth Amendment]. If the States do not conform to the requirements of this clause, if they continue to deny to any person within their jurisdiction the equal protection of the laws, or as the Supreme Court had said, "deny equal justice in its courts," then Congress is here said to have power to enforce the constitutional guarantee by appropriate legislation. That is the power which this bill now seeks to put in exercise. It proposes to enforce the constitutional guarantee against inequality and discrimination by appropriate legislation. It does not seek to confer new rights, nor to place rights conferred by State citizenship under the protection of the United States, but simply to prevent and forbid inequality and discrimination on account of race, color, or previous condition of servitude. Never was there a bill more completely within the constitutional power of Congress. Never was there a bill which appealed for support more strongly to that sense of justice and fair-play which has been said, and in the main with justice, to be a characteristic of the Anglo-Saxon race. The Constitution warrants it; the Supreme Court sanctions it; justice demands it.

Sir, I have replied to the extent of my ability to the arguments which have been presented by the opponents of this measure. I have replied also to some of the legal propositions advanced by gentlemen on the other side; and now that I am about to conclude, I am deeply sensible of the imperfect manner in which I have performed the task. Technically, this bill is to decide upon the civil status of the colored American citizen; a point disputed at the very formation of our present Government, when by a short-sighted policy, a policy repugnant to true republican government, one negro counted as three-fifths of a man. The logical result of this mistake of the framers of the Constitution strengthened the cancer of slavery, which finally spread its poisonous tentacles over the southern portion of the body-politic. To arrest its growth and save the nation we have passed through the harrowing operation of intestine war, dreaded at all times, resorted to at the last extremity, like the surgeon's knife, but absolutely necessary to extirpate the disease which threatened with the life of the nation the overthrow of civil and political liberty on this continent. In that dire extremity the members of the race which I have the honor in part to represent—the race which pleads for justice at your hands to-day, forgetful of their inhuman and brutalizing servitude at the South, their degradation and ostracism at the North—flew willingly and gallantly to the support of the national Government. Their sufferings, assistance, privations, and trials in the swamps and in the rice-fields, their valor on the land and on the sea, is a part of the ever-glorious record which makes up the history of a nation preserved, and might, should I urge the claim, incline you to respect and guarantee their rights and privileges as citizens of our common Republic. But I remember that valor, devotion, and loyalty are not always rewarded according to their just deserts, and that after the battle some who have borne the brunt of the fray may, through neglect or contempt, be assigned to a subordinate place, while the enemies in war may be preferred to the sufferers.

The results of the war, as seen in reconstruction, have settled for-ever the political status of my race. The passage of this bill will deter-mine the civil status, not only of the negro, but of any other class of citizens who may feel themselves discriminated against. It will form the cap-stone of that temple of liberty, begun on this continent under discouraging circumstances, carried on in spite of the sneers of mon-archists and the cavils of pretended friends of freedom, until at last it stands in all its beautiful symmetry and proportions, a building the grandest which the world has ever seen, realizing the most sanguine expectations and the highest hopes of those who, in the name of equal, impartial, and universal liberty, laid the foundation stones.

Questions

1. How does Elliott defend the constitutionality of the Civil Rights Bill?

2. Why does Elliott refer to the "cornerstone speech" of Alexander H. Stephens in making his argument?

CHAPTER 16

America's Gilded Age, 1870–1890

103. Jorgen and Otto Jorgensen, Homesteading in Montana (1908)

Source: Jorgen and Otto Jorgensen, "Boyhood Recollections: A Narrative of Homestead Days in Northeastern Montana," Jorgen Jorgensen family papers, 1921–1938, Small Collection 178, Montana Historical Society Research Center, Archives. Reprinted with permission.

The decades after the Civil War witnessed a flood of migrants moving beyond the Mississippi River to take up farming. Hundreds of thousands of families acquired land under the Homestead Act, and many others purchased it from railroad companies and other private owners. As in earlier westward movements, uprooting one's family to take up land often located far from settled communities required remarkable courage and fortitude. In later interviews, Jorgen Jorgensen and his son Otto, members of a Danish-American family, recalled the decision to move to Montana in 1906. While popular lore celebrated the lone pioneer settler, the Jorgensens' experience illustrates the fact that many homesteaders went West as parts of communities, often organized on an ethnic basis.

═══════════

[JORGEN:] ONE WOULD think that we would have been satisfied to settle down where we were but such was not the case. We had constantly longed for fellowship with other Danes in a Danish congregation in a Danish settlement with a Danish school. There was a Danish

Church in Waupaca [Wisconsin] but that was a distance of seven miles away. Our neighbors were all native Americans. Most of them were uneducated and not too intellectual. They were congenial and friendly enough but we got little satisfaction or enjoyment from fellowship with them. The language was a handicap too because Kristiane [his wife] had not had as good an opportunity to learn it as I who had mixed with other people more. She could make herself understood alright but has since improved a great deal. She reads English books quite well but when it comes to writing I have to do it.

In the meantime we had managed to get all the land under cultivation that I was able to handle without hired help. All we had to do was to plant potatoes in the spring, dig them up in the fall, and haul them to town during the winter which was a little too tame an existence. I have mentioned two reasons why we wanted to move but there was a third. The older girls were growing up, and what if one of them should come home some day with one of these individuals with a foreign background and present him as her sweetheart. This was unthinkable. (Strangely enough after we came to Montana one of the girls actually did come and present an American as her sweetheart but he was a high class individual. He was a lawyer who later became district judge for Sheridan and other counties.)

When E. F. Madsen's call came in "Dannevirke" in 1906 to establish a Danish colony in eastern Montana, I immediately said, "That's where we are going," and Kristiane immediately agreed. I think people thought we were crazy to abandon what was, as far as people could tell, the comfort and security we had for insecurity and a cold, harsh climate. "You'll freeze to death out there," they said and related terrifying experiences of people who had succumbed in snowstorms. But it didn't seem to make much of an impression on us. I was past 50 years of age and if we were to build up another farm it was time to get started.

E. F. Madsen from Clinton, Iowa had been out in Montana on October 6, 1906 to find a place for a new Danish colony and had selected the place where it now is located in the northeast corner of Montana about 25 miles from the Canadian line and close to the Dakota boundary. Madsen named it "Dagman." Its full name is "Dronning Dagmar's Minde" (Queen Dagmar's Memorial), and is the first such colony in the United States. The land is fertile with smooth rolling prairies. The land was not surveyed but could be claimed by anyone over 21 years of age under Squatter's right. The 160 acres allowed was later increased to 320 acres....

[Otto:] My first recollection of any talk of moving or living anywhere else but where we were, was the folks, setting at the kitchen table one night—it must have been in 1906. Mother was fidgeting with something or other on the table, listening to Pa read aloud from the weekly Danish publication, *Dannevirke*, with a bright, faraway look in her eyes; and when he had finished, she said: "Skul' vi?" (should we?) We kids sat around, I for one, with open mouth, sensing something special was in the wind, and when the word Montana was mentioned,—MONTANA!! Montana to me was a magic word! That's where Falsbuts' were going to go! And Falsbuts' boys had thoroughly briefed me on what could be expected there: buffalo, cowboys, and wild horses—Oh boy! Free land, homesteads, Montana and the West! No one has any idea of what those magic words could conjure up in a 10-year-old boy's mind!

As I have grown older, I have often wondered what prompts the pioneering spirit in some people and leaves others completely devoid of it. As the folks became serious about the matter, the idea crystallized, as was evidenced by the preparations such as a new cookstove, a swell big kitchen range, new harnesses, etc. It was now "for sure" that the big adventure was about to become a reality. But it was not until the spring of 1908 that all the difficulties of such an undertaking were overcome. Selling the farm, auction sale, getting, the cash, etc. We didn't sell much—everything was stuffed into the immigrant-car, (special homeseekers rates) and when I say "stuffed" I mean just that! Cows and calves, chickens, pigs, horses, dogs, (no cats). All household goods, all the farming implements, wagons, mower, hayrake, and hayrack. The hayrack was used to double-deck the chickens above the cows.

I have often wondered what Pa's reactions were to all this. He never showed anything, outwardly. I remember when we left the farm for the last time, and we were about to get into the wagon. He was buttoning his coat with one hand and with the other, reached down to stroke the big old gray tom-cat, which was to be left behind; and he said, "Kitty, Kitty!" I was dumbfounded, for I had never seen him do a thing like that before. He straightened up and looked around at the good new house and big new red barn; and in his slow, easy-going and deliberate way, climbed into the wagon. I have often wondered what his innermost thoughts were at that moment. But like so many thousands before him who have pulled up stakes for the unknown future in the West, he left little room for sentiment. In tribute to my father, I think this was his staunchest moment. Of course, the die was cast; the decision had been made some time before, which also took courage—but the final last look at the fruits of 12 to 14 of his best years, brought from him no outward sign of regret. Nor did he, I'm glad to say, ever live to regret it. To turn his back on all this, against the advice of well-meaning neighbors and friends; and at the age of 51 years, take a family of eight children out into the un-tracked prairies fifty miles from the railroad and "nowhere" with measly small capital, took courage and fortitude, to say the least. That kind of spirit and courage, I'm afraid, is fast becoming a thing of the past in these United States.

Questions

1. In what ways do ideas about freedom affect the family's decision to move to Montana?

2. Why do you think Otto believes that the pioneer spirit is "a thing of the past"?

104. Andrew Carnegie, The Gospel of Wealth (1889)

Source: Andrew Carnegie, "Wealth," North American Review (June 1889), pp. 653–64.

One of the richest men in Gilded Age America, the industrialist Andrew Carnegie promoted what he called the Gospel of Wealth, the idea that those who accumulated money had an obligation to use it to promote the advancement of society. He explained his outlook in this article in the *North American Review*, one of the era's most prominent magazines. Carnegie would become famous for practicing what he preached. He helped to fund the creation of public libraries throughout the United States and overseas, and gave money to philanthropies and charities ranging from Carnegie Hall in New York City to the Carnegie Endowment for International Peace. But as an employer, he was tyrannical, strongly opposing labor unions and approving the use of violence against his own workers, including in the Homestead strike that took place three years after the publication of this article.

THE PROBLEM OF our age is the proper administration of wealth, that the ties of brotherhood may still bind together the rich and poor in harmonious relationship. The conditions of human life have not only been changed, but revolutionized, within the past few hundred years. In former days there was little difference between the dwelling, dress, food, and environment of the chief and those of his retainers. The Indians are to-day where civilized man then was. When visiting the Sioux, I was led to the wigwam of the chief. It was like the others in external appearance, and even within the difference was trifling between it and those of the poorest of his braves. The contrast between the palace of the millionaire and the cottage of the laborer with us to-day measures the change which has come with civilization. This change, however, is not to be deplored, but welcomed as highly beneficial. It is well, nay, essential, for the progress of the race that the houses of some should be homes for all that is highest and best in literature and the arts, and for all the refinements of civilization, rather than that none should be so. Much better this great irregularity than universal squalor. Without wealth there can be no Mæcenas. The "good old times" were not good old times. Neither master nor servant was as well situated then as to-day. A relapse to old conditions would be disastrous to both—not the least so to him who serves—and would sweep away civilization with it. But whether the change be for good or ill, it is upon us, beyond our power to alter, and, therefore, to be accepted and made the best of. It is a waste of time to criticize the inevitable....

The growing disposition to tax more and more heavily large estates left at death is a cheering indication of the growth of a salutary change in public opinion. The State of Pennsylvania now takes— subject to some exceptions—one tenth of the property left by its citizens. The budget presented in the British Parliament the other day proposes to increase the death duties; and, most significant of all, the new tax is to be a graduated one. Of all forms of taxation this seems the wisest. Men who continue hoarding great sums all their lives, the proper use of which for public ends would work good to the community from which it chiefly came, should be made to feel that the community, in the form of the State, cannot thus be deprived of its proper share. By taxing estates heavily at death the State marks its condemnation of the selfish millionaire's unworthy life.

It is desirable that nations should go much further in this direction. Indeed, it is difficult to set bounds to the share of a rich man's estate which should go at his death to the public through the agency of the State, and by all means such taxes should be graduated, beginning at nothing upon moderate sums to dependants, and increasing rapidly as the amounts swell....

In bestowing charity, the main consideration should be to help those who will help themselves; to provide part of the means by which those who desire to improve may do so; to give those who desire to rise the aids by which they may rise; to assist, but rarely or never to do all. Neither the individual nor the race is improved by almsgiving. Those worthy of assistance, except in rare cases, seldom require assistance. The really valuable men of the race never do, except in case of accident or sudden change. Every one has, of course, cases of individuals brought to his own knowledge where temporary assistance can do genuine good, and these he will not overlook. But the amount which can be wisely given by the individual for individuals is necessarily limited by his lack of knowledge of the circumstances connected with each. He is the only true reformer who is as careful and as anxious not to aid the unworthy as he is to aid the worthy, and, perhaps, even more so, for in almsgiving more injury is probably done by rewarding vice than by relieving virtue....

The best means of benefiting the community is to place within its reach the ladders upon which the aspiring can rise—free libraries, parks, and means of recreation, by which men are helped in body and mind; works of art, certain to give pleasure and improve the public taste; and public institutions of various kinds, which will improve the general condition of the people; in this manner returning their surplus wealth to the mass of their fellows in the forms best calculated to do them lasting good.

Thus is the problem of rich and poor to be solved. The laws of accumulation will be left free, the laws of distribution free. Individualism will continue, but the millionaire will be but a trustee for the poor, intrusted for a season with a great part of the increased wealth of the community, but administering it for the community far better than it could or would have done for itself. The best minds will thus have reached a stage in the development of the race in which it is clearly seen that there is no mode of disposing of surplus wealth creditable to thoughtful and earnest men into whose hands it flows, save by using it year by year for the general good. This day already dawns. Men may die without incurring the pity of their fellows, still sharers in great business enterprises from which their capital cannot be or has not been withdrawn, and which is left chiefly at death for public uses; yet the day is not far distant when the man who dies leaving behind him millions of available wealth, which was free for him to administer during life, will pass away "unwept, unhonored, and unsung," no matter to what uses he leaves the dross which he cannot take with him. Of such as these the public verdict will then be: "The man who dies thus rich dies disgraced."

Such, in my opinion, is the true gospel concerning wealth, obedience to which is destined some day to solve the problem of the rich and the poor, and to bring "Peace on earth, among men good will."

Questions

1. Why does Carnegie think it is better to build public institutions than to give charity to the poor?

2. Why does Carnegie believe that "the man who dies thus rich dies disgraced"?

105. William Graham Sumner on Social Darwinism (ca. 1880)

Source: Albert G. Keller, ed., The Challenge of Facts and Other Essays by William Graham Sumner *(New Haven, Conn., 1914), pp. 17–27. Keller concludes that the undated essay from which this excerpt is taken was written during the 1880s.*

During the Gilded Age, large numbers of businessmen and middle-class Americans adopted the social outlook known as Social Darwinism. Adherents of this viewpoint borrowed language from Charles Darwin's great work *On the Origin of Species* (1859), which expounded the theory of evolution among plant and animal species, to explain the success and failure of individual human beings and entire social classes. According to Social Darwinists, evolution was as natural a process in human society as in nature, and government must not interfere. Especially misguided, in this view, were efforts to uplift those at the bottom of the social order, such as laws regulating conditions of work or public assistance to the poor.

The era's most influential Social Darwinist was Yale professor William Graham Sumner. For Sumner, freedom required frank acceptance of inequality. The growing influence of Social Darwinism helped to popularize a "negative" definition of freedom as limited government and an unrestrained free market. It also helped to persuade courts, in the name of "liberty of contract," to overturn state laws regulating the behavior of corporations.

MAN IS BORN under the necessity of sustaining the existence he has received by an onerous struggle against nature, both to win what is essential to his life and to ward off what is prejudicial to it. He is born under a burden and a necessity. Nature holds what is essential to him, but she offers nothing gratuitously. He may win for his use what she holds, if he can. Only the most meager and inadequate supply for human needs can be obtained directly from nature. There are trees which may be used for fuel and for dwellings, but labor is required to fit them for this use. There are ores in the ground, but labor is necessary to get out the metals and make tools or weapons. For any real satisfaction, labor is necessary to fit the products of nature for human use. In this struggle every individual is under the pressure of the necessities for food, clothing, shelter, fuel, and every individual brings with him more or less energy for the conflict necessary to supply his needs. The relation, therefore, between each man's needs and each man's energy, or "individualism," is the first fact of human life.

It is not without reason, however, that we speak of a "man" as the individual in question, for women (mothers) and children have special disabilities for the struggle with nature, and these disabilities grow greater and last longer as civilization advances. The perpetuation of the race in health and vigor, and its success as a whole in its struggle to expand and develop human life on earth, therefore, require that the head of the family shall, by his energy, be able to supply not only his own needs, but those of the organisms which are dependent upon him. The history of the human race shows a great variety of experiments in the relation of the sexes and in the organization of the family. These experiments have been controlled by economic circumstances, but, as man has gained more and more control over economic circumstances, monogamy and the family education of children have been more and more sharply developed. If there is one thing in regard to which the student of history and sociology can affirm with confidence that social institutions have made "progress" or grown "better," it is in this arrangement of marriage and the family. All experience proves that monogamy, pure and strict, is the sex relation which conduces most to the vigor and intelligence of the race, and that the family education of children is the institution by which the race as a whole advances most rapidly, from generation to generation, in the struggle with nature.

• • •

The constant tendency of population to outstrip the means of subsistence is the force which has distributed population over the world, and produced all advance in civilization. To this day the two means of escape for an overpopulated country are emigration and an advance in the arts. The former wins more land for the same people; the latter makes the same land support more persons. If, however, either of these means opens a chance for an increase of population, it is evident that the advantage so won may be speedily exhausted if the increase takes place. The social difficulty has only undergone a temporary amelioration, and when the conditions of pressure and competition are renewed, misery and poverty reappear. The victims of them are those who have inherited disease and depraved appetites, or have been brought up in vice and ignorance, or have themselves yielded to vice, extravagance, idleness, and imprudence. In the last analysis, therefore, we come back to vice, in its original and hereditary forms, as the correlative of misery and poverty.

The condition for the complete and regular action of the force of competition is liberty. Liberty means the security given to each man that, if he employs his energies to sustain the struggle on behalf of himself and those he cares for, he shall dispose of the product exclusively as he chooses. It is impossible to know whence any definition or criterion of justice can be derived, if it is not deduced from this view of things; or if it is not the definition of justice that each shall enjoy the fruit of his own labor and self-denial, and of injustice that the idle and the industrious, the self-indulgent and the self-denying, shall share equally in the product.

• • •

Private property, also, which we have seen to be a feature of society organized in accordance with the natural conditions of the struggle for existence produces inequalities between men. The struggle for existence is aimed against nature. It is from her niggardly hand that we have to wrest the satisfactions for our needs, but our fellow-men are our competitors for the meager supply. Competition, therefore, is a law of nature. Nature is entirely neutral; she submits to him who most energetically and resolutely assails her. She grants her rewards to the fittest, therefore, without regard to other considerations of any kind. If, then, there be liberty, men get from her just in proportion to their works, and their having and enjoying are just in proportion to their being and their doing. Such is the system of nature. If we do not like it, and if we try to amend it, there is only one way in which we can do it. We can take from the better and give to the worse. We can deflect the penalties of those who have done ill and throw them on those who have done better. We can take the rewards from those who have done better and give them to those who have done worse. We shall thus lessen the inequalities. We shall favor the survival of the unfittest, and we shall accomplish this by destroying liberty. Let it be understood that we cannot go outside of this alternative: liberty, inequality, survival of the fittest; not-liberty, equality, survival of the unfittest. The former carries society forward and favors all its best members; the latter carries society downwards and favors all its worst members.

• • •

What we mean by liberty is civil liberty, or liberty under law; and this means the guarantees of law that a man shall not be interfered with while using his own powers for his own welfare. It is, therefore, a civil and political status; and that nation has the freest institutions in which the guarantees of peace for the laborer and security for the capitalist are the highest. Liberty, therefore, does not by any means do away with the struggle for existence. We might as well try to do away with the need of eating, for that would, in effect, be the same thing. What civil liberty does is to turn the competition of man with man from violence and brute force into an industrial competition under which men vie with one another for the acquisition of material goods by industry, energy, skill, frugality, prudence, temperance, and other industrial virtues. Under this changed order of things the inequalities are not done away with. Nature still grants her rewards of having and enjoying, according to our being and doing, but it is now the man of the highest training and not the man of the heaviest fist who gains the highest reward. It is impossible that the man with capital and the man without capital should be equal. To affirm that they are equal would be to say that a man who has no tool can get as much food out of the ground as the man who has a spade or a plough; or that the man who has no weapon can defend himself as well against hostile beasts or hostile men as the man who has a weapon. If that were so, none of us would work any more. We work and deny ourselves to get capital, just because, other things being equal, the man who has it is superior, for attaining all the ends of life, to the man who has it not.

• • •

Questions

1. How does Sumner differentiate between the "natural" roles of men and women in society?

2. How does he explain the existence of poverty and social inequality?

106. A Second Declaration of Independence (1879)

Source: Philip S. Foner, We the Other People *(Urbana, 1976), pp. 117–19.*

Not all Americans adhered to the Social Darwinist definition of liberty as frank acceptance of social inequality in an unregulated market. During the Gilded Age, the labor movement presented a very different understanding of freedom. It offered a wide array of programs, from public employment in hard times to currency reform, anarchism, socialism, and the creation of a vaguely defined "cooperative commonwealth." All these ideas arose from the conviction that social conditions in the 1870s and 1880s needed drastic change. One of the most popular demands was for legislation establishing eight hours as a legal day's work. In 1879, Ira Steward, a prominent union leader, drafted a revised version of the Declaration of Independence for a Fourth of July labor picnic in Chicago. He insisted that higher wages and greater leisure time would enable workers to develop new desires, thereby increasing demand for goods and benefiting manufacturers, laborers, and society at large. Steward's program illustrates how, in the aftermath of the Civil War, reformers of all kinds increasingly looked to the government to bring about social change. It also reveals a new sense of identification between American workers and their counterparts overseas.

RESOLVED, THAT THE practical question for an American Fourth of July is not between freedom and slavery, but between wealth and poverty. For if it is true that laborers ought to have as little as possible of the wealth they produce, South Carolina slaveholders were right and the Massachusetts abolitionists were wrong. Because, when the working classes are denied everything but the barest necessities of life, they have no decent use for liberty. . . .

Slavery is . . . the child of poverty, instead of poverty the child of slavery: and freedom is the child of wealth, instead of wealth the child of freedom. The only road, therefore, to universal freedom is the road that leads to universal wealth.

Resolved, That while the Fourth of July was heralded a hundred years ago in the name of Liberty, we now herald this day in behalf of the great economic measure of Eight Hours, or shorter day's work for wageworkers everywhere . . . because more leisure, rest and thought will cultivate habits, customs, and expenditures that mean higher wages: and the world's highest paid laborers now furnish each other with vastly more occupations or days' work than the lowest paid workers can give to one another. . . . If the worker's power to buy increases with his power to do, granaries and warehouses will empty their pockets, and farms and factories fill up with producers. . . .

And we call to the workers of the whole civilized world, especially those of France, Germany, and Great Britain, to join hands with the laborers of the United States in this mighty movement. . . .

Thus shall eight hours prevail; earnings and days' work, wealth, and business prosperity increase, financial reverses be made impossible, and the whole human race emancipated . . . from the capitalist despotism which is made possible and necessary by the poverty of the most of mankind.

On the . . . issue of eight hours, therefore, or less hours, we join hands with all, regardless of politics, nationality, color, religion, or sex; knowing no friends or foes except as they aid or oppose this long-postponed and world-wide movement.

And for the soundness of our political economy, as well as the rectitude of our intentions, we confidently and gladly appeal to the wiser statesmanship of the civilized world.

Questions

1. Why does this declaration appeal to other countries for support?

2. What benefits does the declaration claim will come from shortening the hours of work and increasing wages?

107. Henry George, *Progress and Poverty* (1879)

Source: Henry George, **Progress and Poverty** *[1879] (New York, 1884), pp. 489–96.*

Dissatisfaction with social conditions in the Gilded Age extended well beyond aggrieved workers. Alarmed by fear of class warfare and the growing power of concentrated wealth, social thinkers offered numerous plans for change. Among the most influential was Henry George, whose *Progress and Poverty* became one of the era's great best-sellers. Its extraordinary success testified to what George called "a wide-spread consciousness . . . that there is something *radically* wrong in the present social organization."

George's book began with a famous statement of "the problem" suggested by its title—the expansion of poverty alongside material progress. His solution was the "single tax," which would replace other taxes with a levy on increases in the value of real estate. The single tax would be so high that it would prevent speculation in both urban and rural land, and land would then become available to aspiring businessmen and urban working men seeking to become farmers. Whether or not they believed in George's solution, millions of readers responded to his clear explanation of economic relationships and his stirring account of how the "unjust and unequal distribution of wealth" long thought to be confined to the Old World had made its appearance in the New.

———

THE EVILS ARISING from the unjust and unequal distribution of wealth, which are becoming more and more apparent as modern civilization goes on, are not incidents of progress, but tendencies which must bring progress to a halt; that they will not cure themselves, but, on the contrary, must, unless their cause is removed, grow greater and greater, until they sweep us back into barbarism by the road every previous civilization has trod. But it also shows that these evils are not imposed by natural laws; that they spring solely from social mal-adjustments which ignore natural laws, and that in removing their cause we shall be giving an enormous impetus to progress.

The poverty which in the midst of abundance, pinches and embrutes men, and all the manifold evils which flow from it, spring from a denial of justice. In permitting the monopolization of the natural opportunities which nature freely offers to all, we have ignored the fundamental law of justice—for so far as we can see, when we view things upon a large scale, justice seems to be the supreme law of the universe. But by sweeping away this injustice and asserting the rights of all men to natural opportunities, we shall conform ourselves to the law—we shall remove the great cause of unnatural inequality in the distribution of wealth and power; we shall abolish poverty; tame the ruthless passions of greed; dry up the springs of vice and misery; light in dark places the lamp of knowledge; give new vigor to invention and a fresh impulse to discovery; substitute political strength for political weakness; and make tyranny and anarchy impossible.

The reform I have proposed accords with all that is politically, socially, or morally desirable. It has the qualities of a true reform, for it will make all other reforms easier. What is it but the carrying out in letter and spirit of the truth enunciated in the Declaration of Independence—the "self-evident" truth that is the heart and soul of the Declaration—*"That all men are created equal; that they are endowed by their Creator with certain inalienable rights; that among them are life, liberty, and the pursuit of happiness!"*

These rights are denied when the equal right to land—on which and by which men alone can live—is denied. Equality of political rights will not compensate for the denial of the equal right to the bounty of nature. Political liberty, when the equal right to land is denied, becomes, as population increases and invention goes on, merely the liberty to compete for employment at starvation wages. This is the truth that we have ignored. And so there come beggars in our streets and tramps on our roads; and poverty enslaves men whom we boast are political sovereigns; and want breeds ignorance that our schools cannot enlighten; and citizens vote as their masters dictate; and the demagogue usurps the part of the statesman; and gold weighs in the scales of justice; and in high places sit those who do not pay to civic virtue even the compliment of hypocrisy; and the pillars of the republic that we thought so strong already bend under an increasing strain.

We honor Liberty in name and in form. We set up her statues and sound her praises. But we have not fully trusted her. And with our growth so grow her demands. She will have no half service!

Liberty! it is a word to conjure with, not to vex the ear in empty boastings. For Liberty means Justice, and Justice is the natural law—the law of health and symmetry and strength, of fraternity·and co-operation.

They who look upon Liberty as having accomplished her mission when she has abolished hereditary privileges and given men the ballot, who think of her as having no further relations to the every-day affairs of life, have not seen her real grandeur—to them the poets who have sung of her must seem rhapsodists, and her martyrs fools! As the sun is the lord of life, as well as of light; as his beams not merely pierce the clouds, but support all growth, supply all motion, and call forth from what would otherwise be a cold and inert mass, all the infinite diversities of being and beauty, so is liberty to mankind. It is not for an abstraction that men have toiled and died; that in every age the witnesses of Liberty have stood forth, and the martyrs of Liberty have suffered.

We speak of Liberty as one thing, and virtue, wealth, knowledge, invention, national strength and national independence as other things. But, of all these, Liberty is the source, the mother, the necessary condition. She is to virtue what light is to color; to wealth what sunshine is to grain; to knowledge what eyes are to sight. She is the genius of invention, the brawn of national strength, the spirit of national independence. Where Liberty rises, there virtue grows, wealth increases, knowledge expands, invention multiplies human powers, and in strength and spirit the freer nation rises among her neighbors as Saul amid his brethren—taller and fairer. Where Liberty sinks, there virtue fades, wealth diminishes, knowledge is forgotten, invention ceases, and empires once mighty in arms and arts become a helpless prey to freer barbarians!

• • •

The fiat has gone forth! With steam and electricity, and the new powers born of progress, forces have entered the world that will either compel us to a higher plane or overwhelm us, as nation after nation, as civilization after civilization, have been overwhelmed before. It is the delusion which precedes destruction that sees in the popular unrest with which the civilized world is feverishly pulsing, only the passing effect of ephemeral causes. Between democratic ideas and the aristocratic adjustments of society there is an irreconcilable conflict. Here in the United States, as there in Europe, it may be seen arising. We cannot go on permitting men to vote and forcing them to tramp. We cannot go on educating boys and girls in our public schools and then refusing them the right to earn an honest living. We cannot go on prating of the inalienable rights of man and then denying the inalienable right to the bounty of the Creator.

Questions

1. Why does George write that Americans have not "fully trusted" Liberty?

2. What does he see as the major threats to American freedom?

———

108. Chief Joseph, "Let Me Be a Free Man" (1879)

Source: "An Indian's View of Indian Affairs," North American Review *(April 1879), pp. 415–33.*

In 1879, Chief Joseph, leader of the Nez Percé Indians, delivered a speech in Lincoln Hall, Washington, D.C., to a distinguished audience including President Rutherford B. Hayes. Two years earlier, pursued by troops commanded by General Oliver O. Howard, former head of the Freedmen's Bureau during Reconstruction, Joseph had led his people on a 1,700-mile trek through the Far West. The Indians were seeking to escape to Canada after fights with settlers who had encroached on their tribal lands in Oregon and Idaho. After four months, Howard forced the Indians to surrender, and they were removed to a reservation in Oklahoma.

The speech was delivered in the Nez Percé language and then translated by an interpreter. An unidentified reporter took down the interpreter's version and passed it along to an influential magazine, the *North American Review*, for publication. Whether the words are exactly those delivered by Joseph may be open to question, but the sentiments are certainly his. Speaking in a hall named for the Great Emancipator, he appealed to the ideals of freedom and equal rights before the law. The government eventually transported the surviving Nez Percé to another reservation in Washington Territory. Until his death in 1904, Joseph would unsuccessfully petition successive presidents for his people's right to return to their beloved Oregon homeland.

━━━━━

MY FRIENDS. I have been asked to show you my heart. I am glad to have a chance to do so. I want the white people to understand my people. Some of you think an Indian is like a wild animal. This is a great mistake. I will tell you all about our people, and then you can judge whether an Indian is a man or not. I believe much trouble and blood would be saved if we opened our hearts more. I will tell you in my way how the Indian sees things. The white man has more words to tell you how they look to him, but it does not require many words to speak the truth. What I have to say will come from my heart, and I will speak with a straight tongue. . . .

For a short time we lived quietly. But this could not last. White men had found gold in the mountains around the land of winding water. They stole a great many horses from us, and we could not get them back because we were Indians. The white men told lies for each other. . . . We had no friend who could plead our cause before the war councils. It seemed to me that some of the white men in Wallowa were doing these things on purpose to get up a war. They knew that we were not strong enough to fight them. . . . We gave up some of our country to the white men thinking that we could then have peace. We were mistaken....

I have heard talk and talk, but nothing is done. Good words do not last long unless they amount to something. Words do not pay for my dead people. They do not pay for my country, now overrun by white men.... Good words will not get my people a home where they can live in peace and take care of themselves. I am tired of talk that comes to nothing. It makes my heart sick when I remember all the ... broken promises....

If the white man wants to live in peace with the Indian he can live in peace. There need be no trouble. Treat all men alike. Give them the same law. Give them all an even chance to live and grow. All men were made by the same Great Spirit Chief. They are all brothers. The earth is the mother of all people, and all people should have equal rights upon it. You might as well expect the rivers to run backward as that any man who was born a free man should be contented when penned up and denied liberty to go where he pleases....

When I think of our condition my heart is heavy. I see men of my race treated as outlaws and driven from country to country, or shot down like animals. I know that my race must change. We cannot hold our own with the white men as we are. We only ask an even chance to live as other men live....

Let me be a free man—free to travel, free to stop, free to work, free to trade where I choose, free to choose my own teachers, free to follow the religion of my fathers, free to think and talk and act for myself—and I will obey every law, or submit to the penalty.

Questions

1. How does Chief Joseph define freedom?

2. What are Joseph's main complaints about the treatment of his people?

109. Saum Song Bo, Chinese-American Protest (1885)

Source: **American Missionary** *(October 1885), p. 290.*

The boundaries of freedom, expanded so dramatically in the aftermath of the Civil War, contracted in the late nineteenth century. Blacks were not the only group to find their rights receding. By 1880, 105,000 persons of Chinese descent lived in the United States, nearly all of them on the West Coast. Leaders of both political parties expressed vicious opinions regarding immigrants from China—they were "odious, abominable, dangerous, revolting," declared Republican leader James G. Blaine. Beginning in 1882, Congress excluded immigrants from China from entering the country altogether. Although nonwhites had long been prohibited from becoming naturalized citizens, this was the first time that race had been used to exclude an entire group of people from coming to the United States.

During the mid-1880s, a national campaign sought to raise funds to build the pedestal on which the Statue of Liberty, a gift from France, would rest. Saum Song Bo, a Chinese-American writer, contrasted Americans' celebration of liberty with their actual treatment of the Chinese. He also noted that in their colonies in Southeast Asia, the French themselves were guilty of depriving local residents, including the Chinese, of their liberty.

———

A PAPER WAS presented to me yesterday for inspection, and I found it to be specially drawn up for subscription among my countrymen toward the Pedestal Fund of the Bartholdi Statue of Liberty. Seeing that the heading is an appeal to American citizens, to their love of country and liberty, I feel that my countrymen and myself are honored in being thus appealed to as citizens in the cause of liberty. But the word liberty makes me think of the fact that this country is the land of liberty for men of all nations except the Chinese. I consider it as an insult to us Chinese to call on us to contribute toward building in this land a pedestal for a statue of Liberty. That statue represents Liberty holding a torch which lights the passage of those of all nations who come into this country. But are the Chinese allowed to come? As for the Chinese who are here, are they allowed to enjoy liberty as men of all other nationalities enjoy it? Are they allowed to go about everywhere free from the insults, abuse, assaults, wrongs and injuries from which men of other nationalities are free?

If there be a Chinaman who came to this country when a lad, who has passed through an American institution of learning of the highest grade, who has so fallen in love with American manners and ideas that he desires to make his home in this land, and who, seeing that his countrymen demand one of their own number to be their legal adviser, representative, advocate and protector, desires to study law, can he be a lawyer? By the law of this nation, he, being a Chinaman, cannot become a citizen, and consequently cannot be a lawyer.

And this statue of Liberty is a gift to a people from another people who do not love or value liberty for the Chinese. Are not the Annamese and Tonquinese Chinese, to whom liberty is as dear as to the French? What right have the French to deprive them of their liberty?

Whether this statute against the Chinese or the statue to Liberty will be the more lasting monument to tell future ages of the liberty and greatness of this country, will be known only to future generations.

Liberty, we Chinese do love and adore thee; but let not those who deny thee to us, make of thee a graven image and invite us to bow down to it.

Questions

1. Why does Bo feel that the Chinese do not "enjoy liberty" in the same way as other Americans do?

2. Why does he refer to France's treatment of its colonial subjects in making his argument?

110. Walter Rauschenbusch and the Social Gospel (1912)

Source: Walter Rauschenbusch, Christianizing the Social Order
(New York, 1912), pp. 41–44.

The Baptist clergyman Walter Rauschenbusch, who began preaching in
New York City in 1886, was a bridge between the Gilded Age and the Progressive era of the early twentieth century. Appalled by the low wages
and dire living conditions of his poor parishioners, Rauschenbusch
rejected the idea, common among the era's Protestant preachers, that
poverty arose from individual sins like drinking and sabbath breaking. In
sermons and, in the early twentieth century, in widely read books, he developed what came to be called the Social Gospel. Rauschenbusch insisted that
devout Christians rediscover the "social wealth of the Bible," and especially
Jesus' concern for the poor. Freedom and spiritual self-development, he
argued, required an equalization of wealth and power, and unbridled competition mocked the Christian ideal of brotherhood.

The Social Gospel movement originated as an effort to reform Protestant churches by expanding their appeal in poor urban neighborhoods
and making them more attentive to the era's social ills. Its adherents
established missions and relief programs in urban areas that attempted to
alleviate poverty, combat child labor, and encourage the construction of
better working-class housing.

THE CHIEF PURPOSE of the Christian Church in the past has been
the salvation of individuals. But the most pressing task of the present is not individualistic. Our business is to make over an anti-
quated and immoral economic system; to get rid of laws, customs,
maxims, and philosophies inherited from an evil and despotic past;
to create just and brotherly relations between great groups and
classes of society; and thus to lay a social foundation on which
modern men individually can live and work in a fashion that will not
outrage all the better elements in them. Our inherited Christian faith
dealt with individuals; our present task deals with society.

The Christian Church in the past has taught us to do our work with our eyes fixed on another world and a life to come. But the business before us is concerned with refashioning this present world, making this earth clean and sweet and habitable....

Twenty-five years ago the social wealth of the Bible was almost undiscovered to most of us. We used to plow it six inches deep for crops and never dreamed that mines of anthracite were hidden down below. Even Jesus talked like an individualist in those days and seemed to repudiate the social interest when we interrogated him. He said his kingdom was not of this world; the things of God had nothing to do with the things of Caesar; the poor we would always have with us; and his ministers must not be judges and dividers when Labor argued with Capital about the division of the inheritance. To-day he has resumed the spiritual leadership of social Christianity, of which he was the founder. It is a new tribute to his mastership that the social message of Jesus was the first great possession which social Christianity rediscovered....

With true Christian instinct men have turned to the Christian law of love as the key to the situation. If we all loved our neighbor, we should "treat him right," pay him a living wage, give sixteen ounces to the pound, and not charge so much for beef. But this appeal assumes that we are still living in the simple personal relations of the good old times, and that every man can do the right thing when he wants to do it. But suppose a business man would be glad indeed to pay his young women the $12 a week which they need for a decent living, but all his competitors are paying from $7 down to $5. Shall he love himself into bankruptcy? In a time of industrial depression shall he employ men whom he does not need? And if he does, will his five loaves feed the five thousand unemployed that break his heart with their hungry eyes? If a man owns a hundred shares of stock in a great corporation, how can his love influence its wage scale with that puny stick? The old advice of love breaks down before the hugeness of modern relations. We might as well try to start a stranded ocean liner with the oar which poled our old dory from the mud banks many a time. It is indeed love that we want, but it is socialized love.

Blessed be the love that holds the cup of water to thirsty lips. We can never do without the plain affection of man to man. But what we most need today is not the love that will break its back drawing water for a growing factory town from a well that was meant to supply a village, but a love so large and intelligent that it will persuade an ignorant people to build a system of waterworks up in the hills, and that will get after the thoughtless farmers who contaminate the brooks with typhoid bacilli, and after the lumber concern that is denuding the watershed of its forests. We want a new avatar of love.

Questions

1. Why does Rauschenbusch argue that "the salvation of individuals" is not sufficient to address social problems?

2. What does he urge Christians to do to alleviate poverty?

CHAPTER 17

Freedom's Boundaries, at Home and Abroad, 1890–1900

111. The Populist Platform (1892)

Source: The World Almanac, 1893 *(New York, 1893), pp. 83–85.*

Like industrial workers, small farmers in the late nineteenth century faced increasing economic difficulties. Through the Farmers' Alliance and the People's (or Populist) Party, farmers sought to remedy their condition. The era's greatest political insurgency, the party's major base lay in the cotton and wheat belts of the South and West, but it also sought to appeal to industrial workers.

The Populist platform of 1892, adopted at the party's Omaha convention, remains a classic document of American reform. It spoke of a nation "brought to the verge of moral, political, and material ruin" by political corruption and economic inequality. The platform put forth a long list of proposals to restore democracy and economic opportunity, many of which would be adopted during the next half century, including government control of the currency and a graduated income tax, and asserted that rural and urban workers shared an identity of interest. In addition, Populists called for public ownership of the railroads to guarantee farmers inexpensive access to markets for their crops.

Preamble

The conditions which surround us best justify our co-operation; we meet in the midst of a nation brought to the verge of moral, political, and material ruin. Corruption dominates the ballot-box, the Legislatures, the Congress, and touches even the ermine of the bench. The people are demoralized; most of the States have been compelled to isolate the voters at the polling places to prevent universal intimidation and bribery. The newspapers are largely subsidized or muzzled, public opinion silenced, business prostrated, homes covered with mortgages, labor impoverished, and the land concentrating in the hands of capitalists. The urban workmen are denied the right to organize for self-protection, imported pauperized labor beats down their wages, a hireling standing army, unrecognized by our laws, is established to shoot them down, and they are rapidly degenerating into European conditions. The fruits of the toil of millions are boldly stolen to build up colossal fortunes for a few, unprecedented in the history of mankind; and the possessors of those, in turn, despise the Republic and endanger liberty. From the same prolific womb of governmental injustice we breed the two great classes—tramps and millionaires.

The national power to create money is appropriated to enrich bondholders; a vast public debt payable in legal tender currency has been funded into gold-bearing bonds, thereby adding millions to the burdens of the people.

Silver, which has been accepted as coin since the dawn of history, has been demonetized to add to the purchasing power of gold by decreasing the value of all forms of property as well as human labor, and the supply of currency is purposely abridged to fatten usurers, bankrupt enterprise, and enslave industry. A vast conspiracy against mankind has been organized on two continents, and it is rapidly taking possession of the world. If not met and overthrown at once it forebodes terrible social convulsions, the destruction of civilization, or the establishment of an absolute despotism.

We have witnessed for more than a quarter of a century the struggles of the two great political parties for power and plunder, while grievous wrongs have been inflicted upon the suffering people. We charge that the controlling influences dominating both these parties have permitted the existing dreadful conditions to develop without serious effort to prevent or restrain them. Neither do they now promise us any substantial reform. They have agreed together to ignore, in the coming campaign, every issue but one. They propose to drown the outcries of a plundered people with the uproar of a sham battle over the tariff, so that capitalists, corporations, national banks, rings, trusts, watered stock, the demonetization of silver and the oppressions of the usurers may all be lost sight of. They propose to sacrifice our homes, lives, and children on the altar of mammon; to destroy the multitude in order to secure corruption funds from the millionaires.

Assembled on the anniversary of the birthday of the nation, and filled with the spirit of the grand general and chief who established our independence, we seek to restore the government of the Republic to the hands of "the plain people," with which class it originated. We assert our purposes to be identical with the purposes of the National Constitution; to form a more perfect union and establish justice, insure domestic tranquillity, provide for the common defence, promote the general welfare, and secure the blessings of liberty for ourselves and our posterity.

We declare that this Republic can only endure as a free government while built upon the love of the whole people for each other and for the nation; that it cannot be pinned together by bayonets; that the civil war is over, and that every passion and resentment which grew out of it must die with it, and that we must be in fact, as we are in name, one united brotherhood of free men.

Our country finds itself confronted by conditions for which there is no precedent in the history of the world; our annual agricultural productions amount to billions of dollars in value, which must, within a few weeks or months, be exchanged for billions of dollars' worth of commodities consumed in their production; the existing currency supply is wholly inadequate to make this exchange; the results are falling prices, the formation of combines and rings, the impoverishment of the producing class. We pledge ourselves that if given power we will labor to correct these evils by wise and reasonable legislation, in accordance with the terms of our platform.

We believe that the power of government—in other words, of the people—should be expanded (as in the case of the postal service) as rapidly and as far as the good sense of an intelligent people and the teachings of experience shall justify, to the end that oppression, injustice, and poverty shall eventually cease in the land.

While our sympathies as a party of reform are naturally upon the side of every proposition which will tend to make men intelligent, virtuous, and temperate, we nevertheless regard these questions, important as they are, as secondary to the great issues now pressing for solution, and upon which not only our individual prosperity but the very existence of free institutions depend; and we ask all men to first help us to determine whether we are to have a republic to administer before we differ as to the conditions upon which it is to be administered, believing that the forces of reform this day organized will never cease to move forward until every wrong is remedied and equal rights and equal privileges securely established for all the men and women of this country.

PLATFORM

We declare, therefore—

First.—That the union of the labor forces of the United States this day consummated shall be permanent and perpetual; may its spirit enter into all hearts for the salvation of the Republic and the uplifting of mankind.

Second.—Wealth belongs to him who creates it, and every dollar taken from industry without an equivalent is robbery. "If any will not work, neither shall he eat." The interests of rural and civic labor are the same; their enemies are identical.

Third.—We believe that the time has come when the railroad corporations will either own the people or the people must own the railroads, and should the government enter upon the work of owning and managing all railroads, we should favor an amendment to the Constitution by which all persons engaged in the government service shall be placed under a civil-service regulation of the most rigid character, so as to prevent the increase of the power of the national administration by the use of such additional government employees.

Finance.—We demand a national currency, safe, sound, and flexible, issued by the general government only, a full legal tender for all debts, public and private, and that without the use of banking corporations, a just, equitable, and efficient means of distribution direct to the people, at a tax not to exceed 2 per cent per annum, to be provided as set forth in the sub-treasury plan of the Farmers' Alliance, or a better system; also by payments in discharge of its obligations for public improvements.

1. We demand free and unlimited coinage of silver and gold at the present legal ratio of 16 to 1.

2. We demand that the amount of circulating medium be speedily increased to not less than $50 per capita.

3. We demand a graduated income tax.

4. We believe that the money of the country should be kept as much as possible in the hands of the people, and hence we demand that all State and national revenues shall be limited to the necessary expenses of the government, economically and honestly administered.

5. We demand that postal savings banks be established by the government for the safe deposit of the earnings of the people and to facilitate exchange.

Transportation.—Transportation being a means of exchange and a public necessity, the government should own and operate the railroads in the interest of the people. The telegraph, telephone, like the post-office system, being a necessity for the transmission of news, should be owned and operated by the government in the interest of the people.

Land.—The land, including all the natural sources of wealth, is the heritage of the people, and should not be monopolized for speculative purposes, and alien ownership of land should be prohibited.

All land now held by railroads and other corporations in excess of their actual needs, and all lands now owned by aliens should be reclaimed by the government and held for actual settlers only.

Questions

1. How does the Omaha platform identify the main threats to American liberty?

2. How did the Populists seek to rethink the relationship between government power and freedom?

---

112. William Birney, "Deporting Mohammedans" (1897)

Source: Washington Post, *November 21, 1897.*

The 1890s were a decade of heightened anxiety over immigration, particularly as newcomers from the traditional sources—countries of northern and western Europe—were outnumbered by those from southern and eastern Europe, considered by many Americans less "fit" for American citizenship. Small numbers also arrived from the Ottoman Empire, where Islam was the predominant religion, sparking concern among American Protestants. Long before presidential candidate Donald Trump in 2016 called for a "complete shutdown" of Muslim immigration to the United States, federal officials excluded a group of Muslims from entering the country. William Birney, an ardent abolitionist and a Union general in the Civil War, protested the action in a letter to the *Washington Post.*

FIVE MEN AND a lad of fifteen, immigrants from Turkey, passengers on the *Caledonia*, have been held in custody at New York since last Monday and are to be deported, by order of the United States Supervisors of Immigration. The cause of this imprisonment and banishment is that the newcomers, on being questioned by a subordinate official, admitted they were Mohammedans....

Where is this sort of thing to end?... If the principle should be approved, it may be applied to any persons whose opinions the officials of the time may think dangerous, to Jews, Catholics, Mormons, Cubans, Spaniards, and even to bankers and bosses. It would be risky for [political bosses] Croker or Platt or Hanna or [J. P.] Morgan to leave the country; he might not get back again.

This deportation by order of a board, because of religion, is too absurd to be tolerated by the authorities. It follows close on the president's Thanksgiving proclamation in which he recommended all persons (including, of course, Jews, Mormons, Spiritualists, Mohammedans, and Christian Scientists) to meet "in their respective places of worship" and offer thanks. Congress has no right to legislate for or against any religious sect or to banish any. It is the glory of our country that a man may believe anything but if he injures other people, the law takes hold of him. If anyone commits bigamy, he is punishable.

There are Mohammedans in the United States. Some of them are missionaries sent to New York to convert the people. If we deport Mohammedans, the Sultan may retort by deporting American missionaries—whom he regards as a demoralizing and dangerous class. If he should, what can we say against it?

If we let Mohammedan immigrants alone, showing ourselves civilized and kind-hearted, they will soon become Americans in feeling and habits.

Questions

1. Why does Birney think that the action of the immigration officials sets a dangerous precedent?

2. Why does he think that toleration is likely to promote immigrant assimilation?

113. W. E. B. Du Bois, "Your Country?" (1903)

Source: W. E. B. Du Bois, The Souls of Black Folk *(Chicago, 1903), pp. 262–63.*

The most powerful call for equal rights for black Americans at the turn of the twentieth century came from the pen of the black educator and activist W. E. B. Du Bois. Du Bois's life spanned the history of the civil rights movement—he was born during Reconstruction and died on the eve of the March on Washington of 1963. The unifying theme of Du Bois's career was his effort to reconcile the contradiction between "American freedom for whites and the continuing subjugation of Negroes."

In *The Souls of Black Folk,* a collection of essays on African-American history and the state of American race relations, Du Bois sought to revive the abolitionist tradition of agitation for basic civil, political, and educational rights. He ended the book with a chapter on the "sorrow songs"—slave spirituals that beautifully expressed longings for freedom. At the conclusion, in poetic language, he criticized the prevailing belief in white supremacy and pointed out that blacks had been an integral part of American life from the very beginning of European settlement. He would go on to help found the National Association for the Advancement of Colored People.

THROUGH ALL THE sorrow of the Sorrow Songs there breathes a hope—a faith in the ultimate justice of things. The minor cadences of despair change often to triumph and calm confidence. Sometimes it is faith in life, sometimes a faith in death, sometimes assurance of boundless justice in some fair world beyond. But whichever it is, the meaning is always clear: that sometime, somewhere, men will judge men by their souls and not by their skins. Is such a hope justified? Do the Sorrow Songs sing true?

The silently growing assumption of this age is that the probation of races is past, and that the backward races of today are of proven inefficiency and not worth the saving. Such an assumption is the arrogance of peoples irreverent toward time and ignorant of the deeds of men. A thousand years ago such an assumption, easily possible, would have made it difficult for the Teuton to prove his right to life. Two thousand years ago such dogmatism, readily welcome, would have scouted the idea of blond races ever leading civilization. So woefully unorganized is sociological knowledge that the meaning of progress, the meaning of "swift" and "slow" in human doing, and the limits of human perfectability, are veiled, unanswered sphinxes on the shores of science. Why should Aeschylus have sung two thousand years before Shakespeare was born? Why has civilization flourished in Europe, and flickered, flamed, and died in Africa? So long as the world stands meekly dumb before such questions, shall this nation proclaim its ignorance and unhallowed prejudices by denying freedom of opportunity to those who brought the Sorrow Songs to the Seats of the Mighty?

Your country? How came it yours? Before the Pilgrims landed we were here. Here we have brought our three gifts and mingled them with yours: a gift of story and song—soft, stirring melody in an ill-harmonized and unmelodious land; the gift of sweat and brawn to beat back the wilderness, conquer the soil, and lay the foundations of this vast economic empire two hundred years earlier than your weak hands could have done it; the third, a gift of the Spirit. Around us the history of the land has centred for thrice a hundred years; out of the nation's heart we have called all that was best to throttle and subdue all that was worst; fire and blood, prayer and sacrifice, have billowed over this people, and they have found peace only in the altars of the God of Right. Nor has our gift of the Spirit been merely passive. Actively we have woven ourselves with the very warp and woof of this nation,—we fought their battles, shared their sorrow, mingled our blood with theirs, and generation after generation have pleaded with a headstrong, careless people to despise not Justice, Mercy, and Truth, lest the nation be smitten with a curse. Our song, our toil, our cheer, and warning have been given to this nation in blood-brotherhood. Are not these gifts worth the giving? Is not this work and striving? Would America have been America without her Negro people?

Questions

1. In what ways does Du Bois criticize and in what ways does he seem to embrace the idea of inborn racial characteristics and abilities?

2. How does Du Bois appeal to both American and world history to bolster his claim to inclusion and equality for black Americans?

114. Ida B. Wells, *Crusade for Justice* (ca. 1892)

Source: Ida B. Wells, "The Crusade for Justice," from The Crusade for Justice: The Autobiography of Ida B. Wells, *ed. Alfreda M. Duster, pp. 47–52, 64–71, 78–81. Copyright © 1970 The University of Chicago. Reprinted by permission of the University of Chicago Press.*

Racial segregation was only one part of a comprehensive system of racial inequality that was firmly put into place during the 1890s. Blacks who sought to challenge the system or who refused to accept the demeaning treatment that was a daily feature of southern life faced not only overwhelming political and legal power but also the threat of violent reprisal. In every year between 1883 and 1905, more than fifty people, the vast majority of them black men, were lynched in the South—that is, murdered by a mob. Lynching continued well into the twentieth century.

Many victims of lynchings were accused after their deaths of having raped a white woman. Many white southerners considered preserving the purity of white womanhood a justification for extralegal vengeance. Yet, in nearly all cases, as Ida B. Wells argued in a newspaper editorial after a Memphis lynching in 1892, the charge of rape was a "bare lie." Born a slave

in Mississippi in 1862, Wells had become a schoolteacher and an editor.
Her essay condemning the lynching of three black men in Memphis led a
mob to destroy her newspaper, the *Memphis Free Press*, while she was out of
the city. Wells remained in the North, where she became the nation's leading antilynching crusader. In her autobiography, which remained unpub-
lished until 1970, Wells described the Memphis lynching and the
beginnings of the antilynching movement.

WHILE I WAS thus carrying on the work of my newspaper, . . . there
came the lynching in Memphis which changed the whole course of
my life. . . .

Thomas Moss, Calvin McDowell, and Henry Stewart owned and
operated a grocery store in a thickly populated suburb. . . . There was
already a grocery owned and operated by a white man who hitherto
had had a monopoly on the trade of this thickly populated colored
suburb. Thomas's grocery changed all that, and he and his associ-
ates were made to feel that they were not welcome by the white grocer. . . .

One day some colored and white boys quarreled over a game of
marbles and the colored boys got the better of the fight which followed. . . . Then the challenge was issued that the vanquished whites
were coming on Saturday night to clean out [Thomas's] Colored People's Grocery Company. . . . Accordingly the grocery company armed
several men and stationed them in the rear of the store on that fatal
Saturday night, not to attack but repel a threatened attack. . . . The
men stationed there had seen several white men stealing through
the rear door and fired on them without a moment's pause. Three of
these men were wounded, and others fled and gave the alarm. . . .
Over a hundred colored men were dragged from their homes and
put in jail on suspicion.

All day long on that fateful Sunday white men were permitted
in the jail to look over the imprisoned black men. . . . The mob took
out of their cells Thomas Moss, Calvin McDowell, and Henry

Stewart, the three officials of the People's Grocery Company. They were loaded on a switch engine of the railroad which ran back of the jail, carried a mile north of the city limits, and horribly shot to death. One of the morning papers held back its edition in order to supply its readers with the details of that lynching.... The mob took possession of the People's Grocery Company, helping themselves to food and drink, and destroyed what they could not eat or steal. The creditors had the place closed and a few days later what remained of the stock was sold at auction. Thus, with the aid of city and county authorities and the daily papers, that white grocer had indeed put an end to his rival Negro grocer as well as to his business....

Like many another person who had read of lynchings in the South, I had accepted the idea meant to be conveyed—that although lynching was irregular and contrary to law and order, unreasoning anger over the terrible crime of rape led to the lynching; that perhaps the brute deserved death anyhow and the mob was justified in taking his life.

But Thomas Moss, Calvin McDowell and Henry Stewart had been lynched in Memphis, one of the leading cities of the South, in which no lynching had taken place before, with just as much brutality as other victims of the mob; and they had committed no crime against white women. This is what opened my eyes to what lynching really was. An excuse to get rid of Negroes who were acquiring wealth and property and thus keep the race terrorized and "keep the nigger down." I then began an investigation of every lynching I read about. I stumbled on the amazing record that every case of rape reported ... became such only when it became public.

Many cases were like that of the lynching which happened in Tunica County, Mississippi. The Associated Press reporter said, "The big burly brute was lynched because he had raped the seven-year-old daughter of the sheriff." I visited the place afterward and saw the girl, who was a grown woman more than seventeen years old. She had been found in the lynched Negro's cabin by her father, who had led the mob against him in order to save his daughter's reputation. That Negro was a helper on the farm....

It was with these and other stories in mind in that last week in May 1892 that I wrote the following editorial:

> Eight Negroes lynched since last issue of the *Free Speech*. They were charged with killing white men and five with raping white women. Nobody in this section believes the old thread-bare lie that Negro men assault white women. If Southern white men are not careful they will overreach themselves and a conclusion will be drawn which will be very damaging to the moral reputation of their women.

This editorial furnished at last the excuse for doing what the white leaders of Memphis had long been wanting to do: put an end to the *Free Speech*....

Having lost my paper, had a price put on my life, and been made an exile from home for hinting at the truth, I felt that I owed it to myself and to my race to tell the whole truth now that I was where I could do so freely. Accordingly, the fourth week in June, the *New York Age* had a seven-column article on the front page giving names, dates and places of many lynchings for alleged rape. This article showed conclusively that my editorial in the *Free Speech* was based on facts of illicit association between black men and white women.

Such relationships between white men and colored women were notorious, and had been as long as the two races had lived together in the South....

• • •

The more I studied the situation, the more I was convinced that the Southerner had never gotten over his resentment that the Negro was no longer his plaything, his servant, and his source of income. The federal laws for Negro protection passed during Reconstruction had been made a mockery by the white South where it had not secured their repeal. This same white South had secured political control of its several states, and as soon as white southerners came

into power they began to make playthings of Negro lives and property. This still seemed not enough "to keep the nigger down."

Here came lynch law to stifle Negro manhood which defended itself,
and the burning alive of Negroes who were weak enough to accept
favors from white women. The many unspeakable and unprintable
tortures to which Negro rapists (?) of white women were subjected
were for the purpose of striking terror into the hearts of other Negroes
who might be thinking of consorting with willing white women.

I found that in order to justify these horrible atrocities to the
world, the Negro was branded as a race of rapists, who were especially after white women. I found that white men who had created a
race of mulattoes by raping and consorting with Negro women were
still doing so wherever they could; these same white men lynched,
burned and tortured Negro men for doing the same thing with white
women; even when the white women were willing victims.

That the entire race should be branded as moral monsters and
despoilers of white womanhood and childhood was bound to rob us
of all the friends we had and silence any protests that they might
make for us. For all these reasons it seemed a stern duty to give the
facts I had collected to the world....

About two months after my appearance in the columns in the
New York Age, two colored women remarked on my revelations during a visit with each other and said they thought that the women of
New York and Brooklyn should do something to show appreciation
of my work and to protest the treatment which I had received.... A
committee of two hundred and fifty women was appointed, and they
stirred up sentiment throughout the two cities which culminated
in a testimonial at Lyric Hall on 5 October 1892.

This testimonial was conceded by the oldest inhabitants to be the
greatest demonstration ever attempted by race women for one of their
number.... The leading colored women of Boston and Philadelphia
had been invited to join in this demonstration, and they came, a bril-
liant array ... behind a lonely, homesick girl who was an exile because
she had tried to defend the manhood of her race....

So many things came out of that wonderful testimonial.

First it was the beginning of the club movement among the colored women in this country. The women of New York and Brooklyn decided to continue that organization, which they called the Women's Loyal Union. These were the first strictly women's clubs organized in those cities. Mrs. Ruffin of Boston, who came over to that testimonial . . . called a meeting of the women at her home to meet me, and they organized themselves into the Woman's Era Club of that city. Mrs. Ruffin had been a member of the foremost clubs among white women in Boston for years, but this was her first effort to form one among colored women. . . .

Second, that testimonial was the beginning of public speaking for me. I have already said that I had not before made speeches, but invitations came from Philadelphia, Wilmington, Delaware, Chester, Pennsylvania, and Washington, D.C. . . .

In Philadelphia . . . Miss Catherine Impey of Street Somerset, England, was visiting Quaker relatives of hers in the city and at the same time was trying to learn what she could about the color question in this country. She was the editor of *Anti-Caste*, a magazine published in England in behalf of the natives of India, and she was therefore interested in the treatment of darker races everywhere. . . . The third great result of that wonderful testimonial in New York the previous month [followed]. . . . The interview between Miss Impey and myself resulted in an invitation to England and the beginning of the worldwide campaign against lynching.

Questions

1. What social conditions gave rise to the Memphis lynching?

2. What does Wells see as the contributions of the antilynching movement?

115. Frances E. Willard, *Women and Temperance* (1883)

Source: Frances E. Willard, Women and Temperance *(Hartford, Conn., 1883), pp. 43–46.*

Founded in 1874, the Woman's Christian Temperance Union (WCTU) grew to become the era's largest female organization, with a membership of 150,000 by 1890. Under the banner of Home Protection, it moved from demanding the prohibition of alcoholic beverages (blamed for leading men to squander their wages on drink and treat their wives abusively) to a comprehensive program of economic and political reform including the right to vote. Women, insisted Frances Willard, the group's president, must abandon the idea that "weakness" and dependence were their nature and join assertively in movements to change society.

———

TO HELP FORWARD the coming of Christ into all departments of life, is, in its last analysis, the purpose and aim of the W. C. T. U. For we believe this correlation of New Testament religion with philanthropy, and of the church with civilization, is the perpetual miracle which furnishes the only sufficient antidote to current skepticism. Higher toward the zenith climbs the Sun of Righteousness, making circle after circle of human endeavor and achievement warm and radiant with the healing of its beams. First of all, in our gospel temperance work, this heavenly light penetrated the gloom of the individual, tempted heart (that smallest circle, in which all others are involved), illumined its darkness, melted its hardness, made it a sweet and sunny place—a temple filled with the Holy Ghost.

Having thus come to the heart of the drinking man in the plenitude of his redeeming power, Christ entered the next wider circle, in which two human hearts unite to form a home, and here, by the revelation of her place in His kingdom, He lifted to an equal level with her husband the gentle companion who had supposed herself happy in being the favorite vassal of her liege lord. "There is neither male nor female in Christ Jesus;" this was the "open sesame," a declaration utterly opposed to all custom and tradition, but so steadily the light has shone, and so kindly has it made the heart of man, that without strife of tongues, or edict of sovereigns, it is coming now to pass that in proportion as any home is really Christian, the husband and the wife are peers in dignity and power. There are no homes on earth where woman is "revered, beloved," and individualized in character and work, so thoroughly as the fifty thousand in America where "her children arise up and call her blessed, her husband also, and he praiseth her" because of her part in the work of our W. C. T. U.

• • •

But the modern temperance movement, born of Christ's gospel and cradled at His altars, is rapidly filling one more circle of influence, wide as the widest zone of earthly weal or woe, and that is government. "The government shall be upon His shoulder." "Unto us a King is given." "He shall reign whose right it is." "He shall not fail, nor be discouraged until he hath set judgment in the earth." "For at the name of Jesus every knee shall bow, and every tongue confess that Christ is Lord to the glory of God the Father." "Thy kingdon come, thy will be done *on earth*." Christ shall reign—not visibly, but invisibly; not in form, but in fact; not in substance, but in essence, and the day draws nigh! Then surely the traffic in intoxicating liquors as a drink will no longer be protected by the statute book, the lawyer's plea, the affirmation of the witness, and decision of the judge. And since the government is, after all, a circle that include all hearts, all homes, all churches, all societies, does it not seem as if intelligent loyalty to Christ the King would cause each heart that loves Him to feel in duty bound to use all the power it could gather to itself in helping choose the framers of these more righteous laws? But let it be remembered that for every Christian man who has a voice in making and enforcing laws there are at least two Christian women who have no voice at all. Hence, under such circumstances as now exist, His militant army must ever be powerless to win those legislative battles which, more than any others, affect the happiness of aggregate humanity. But the light gleams already along the sunny hilltops of the nineteenth century of grace. Upon those who in largest numbers love Him who has filled their hearts with peace and their homes with blessing, slowly dawns the consciousness that they may—nay, better still, *they ought to*—ask for power to help forward the coming of their Lord in government—to throw the safeguard of their prohibition ballots around those who have left the shelter of their arms only to be entrapped by the saloons that bad men legalize and set along the streets.

Questions

1. What religious convictions inspire Willard's crusade against liquor?

2. Why does Willard believe that women should enjoy the right to vote?

116. Josiah Strong, *Our Country* (1885)

Source: Josiah Strong, **Our Country: Its Possible Future and Its Present Crisis** *(New York, 1885), pp. 174–77.*

With the annexation of Puerto Rico and the Philippines as a result of the Spanish-American War, the United States emerged for the first time as ruler of an overseas empire. Of course, the roots of American expansionism lay deep in the nation's history. Before the Civil War, many Americans had believed in the doctrine of manifest destiny. In 1885 the Congregational minister Josiah Strong published *Our Country*, a work that achieved great popularity with its combination of the Social Gospel—a desire, grounded in religious belief, to solve the nation's social problems—and an updated version of manifest destiny and American expansionism strongly connected to ideas of racial superiority and a Christian missionary impulse. Strong's writings showed how evangelical Christianity could provide a strong underpinning for American empire.

WHAT IS THE significance of such facts? These tendencies infold the future; they are the mighty alphabet with which God writes his prophecies. May we not, by a careful laying together of the letters, spell out something of his meaning? It seems to me that God, with infinite wisdom and skill, is training the Anglo-Saxon race for an hour sure to come in the world's future. Heretofore there has always been in the history of the world a comparatively unoccupied land westward, into which the crowded countries of the East have poured their surplus populations. But the widening waves of migration, which millenniums ago rolled east and west from the valley of the Euphrates, meet to-day on our Pacific coast. There are no more new worlds. The unoccupied arable lands of the earth are limited, and will soon be taken. The time is coming when the pressure of population on the means of subsistence will be felt here as it is now felt in Europe and Asia. Then will the world enter upon a new stage of its history— *the final competition of races, for which the Anglo-Saxon is being schooled.*

Long before the thousand millions are here, the mighty *centrifugal* tendency, inherent in this stock and strengthened in the United States, will assert itself. Then this race of unequaled energy, with all the majesty of numbers and the might of wealth behind it— the representative, let us hope, of the largest liberty, the purest Christianity, the highest civilization—having developed peculiarly aggressive traits calculated to impress its institutions upon mankind, will spread itself over the earth. If I read not amiss, this powerful race will move down upon Mexico, down upon Central and South America, out upon the islands of the sea, over upon Africa and beyond. And can any one doubt that the result of this competition of races will be the "survival of the fittest"? ... "Nothing can save the inferior race but a ready and pliant assimilation. Whether the feebler and more abject races are going to be regenerated and raised up, is already very much of a question. What if it should be God's plan to people the world with better and finer material? Certain it is, whatever expectations we may indulge, that there is a tremendous overbearing surge of power in the Christian nations, which, if the others are not speedily raised to some vastly higher capacity, will inevitably submerge and bury them forever. These great populations of Christendom—what are they doing, but throwing out their colonies on every side, and populating themselves, if I may so speak, into the possession of all countries and climes?" To this result no war of extermination is needful; the contest is not one of arms, but of vitality and of civilization. . . .

Some of the stronger races, doubtless, may be able to preserve their integrity: but, in order to compete with the Anglo-Saxon, they will probably be forced to adopt his methods and instruments, his civilization and his religion.

Questions

1. How does Strong justify the idea of world domination by Anglo-Saxons?

2. What does he believe "inferior" races need to do to avoid extinction?

---

117. Emilio Aguinaldo on American Imperialism in the Philippines (1899)

Source: "Aguinaldo's Case against the United States," North American Review, *no. 514 (September 1899), pp. 425–32.*

President McKinley's decision to annex the Philippines rather than grant it independence led inexorably to a long, bloody war against Filipino nationalists, led by Emilio Aguinaldo. During the 1890s, Aguinaldo had served in local government under Spanish rule, but in 1895 he joined the movement that launched an armed uprising for Philippine independence. He was exiled in 1897 but, with American encouragement, returned to the islands in 1898 after the outbreak of the Spanish-American War and declared himself president. A believer in the ideals of the American Declaration of Independence, Aguinaldo was bitterly disappointed that McKinley did not recognize the Filipinos' right to self-government. In

1899 he explained his reasons for opposing American imperialism in an article in a widely read magazine, the *North American Review*. He contrasted American traditions of self-government with the refusal to grant this right to the Philippines and chastised the United States for misunderstandings about the people of the islands. Not until 1903, after a war that took the lives of more than 4,000 American soldiers and 100,000 Filipinos, was American control of the Philippines secured. Aguinaldo himself lived until 1964.

We Filipinos have all along believed that if the American nation at large knew exactly, as we do, what is daily happening in the Philippine Islands, they would rise en masse, and demand that this barbaric war should stop. There are other methods of securing sovereignty—the true and lasting sovereignty that has its foundation in the hearts of the people.... And, did America recognize this fact, she would cease to be the laughing stock of other civilized nations, as she became when she abandoned her traditions and set up a double standard of government—government by consent in America, government by force in the Philippine Islands....

You have been deceived all along the line. You have been greatly deceived in the personality of my countrymen. You went to the Philippines under the impression that their inhabitants were ignorant savages.... We have been represented by your popular press as if we were Africans or Mohawk Indians. We smile, and deplore the want of ethnological knowledge on the part of our literary friends. We are none of these. We are simply Filipinos.... In the struggle for liberty which we have ever waged, the education of the masses has been slow; but we are not, on that account, an uneducated people....

You repeat constantly the dictum that we cannot govern ourselves.... With equal reason, you might have said the same thing some fifty or sixty years ago of Japan; and, little over a hundred years ago, it was extremely questionable, when you, also, were rebels against the English Government, if you could govern yourselves.... Now, the moral of all this obviously is: Give us the chance; treat us exactly as you demanded to be treated at the hands of England when you rebelled against her autocratic methods.

Now, here is a unique spectacle—the Filipinos fighting for liberty, the American people fighting them to give them liberty. The two peoples are fighting on parallel lines for the same object. We know that parallel lines never meet. Let us look back to discover the point at which the lines separated.... You declared war with Spain for the sake of Humanity. You announced to the world that your program was to set Cuba free, in conformity with your constitutional principles....

You entered into an alliance with our chiefs at Hong Kong and at Singapore, and you promised us your aid and protection in our attempt to form a government on the principles and after the model of the government of the United States.... In combination with our forces, you compelled Spain to surrender.... Joy abounded in every heart, and all went well ... until ... the Government at Washington ... commenc[ed] by ignoring all promises that had been made and end[ed] by ignoring the Philippine people, their personality and rights, and treating them as a common enemy.... In the face of the world you emblazon humanity and Liberty upon your standard, while you cast your political constitution to the winds and attempt to trample down and exterminate a brave people whose only crime is that they are fighting for their liberty.

Questions

1. Why does Aguinaldo think that the United States is betraying its own values?

2. In what ways does Aguinaldo think that Americans misunderstand the Filipinos?

CHAPTER 18

The Progressive Era, 1900-1916

118. Manuel Gamio on a Mexican-American Family and American Freedom (ca. 1926)

Source: Manuel Gamio, "The Santella Family," Mexican Immigration to the United States, 1926–1928, *Gamio Collection, Bancroft Library, University of California at Berkeley. Reprinted with permission of the Bancroft Library.*

The early twentieth century was a period of massive immigration to the United States. Most of the newcomers arrived from southern and eastern Europe, but between 1900 and 1930, some one million Mexicans also entered the country. Like their predecessors, the new immigrants arrived imagining the United States as a land of freedom, where all persons worshiped as they pleased, enjoyed economic opportunity, and had been emancipated from the oppressive social hierarchies of their homelands.

During the 1920s, the sociologist Manuel Gamio conducted interviews of Mexican-American immigrants in Los Angeles. This excerpt from his report on the Santella family, one better off and "whiter" than most Mexican immigrants, reveals the intergenerational tensions that American freedom inspired within immigrant families.

———

THE FOLLOWING INFORMATION concerning the Santella family was obtained by conversation with them and by observing them for it has been a long time that we have known them.

In 1915, on account of the Mexican revolution, which was at its height, Mr. Santella, his wife and his children, who are seven, five girls and two boys, came to the United States, going to live in San Antonio, Texas. As they are a well-to-do family they lived with every comfort possible in a house which was rented to them on San Pedro Street. I understand that they own a number of pieces of property in Mexico City, among them the private residence of the family, which according to the picture which I have before me is a beautiful colonial style building. On San Pedro Street live the wealthiest class of the Mexican colony, or rather, a number of the wealthier members who make up a sort of "high society" in the midst of the great majority of the Mexican colony, which is made up of persons of the working classes.

• • •

After five years of residence in San Antonio all the members of the family talked English and had conformed to the American customs with the exception of the father and the mother. The eldest of the young women married a young American who was manager of a jewelry shop. Two years later the youngest married a brother of this American. This other man was an employee of the same jewelry shop. It seems that these marriages didn't please the father for he constantly declared at the time that these young men didn't "belong to society." The brother who went to Europe returned to San Antonio, Texas, and later moved to Los Angeles, California, where he married a young American girl.

The other male member of the family is much given to the radio and occupies himself with the selling and buying of them, their installation, etc., but he doesn't help the family in any way and he is supported by his father.

The musician has met with good success during his stay in Los Angeles for he is director of the symphonic orchestra of the "Figueroa" theatre located in one of the colonies in Los Angeles. He also has made several adaptations of music for the theatre and movies and has composed several pieces, all of which has given him a certain amount of name and a good place among the artistic elements of Los Angeles.

Before going on we ought to say that this family is white for the grandparents of the father were French and those of the mother were Spaniards. Two of the sisters are blondes and the others are brunettes; the brothers are dark.

Tired of living in San Antonio and of seeing himself obliged to continuously travel between Mexico and the United States, the father decided to permanently return to Mexico in order to be able to watch over his interests there, letting his wife choose the place where she would rather live. The mother with her unmarried daughter and her son decided to come to live in Los Angeles, where they are now living. They live in an apartment in a residence on South Bronson Street, which leads to Hollywood. Their relations are largely with Americans. The family owns a Buick automobile, which the young ladies run.

The father, therefore, lives in Mexico City, where the members of the family only go for visits. The mother lives with her three unmarried daughters and her son. The married son lives in a house that faces the family and the two married daughters live in San Antonio, Texas.

The daughters have worked at different times in Los Angeles against the will of their parents, they say, in the movies as extras representing Spanish types.

The mother says that she likes life in the United States, for the comfort that there is, the quietness and because she finds less danger for her daughters. Here she goes with freedom to the grocery store, clothing store or wherever it may be and buys whatever she wishes without anyone paying attention to her. She lives as she wants and without as many social obligations as in Mexico, where she had to follow such and such a custom, have a great number of servants, and always having to meet a great number of social requirements which bothered her a great deal. She says, nevertheless, that she doesn't like the American customs in the matter of the liberty and way of behaving of the young women of this country, [the] customs and ways of being by which her daughters have been influenced and which greatly concerns her. On the other hand, she likes this country for the progress which it has made and she says that she only likes to go back to Mexico for visits. And since her daughters have married she considers herself obligated to live here in order to help them in everything possible and above all else it happens that the climate of Los Angeles is very good for her.

The youngest of the girls was studying in a high school in San Antonio and later continued her studies in Los Angeles but a little after arriving in this city she entered into relations with a young Englishman who is now her fiancé and she will be married to him within a few months. She quit school on account of this and also wishing to be independent and earn herself the money needed for her clothes and other wants she decided to go to work in spite of the opposition of her father and mother. She is now the secretary of a doctor. She receives the patients who come to his clinic, answers the telephone calls and takes charge of answering the correspondence of her chief for she knows shorthand and typewriting. She receives $20.00 a week for this work with which she buys her dresses, shoes, etc. This young lady who is seventeen years old is the most Americanized of all according to what her mother and sisters say.

Questions

1. What evidence does the report provide about the spread of consumer culture in early twentieth-century America?

2. What differences in attitudes toward Americanization and gender relations within the Santella family are revealed in Gamio's report?

119. Charlotte Perkins Gilman, *Women and Economics* (1898)

Source: Charlotte Perkins Gilman, Women and Economics *(Boston, 1898), pp. 20–21, 152–57, 210–11.*

During the Progressive era, the working woman—immigrant and native, working class and professional—became a symbol of female emancipation. The growing number of younger women who desired a lifelong career, wrote Charlotte Perkins Gilman in her influential book *Women and Economics*, offered evidence of a "spirit of personal independence" that pointed to a coming transformation of both economic and family life. In the home, Gilman argued, women experienced not fulfillment but oppression, and the housewife was an unproductive parasite, little more than a servant to her husband and children. By condemning women to a life of domestic drudgery, prevailing gender norms made them incapable of contributing to society or enjoying freedom in any meaningful sense of the word. Gilman devised plans for communal nurseries, cafeterias, and laundries to help free married women from "house service." Her writings had a strong impact on the first generation of twentieth-century feminists.

IT IS NOT motherhood that keeps the housewife on her feet from dawn till dark; it is house service, not child service. Women work longer and harder than most men, and not solely in maternal duties. The savage mother carries the burdens, and does all menial service for the tribe. The peasant mother toils in the fields, and the working-man's wife in the home. Many mothers, even now, are wage-earners for the family, as well as bearers and rearers of it. And the women who are not so occupied, the women who belong to rich men,—here perhaps is the exhaustive devotion to maternity which is supposed to justify an admitted economic dependence. But we do not find it even among these. Women of ease and wealth provide for their children better care than the poor woman can; but they do not spend more time upon it themselves, nor more care and effort. They have other occupation.

• • •

The working power of the mother has always been a prominent factor in human life. She is the worker *par excellence*, but her work is not such as to affect her economic status. Her living, all that she gets,—food, clothing, ornaments, amusements, luxuries,—these bear no relation to her power to produce wealth, to her services in the house, or to her motherhood. These things bear relation only to the man she marries, the man she depends on,—to how much he has and how much he is willing to give her.

• • •

A truer spirit is the increasing desire of young girls to be independent, to have a career of their own, at least for a while, and the growing objection of countless wives to the pitiful asking for money, to the beggary of their position. More and more do fathers give their daughters, and husbands their wives, a definite allowance,—a separate bank account,—something which they can play is all their own. The spirit of personal independence in the women of to-day is sure proof that a change has come.

For a while the introduction of machinery which took away from the home so many industries deprived woman of any importance as an economic factor; but presently she arose, and followed her lost wheel and loom to their new place, the mill. To-day there is hardly an industry in the land in which some women are not found. Everywhere throughout America are women workers outside the unpaid labor of the home, the last census giving three million of them. This is so patent a fact, and makes itself felt in so many ways by so many persons, that it is frequently and widely discussed. Without here going into its immediate advantages or disadvantages from an industrial point of view, it is merely instanced as an undeniable proof of the radical change in the economic position of women that is advancing upon us. She is assuming new relations from year to year before our eyes; but we, seeing all social facts from a personal point of view, have failed to appreciate the nature of the change.

• • •

The growing individualization of democratic life brings inevitable change to our daughters as well as to our sons. Girls do not all like to sew, many do not know how. Now to sit sewing together, instead of being a harmonizing process, would generate different degrees of restlessness, of distaste, and of nervous irritation. And, as to the reading aloud, it is not so easy now to choose a book that a well-educated family of modern girls and their mother would all enjoy together. As the race become more specialized, more differentiated, the simple lines of relation in family life draw with less force, and the more complex lines of relation in social life draw with more force; and this is a perfectly natural and desirable process for women as well as for men.

• • •

Economic independence for women necessarily involves a change in the home and family relation. But, if that change is for the advantage of individual and race, we need not fear it. It does not involve a change in the marriage relation except in withdrawing the element of economic dependence, nor in the relation of mother to child save to improve it. But it does involve the exercise of human faculty in women, in social service and exchange rather than in domestic service solely. This will of course require the introduction of some other form of living than that which now obtains. It will render impossible the present method of feeding the world by means of millions of private servants, and bringing up children by the same hand.

It is a melancholy fact that the vast majority of our children are reared and trained by domestic servants,—generally their mothers, to be sure, but domestic servants by trade. To become a producer, a factor in the economic activities of the world, must perforce interfere with woman's present status as a private servant. House mistress she may still be, in the sense of owning and ordering her home, but housekeeper or house-servant she may not be—and be anything else. Her position as mother will alter, too. Mother in the sense of bearer and rearer of noble children she will be, as the closest and dearest, the one most honored and best loved; but mother in the sense of exclusive individual nursery-maid and nursery-governess she may not be—and be anything else.

Questions

1. Why does Gilman foresee a "radical change in the economic position of women"?

2. What changes in family life does she envision as a result of the growing economic independence of women?

120. John A. Ryan, *A Living Wage* (1912)

Source: John A. Ryan, A Living Wage: Its Ethical and Economic Aspects *(New York, 1912), pp. 67–73, 297–301.*

During the Progressive era, the ideas of "industrial freedom" and "industrial democracy," which had entered the political vocabulary during the Gilded Age, moved to the center of political discussion. They had many meanings, including improving the general standard of living and working conditions, and empowering workers to participate in economic decision making via strong unions. In any form, these terms challenged traditional definitions of freedom, as well as the idea of the inviolability of private property. The government, Progressives believed, had the right to expand liberty by regulating economic activity in the public interest.

One of the era's foremost advocates of social justice was John A. Ryan, a Roman Catholic priest and professor at Catholic University in Washington, D.C. In 1891, Pope Leo XIII had called on Catholics to engage in social activism on behalf of industrial workers. Ryan became the leading proponent of the idea that all persons had a natural right not simply to subsistence but to a "living wage," which would enable them to share in the fruits of modern technology. His book on the subject helped to popularize the idea and influenced legislation of the Progressive era and New Deal establishing minimum wage levels. Ryan would become so close to President Franklin D. Roosevelt during the 1930s that he was known as the "Right Reverend New Dealer."

———

THE RIGHT TO a Living Wage is derived from the right to live from the bounty of the earth. The latter right acknowledged by most nations and insisted upon by Christianity. It is evident from a view of man's nature and his relation to the earth. It is superior to and limits the right of private ownership. Meaning a decent livelihood. Its rational basis is the sacredness of personality. Men have not natural rights to equal amounts of goods; for they are unequal both in individual needs and productive powers. Nor rights to equal satisfaction of the totality of their needs. . . .

A man's natural rights are as many and as extensive as are the liberties, opportunities and possessions that are required for the reasonable maintenance and development of his personality. They may all be reduced to the right to a reasonable amount of external liberty of action. Some of them, for instance the right to live and the right to marry, are original and primary, inhering in all persons of whatever condition; others are derived and secondary, occasioned and determined by the particular circumstances of particular persons. To the latter class belongs the right to a Living Wage. It is not an original and universal right; for the receiving of wages supposes that form of industrial organization known as the wage system, which has not always existed and is not essential to human welfare. Even today there are millions of men who get their living otherwise than by wages, and who, therefore, have no juridical title to wages of any kind or amount. The right to a Living Wage is evidently a derived right which is measured and determined by existing social and industrial institutions. . . .

Private property is morally legitimate because it is the method that best enables man to realize his natural right to use the gifts of material nature for the development of his personality. It is, therefore, merely a means, and its scope is determined and limited by the end which it promotes, and which is its sole justification. The private right of any and every individual must be interpreted consistently with the common rights of all.... Hence a man's right to a superfluous loaf which is his by a title of private ownership does not absolve him from the crime of injustice when he withholds it from his starving fellow man....

So much for the right to subsistence, to a bare livelihood. By a *decent* livelihood is meant that amount of the necessities and comforts of life that is in keeping with the dignity of a human being. It has no precise relation to the conventional standard of living that may prevail within any social or industrial class, but describes rather that minimum of conditions which the average person of a given age or sex must enjoy in order to live as a human being should live ... in a reasonable degree of comfort.... He must have food, clothing and shelter. He must have opportunity to develop within reasonable limits all his faculties, physical, intellectual, moral, and spiritual....

The obligation of providing the laborer with a Living Wage ... rests upon the State.... Negatively, liberty is the absence of restraint; positively, it is the power to act and to enjoy.... The absence of State intervention means the presence of insuperable obstacles to real and effective liberty.... [Such legislation] would secure a wider measure of freedom in larger economic opportunity.... The State has both the right and the duty to compel all employers to pay a Living Wage.

Questions

1. How does Ryan justify the idea that people have a right to a Living Wage?

2. Why does he see governmental action to promote a Living Wage as an expansion of liberty rather than a threat to it?

121. The Industrial Workers of the World and the Free Speech Fights (1909)

Source: Elizabeth Gurley Flynn, "The Free-Speech Fight at Spokane,"
International Socialist Review, *vol. 16 (December 1909), pp. 483–89.*

The most prominent union of the Progressive era, the American Federation of Labor mainly represented the most privileged American workers—skilled industrial and craft laborers, nearly all of them white, male, and native born. In 1905, a group of unionists who rejected the AFL's exclusionary policies formed the Industrial Workers of the World (IWW), which sought to mobilize the immigrant factory labor force, migrant timber and agricultural workers, women, blacks, and even the despised Chinese.

But what really attracted attention to the IWW was its battle for freedom of speech. Lacking union halls, its organizers relied on songs, street theater, impromptu organizing meetings, and street corner gatherings to spread their message and attract support. In response to IWW activities, officials in Los Angeles, Spokane, Denver, and more than a dozen other cities limited or prohibited outdoor meetings. To arouse popular support, the IWW filled the jails with members who defied local law by speaking in public. In nearly all the free-speech fights, the IWW eventually forced local officials to give way. "Whether they agree or disagree with its methods or aims," wrote one journalist, "all lovers of liberty everywhere owe a debt to this organization for . . . [keeping] alight the fires of freedom."

THE WORKING CLASS of Spokane are engaged in a terrific conflict, one of the most vital of the local class struggles. It is a fight for more than free speech. It is to prevent the free press and labor's right to organize from being throttled. The writers of the associated press newspapers have lied about us systematically and unscrupulously. It is only through the medium of the Socialist and labor press that we can hope to reach the ear of the public.

The struggle was precipitated by the I.W.W. and it is still doing the active fighting, namely, going to jail. But the principles for which we are fighting have been endorsed by the Socialist Party and the Central Labor Council of the A.F. of L. [American Federation of Labor].

The I.W.W. in Spokane is composed of "floaters," men who drift from harvest fields to lumber camps from east to west. They are men without families and are fearless in defense of their rights but as they are not the "home guard" with permanent jobs, they are the type upon whom the employment agents prey. With alluring signs detailing what short hours and high wages men can get in various sections, usually far away, these leeches induce the floater to buy a job, paying exorbitant rates, after which they are shipped out a thousand miles from nowhere. The working man finds no such job as he expected but one of a few days' duration until he is fired to make way for the next "easy mark."

The I.W.W. since its inception in the northwest has carried on a determined, relentless fight on the employment sharks and as a result the business of the latter has been seriously impaired. Judge Mann in the court a few days ago remarked: "I believe all this trouble is due to the employment agencies," and he certainly struck the nail on the head. "The I.W.W. must go," the sharks decreed last winter and a willing city council passed an ordinance forbidding all street meetings within the fire limits. This was practically a suppression of free speech because it stopped the I.W.W. from holding street meetings in the only districts where working men congregate. In August the Council modified their decision to allow religious bodies to speak on the streets, thus frankly admitting their discrimination against the I.W.W.

The I.W.W. decided that fall was the most advantageous time for the final conflict because the members of the organization drift back into town with their "stake" to tide them over the winter.

A test case was made about three weeks ago when Fellow Worker Thompson spoke on the street. At his trial on November 2nd the ordinance of August was declared unconstitutional by Judge Mann. He made a flowery speech in which he said that the right of free speech was "God given" and "inalienable," but with the consistency common to legal lights ruled that the *first ordinance* was now in vogue.

Members of the Industrial Workers of the World thereupon went out on the street and spoke. They were all arrested and to our surprise the next morning were charged with disorderly conduct, which came under another ordinance. It looked as if the authorities hardly dared to fight it out on the ordinance forbidding free speech. From that time on, every day has witnessed the arrests of many members of the Industrial Workers of the World, Socialists and W.F. of M. [Western Federation of Miners] men.

On the third of November the headquarters of the I.W.W. was raided by Chief of Police Sullivan and his gang. They arrested James Wilson, editor of the *Industrial Worker,* James P. Thompson, local organizer, C. L. Filigno, local secretary, and A. E. Cousins, associate editor, on a charge of criminal conspiracy. E. J. Foote, acting editor of the *Industrial Worker,* was arrested out of the lawyer's office on the next day. The idea of the police was presumably to get "the leaders," as they are ignorant enough to suppose that by taking a few men they can cripple a great organization. The arrest of these men is serious, however, as they are charged with a state offense and are liable to be railroaded to the penitentiary for five years.

The condition of the city jail is such that it cannot be described in decent language. Sufficient to say, that the boys have been herded twenty-eight to thirty at a time in a 6×8 cell known as the sweat box. The steam has been turned on full blast until the men were ready to drop from exhaustion. Several have been known to faint before being removed. Then they were placed in an ice-cold cell and as a result of this inhuman treatment several are now in so precarious a condition that we fear they will die. After this preliminary punishment they were ordered to work on the rock pile and when they refused were placed on a diet of bread and water. Many of the boys, with a courage that is remarkable, refused even that. This is what the capitalist press sneeringly alluded to as a "hunger strike." The majority has been sentenced to thirty days. Those who repeated the terrible crime of saying "Fellow Workers" on the street corner were given thirty days, one hundred dollars' fine and costs. The trials have given additional proof to our much-disputed charge that justice in the United States is a farce. Fellow Worker Little was asked by the Judge what he was doing when arrested. He answered "reading the Declaration of Independence." "Thirty days," said the Judge. The next fellow worker had been reading extracts from the *Industrial Worker* and it was thirty days for him. We are a "classy" paper ranked with the Declaration of Independence as too incendiary for Spokane.

A case in point illustrates how "impartial" the court is. A woman from a notorious resort in this city which is across the street from the city hall and presumably operated under police protection appeared and complained against a colored soldier charged with disorderly conduct. The case was continued. The next case was an I.W.W. speaker. The Judge without any preliminaries asked "were you speaking on the street?" When the defendant replied "Yes" the Judge sternly ordered thirty days, one hundred dollars' fine and costs.

Fellow Worker Knust, one of our best speakers, was brutally beaten by an officer and he is at present in the hospital. Mrs. Frenette, one of our women members, was also struck by an officer. Some of the men inside the jail have black eyes and bruised faces. One man has a broken jaw, yet these men were not in such a condition when they were arrested.

Those serving sentence have been divided into three groups, one in the city jail, another in an old abandoned and partly wrecked schoolhouse and the third at Fort Wright, guarded by negro soldiers. These outrages are never featured in the local leading papers. It might be detrimental to the Washington Water Power–owned government. The usual lies about the agitators being ignorant foreigners, hoboes and vags [vagrants] are current. Assuming that most of those arrested were foreigners, which is not the case, there are 115 foreigners and 136 Americans, it would certainly reflect little credit on American citizens that outsiders have to do the fighting for what is guaranteed in the American constitution. Most of the boys have money. They are not what could be called "vags," although that would not be to their discredit, but they do not take their money to jail with them. They believe in leading a policeman not into temptation. They are intelligent, level-headed working men fighting for the rights of their class.

The situation assumed such serious proportions that a committee of the A.F. of L., the Socialist Party and the I.W.W. went before the City Council requesting the repeal of the present ordinance and the passage of one providing for orderly meetings at reasonable hours. All of these committees, without qualification, endorsed free speech and made splendid talks before the Council. Two gentlemen appeared against us. One was an old soldier over 70 years of age with strong prejudices against the I.W.W. and the other president of the Fidelity National Bank of Spokane; yet these two presumably carried more weight than the twelve thousand five hundred citizens the three committees collectively represented. We were turned down absolutely and a motion was passed that no further action would be taken upon the present ordinance until requests came from the Mayor and Chief of Police. The Mayor, on the strength of this endorsement by a body of old fogies who made up all the mind they possess years ago, called upon the acting governor for the militia. His request was refused, however, and the acting governor is quoted as saying that he saw no disturbance.

The "Industrial Worker" appeared on time yesterday much to the chagrin and amazement of the authorities. Perhaps they now understand that every member in turn will take their place in the editorial chair before our paper will be suppressed.

The organization is growing by leaps and bounds. Men are coming in from all directions daily to go to jail that their organization may live.

Questions

1. Why was freedom of speech so important to labor organizations like the IWW?

2. What does the IWW's experience reveal about the status of civil liberties in early-twentieth-century America?

122. Margaret Sanger on "Free Motherhood," from *Woman and the New Race* (1920)

Source: Margaret Sanger, "Free Motherhood," from Woman and the New Race, *1920. Reprinted with permission of Alexander Sanger, executor of the estate of Margaret Sanger.*

The word "feminism" entered the political vocabulary for the first time in the years before World War I. It expressed not only traditional demands such as the right to vote and greater economic opportunities for women but also a quest for free sexual expression and reproductive choice as essential to women's emancipation. The law banned not only the sale of birth-control devices but also distributing information about them.

More than any other individual, Margaret Sanger, one of eleven children of an Irish-American working-class family, placed the issue of birth control at the heart of the new feminism. She began openly advertising birth-control devices in her own journal, *The Woman Rebel.* In 1916, Sanger opened a clinic in a working-class neighborhood of Brooklyn and began distributing contraceptive devices to poor Jewish and Italian women, an action for which she was sentenced to a month in prison. Like the IWW free-speech fights, Sanger's experience revealed how laws set rigid limits to Americans' freedom of expression.

THE MOST FAR-REACHING social development of modern times is the revolt of woman against sex servitude. The most important force in the remaking of the world is a free motherhood. Beside this force, the elaborate international programmes of modern statesmen are weak and superficial. Diplomats may formulate leagues of nations and nations may pledge their utmost strength to maintain them, statesmen may dream of reconstructing the world out of alliances, hegemonies and spheres of influence, but woman, continuing to produce explosive populations, will convert these pledges into the proverbial scraps of paper; or she may, by controlling birth, lift motherhood to the plane of a voluntary, intelligent function, and remake the world. When the world is thus remade, it will exceed the dream of statesman, reformer and revolutionist.

• • •

Most women who belong to the workers' families have no accurate or reliable knowledge of contraceptives, and are, therefore, bringing children into the world so rapidly that they, their families and their class are overwhelmed with numbers. Out of these numbers ... have grown many of the burdens with which society in general is weighted; out of them have come, also, the want, disease, hard living conditions and general misery of the workers.

The women of this class are the greatest sufferers of all. Not only do they bear the material hardships and deprivations in common with the rest of the family, but in the case of the mother, these are intensified. It is the man and the child who have first call upon the insufficient amount of food. It is the man and the child who get the recreation, if there is any to be had, for the man's hours of labor are usually limited by law or by his labor union.

It is the woman who suffers first from hunger, the woman whose clothing is least adequate, the woman who must work all hours, even though she is not compelled, as in the case of millions, to go into a factory to add to her husband's scanty income. It is she, too, whose health breaks first and most hopelessly, under the long hours of work, the drain of frequent childbearing, and often almost constant nursing of babies. There are no eight-hour laws to protect the mother against overwork and toil in the home; no laws to protect her against ill health and the diseases of pregnancy and reproduction. In fact there has been almost no thought or consideration given for the protection of the mother in the home of the workingman.

• • •

The basic freedom of the world is woman's freedom. A free race cannot be born of slave mothers. A woman enchained cannot choose but give a measure of that bondage to her sons and daughters. No woman can call herself free who does not own and control her body. No woman can call herself free until she can choose consciously whether she will or will not be a mother.

It does not greatly alter the case that some women call themselves free because they earn their own livings, while others profess freedom because they defy the conventions of sex relationship. She who earns her own living gains a sort of freedom that is not to be undervalued, but in quality and in quantity it is of little account beside the untrammeled choice of mating or not mating, of being a mother or not being a mother. She gains food and clothing and shelter, at least, without submitting to the charity of her companion, but the earning of her own living does not give her the development of her inner sex urge, far deeper and more powerful in its outworkings than any of these externals. In order to have that development, she must still meet and solve the problem of motherhood.

With the so-called "free" woman, who chooses a mate in defiance of convention, freedom is largely a question of character and audacity. If she does attain to an unrestricted choice of a mate, she is still in a position to be enslaved through her reproductive powers. Indeed, the pressure of law and custom upon the woman not legally married is likely to make her more of a slave than the woman fortunate enough to marry the man of her choice.

• • •

Voluntary motherhood implies a new morality—a vigorous, constructive, liberated morality. That morality will, first of all, prevent the submergence of womanhood into motherhood. It will set its face against the conversion of women into mechanical maternity and toward the creation of a new race.

Woman's role has been that of an incubator and little more. She has given birth to an incubated race. She has given to her children what little she was permitted to give, but of herself, of her personality, almost nothing. In the mass, she has brought forth quantity, not quality. The requirement of a male dominated civilization has been numbers. She has met that requirement.

It is the essential function of voluntary motherhood to choose its own mate, to determine the time of childbearing and to regulate strictly the number of offspring. Natural affection upon her part, instead of selection dictated by social or economic advantage, will give her a better fatherhood for her children. The exercise of her right to decide how many children she will have and when she shall have them will procure for her the time necessary to the development of other faculties than that of reproduction. She will give play to her tastes, her talents and her ambitions. She will become a full-rounded human being.

• • •

A free womanhood turns of its own desire to a free and happy motherhood, a motherhood which does not submerge the woman, but, which is enriched because she is unsubmerged. When we voice, then, the necessity of setting the feminine spirit utterly and absolutely free, thought turns naturally not to rights of the woman, nor indeed of the mother, but to the rights of the child—of all children in the world. For this is the miracle of free womanhood, that in its freedom it becomes the race mother and opens its heart in fruitful affection for humanity.

Questions

1. How does Sanger define "free womanhood"?

2. How does she believe access to birth control will change women's lives?

123. Mary Church Terrell, "What It Means to Be Colored in the Capital of the United States" (1906)

Source: The Independent, *January 24, 1907, pp. 181–86.*

The daughter of slaves, Mary Church Terrell was born in 1863, the year of the Emancipation Proclamation, and became one of the nation's most prominent black women. A high school teacher in Washington, D.C., who lost her job after marrying because of a local law barring married women from teaching, she went on to serve on the city's Board of Education and later became a founder of the NAACP. At the age of eighty-six, she led a protest campaign that in 1953 finally achieved the desegregation of the city's restaurants.

In 1906, Terrell delivered a speech to a women's club in Washington in which she outlined some of the numerous forms of prejudice and humiliation faced daily by African-Americans in the nation's capital. But despite the numerous reforms of the Progressive era, the bonds of segregation were drawn ever tighter during these years.

WASHINGTON, D.C., HAS been called "The Colored Man's Paradise." Whether this sobriquet was given to the national capital in bitter irony by a member of the handicapped race, as he reviewed some of his own persecutions and rebuffs, or whether it was given immediately after the war by an ex-slaveholder who for the first time in his life saw colored people walking about like free men, minus the overseer and his whip, history saith not. It is certain that it would be difficult to find a worse misnomer for Washington than "The Colored Man's Paradise" if so prosaic a consideration as veracity is to determine the appropriateness of a name.

For fifteen years I have resided in Washington, and while it was far from being a paradise for colored people when I first touched these shores it has been doing its level best ever since to make conditions for us intolerable. As a colored woman I might enter Washington any night, a stranger in a strange land, and walk miles without finding a place to lay my head. Unless I happened to know colored people who live here or ran across a chance acquaintance who could recommend a colored boarding-house to me, I should be obliged to spend the entire night wandering about. Indians, Chinamen, Filipinos, Japanese and representatives of any other dark race can find hotel accommodations, if they can pay for them. The colored man alone is thrust out of the hotels of the national capital like a leper.

As a colored woman I may walk from the Capitol to the White House, ravenously hungry and abundantly supplied with money with which to purchase a meal, without finding a single restaurant in which I would be permitted to take a morsel of food, if it was patronized by white people, unless I were willing to sit behind a screen. As a colored woman I cannot visit the tomb of the Father of this country, which owes its very existence to the love of freedom in the human heart and which stands for equal opportunity to all, without being forced to sit in the Jim Crow section of an electric car which starts from the very heart of the city—midway between the Capitol and the White House. If I refuse thus to be humiliated, I am cast into jail and forced to pay a fine for violating the Virginia laws....

As a colored woman I may enter more than one white church in Washington without receiving that welcome which as a human being I have the right to expect in the sanctuary of God....

Unless I am willing to engage in a few menial occupations, in which the pay for my services would be very poor, there is no way for me to earn an honest living, if I am not a trained nurse or a dressmaker or can secure a position as teacher in the public schools, which is exceedingly difficult to do. It matters not what my intellectual attainments may be or how great is the need of the services of a competent person, if I try to enter many of the numerous vocations in which my white sisters are allowed to engage, the door is shut in my face.

From one Washington theater I am excluded altogether. In the remainder certain seats are set aside for colored people, and it is almost impossible to secure others.... If I possess artistic talent, there is not a single art school of repute which will admit me....

With the exception of the Catholic University, there is not a single white college in the national capitol to which colored people are admitted.... A few years ago the Columbian Law School admitted colored students, but in deference to the Southern white students the authorities have decided to exclude them altogether.

Some time ago a young woman who had already attracted some attention in the literary world by her volume of short stories answered an advertisement which appeared in a Washington newspaper, which called for the services of a skilled stenographer and expert typewriter.... The applicants were requested to send specimens of their work and answer certain questions concerning their experience and their speed before they called in person. In reply to her application the young colored woman ... received a letter from the firm stating that her references and experience were the most satisfactory that had been sent and requesting her to call. When she presented herself there was some doubt in the mind of the man to whom she was directed concerning her racial pedigree, so he asked her point-blank whether she was colored or white. When she confessed the truth the merchant expressed ... deep regret that he could not avail himself of the services of so competent a person, but frankly admitted that employing a colored woman in his establishment in any except a menial position was simply out of the question....

Not only can colored women secure no employment in the Washington stores, department and otherwise, except as menials, and such positions, of course, are few, but even as customers they are not infrequently treated with discourtesy both by the clerks and the proprietor himself....

Although white and colored teachers are under the same Board of Education and the system for the children of both races is said to be uniform, prejudice against the colored teachers in the public schools is manifested in a variety of ways. From 1870 to 1900 there was a colored superintendent at the head of the colored schools. During all that time the directors of the cooking, sewing, physical culture, manual training, music and art departments were colored people. Six years ago a change was inaugurated. The colored superintendent was legislated out of office and the directorships, without a single exception, were taken from colored teachers and given to the whites.... Now, no matter how competent or superior the colored teachers in our public schools may be, they know that they can never rise to the height of a directorship, can never hope to be more than an assistant and receive the meager salary therefore, unless the present regime is radically changed....

And so I might go on citing instance after instance to show the variety of ways in which our people are sacrificed on the altar of prejudice in the Capital of the United States and how almost insurmountable are the obstacles which block his path to success.... It is impossible for any white person in the United States, no matter how sympathetic and broad, to realize what life would mean to him if his incentive to effort were suddenly snatched away. To the lack of incentive to effort, which is the awful shadow under which we live, may be traced the wreck and ruin of scores of colored youth. And surely nowhere in the world do oppression and persecution based solely on the color of the skin appear more hateful and hideous than in the capital of the United States, because the chasm between the principles upon which this Government was founded, in which it still professes to believe, and those which are daily practiced under the protection of the flag, yawn so wide and deep.

Questions

1. Why does Terrell believe that "persecution based solely on the color of the skin" is more "hideous" in Washington, D.C., than anywhere else in the world?

2. To what extent are the inequalities Terrell discusses the result of governmental action and to what extent the decisions of private individuals and businesses?

124. Woodrow Wilson and the New Freedom (1912)

Source: Woodrow Wilson, republished with permission of Princeton University Press, from The Papers of Woodrow Wilson, Vol. 25, August—November 1912, *ed. Arthur Link, 1978; permission conveyed through Copyright Clearance Center, Inc.*

The four-way presidential contest of 1912 between President William Howard Taft, former president Theodore Roosevelt, Woodrow Wilson, and Socialist Eugene V. Debs became a national debate on the relationship between political and economic freedom in the age of big business. Public attention focused particularly on the battle between Wilson, the Democratic candidate, and Roosevelt, running as the standard-bearer of the new Progressive Party, over the role of the federal government in securing economic freedom. Both believed increased government action was necessary to preserve individual freedom, but they differed about the dangers of increasing the government's power and the inevitability of economic concentration. Wilson called his approach the New Freedom. He envisioned the federal government strengthening antitrust laws, protecting the right of workers to unionize, and actively encouraging small businesses. Wilson feared big government as much as the power of the corporations. He warned that corporations were as likely to corrupt government as to be managed by it, a forecast that proved remarkably accurate.

YOU HAVE IN this new party [the Progressive Party] two things—a political party and a body of social reformers. Will the political party contained in it be serviceable to the social reformers? I do not think that I am mistaken in picking out as the political part of that platform the part which determines how the government is going to stand related to the central problems upon which its freedom depends. The freedom of the Government of the United States depends upon getting separated from, disentangled from, those interests which have enjoyed, chiefly enjoyed, the patronage of that government. Because the trouble with the tariff is not that it has been protective, for in recent years it has been much more than protective. It has been one of the most colossal systems of deliberate patronage that has ever been conceived. And the main trouble with it is that the protection stops where the patronage begins, and that if you could lop off the patronage, you would have taken away most of the objectionable features of the so-called protection.

This patronage, this special privilege, these favors doled out to some persons and not to all, have been the basis of the control which has been set up over the industries and over the enterprises of this country by great combinations. Because we forgot, in permitting a regime of free competition to last so long, that the competitors had ceased to be individuals or small groups of individuals, and it had come to be a competition between individuals or small groups on the one hand and enormous aggregations of individuals and capital on the other; and that, after that contrast in strength had been created in fact, competition, free competition, was out of the question, that it was then possible for the powerful to crush the weak.

That isn't competition; that is warfare. And because we did not check the free competition soon enough, because we did not check it at the point where pigmies entered the field against giants, we have created a condition of affairs in which the control of industry, and to a large extent the control of credit in this country, upon which industry feeds and in which all new enterprises must be rooted, is in the hands of a comparatively small and very compact body of men. These are the gentlemen who have in some instances, perhaps in more than have been exhibited by legal proof, engaged in what we are now expected to call "unreasonable combinations in restraint of trade." They have indulged themselves beyond reason in the exercise of that power which makes competition practically impossible.

Very well then, the test of our freedom for the next generation lies here. Are we going to take that power away from them, or are we going to leave it with them? You can take it away from them if you regulate competition and make it impossible for them to do some of the things which they have been doing. You leave it with them if you legitimatize and regulate monopoly. And what the platform of the new party proposes to do is exactly that.

It proposes to start where we are, and, without altering the established conditions of competition, which are conditions which affect it. We shall say what these giants shall do and to what the pigmies shall submit, and we shall do that not by law, for if you will read the plank in its candid statement—for it is perfectly candid—you will find that it rejects regulation by law and proposes a commission which shall have the discretion itself to undertake what the plank calls "constructive regulation." It shall make its rules as it goes along. As it handles these giants, so shall it shape its course. That, gentlemen, is nothing more than a legitimatized continuation of the present order of things, with the alliance between the great interests and the government open instead of covert.

• • •

Liberty has never come from the government. Liberty has always come from the subjects of the government. The history of liberty is a history of resistance. The history of liberty is a history of the limitation of governmental power, not the increase of it. Do these gentlemen dream that in the year 1912 we have discovered a unique exception to the movement of human history? Do they dream that the whole character of those who exercise power has changed, that it is no longer a temptation? Above all things else, do they dream that men are bred great enough now to be a Providence over the people over whom they preside?

• • •

[Theodore Roosevelt believes that] big business and the government could live on amicable terms with one another. . . .

Now, I say that in that way lies no thoroughfare for social reform, and that those who are hopeful of social reform through the instrumentality of that party ought to realize that in the very platform itself is supplied the demonstration that it is not a serviceable instrument. They do propose to serve civilization and humanity, but they can't serve civilization and humanity with that kind of government.

Questions

1. Why does Wilson say, "The history of liberty is a history of the limitation of governmental power"?

2. How does he propose to protect "our freedom for the next generation"?

---

125. John Mitchell, Industrial Liberty (1910)

Source: John Mitchell, "The Workingman's Conception of Industrial Liberty," **American Federationist,** *May 1910, pp. 405–10.*

During the Progressive era, the ideas of "industrial freedom" and "industrial democracy," which had entered the political vocabulary in the Gilded Age, moved to the center of political discussion. Lack of "industrial freedom" was widely believed to lie at the root of the widely discussed "labor problem." Many Progressives believed that the key to increasing industrial freedom lay in empowering workers to participate in economic decision making via strong unions. Workers deserved a voice not only in establishing wages and working conditions but in such managerial decisions as the relocation of factories, layoffs, and the distribution of profits.

In the document below, John Mitchell, head of the United Mine Workers of America union, pointedly contrasts workers' understanding of "industrial liberty" with prevailing laissez-faire definitions of freedom inherited from the Gilded Age and enforced by the courts during the Progressive era. Workers, he observes, "feel that they are being guaranteed the liberties they do not want and denied the liberty that is of real value to them."

WHILE THE DECLARATION of Independence established civil and political liberty, it did not, as you all know, establish industrial liberty. For nearly one hundred years following the Declaration of Independence, chattel slavery was a recognized and legal institution in our civilization. And real industrial liberty was not even established with the abolition of chattel slavery; because liberty means more than the right to choose the field of one's employment. He is not a free man whose family must buy food today with the money that is earned tomorrow. He is not really free who is forced to work unduly long hours and for wages so low that he can not provide the necessities of life for himself and his family; who must live in a crowded tenement and see his children go to work in the mills, the mines, and the factories before their bodies are developed and their minds trained. To have freedom a man must be free from the harrowing fear of hunger and want; he must be in such a position that by the exercise of reasonable frugality he can provide his family with all of the necessities and the reasonable comforts of life. He must be able to educate his children and to provide against sickness, accident, and old age. . . .

A number of years ago the legislatures of several coal producing States enacted laws requiring employers to pay the wages of their workmen in lawful money of the United States and to cease the practice of paying wages in merchandise. From time immemorial it had been the custom of coal companies to conduct general supply stores, and the workingmen were required, as a condition of employment, to accept products in lieu of money in return for services rendered. This system was a great hardship to the workmen. . . . The question of the constitutionality of this legislation was carried into the courts and by the highest tribunal it was declared to be an invasion of the workman's liberty to deny him the right to accept merchandise in lieu of money as payment of his wages. . . . [This is] typical of hundreds of instances in which laws that have been enacted for the protection of the workingmen have been declared by the courts to be unconstitutional, on the grounds that they invaded the liberty of the working people. To understand the attitude of the workingmen in matters of this kind, it is necessary to bear in mind that all this legislation was championed by them and was enacted at their solicitation, and when courts declare such laws unconstitutional—basing their decisions on the hypothesis that the liberty of the workingmen is invaded—is it not natural that the workingmen should feel that they are being guaranteed the liberties they do not want and denied the liberty that is of real value to them? May they not exclaim, with Madame Roland [of the French Revolution], "O Liberty! Liberty! How many crimes are committed in thy name!" ...

The labor movement is primarily and fundamentally a moral movement. While attention is attracted to it by its strikes and its struggles yet the battles it fights in defense of the poor and the helpless are but phases of the great movement which is making for the physical, the mental, and the moral uplift of the people. Behind and above the demand for higher wages and shorter hours stands the greater movement for better men, for happier women, and for joyous children, for homes, for books, for pictures and music, for the things that make for culture and refinement. The labor movement stands for the essential principles of religion and morality; for temperance; for decency; and for dignity.

Questions

1. Why does Mitchell say that the labor movement is essentially a "moral movement"?

2. What would be necessary to establish "real industrial liberty" as understood by Mitchell?

CHAPTER 19

Safe for Democracy: The United States and World War I, 1916–1920

126. Woodrow Wilson, A World "Safe for Democracy" (1917)

Source: 65th Congress, 1st Session, Senate Document No. 5.

More than any other individual in the early twentieth century, President Woodrow Wilson articulated a new vision of America's relationship to the rest of the world. His foreign policy, called by historians "liberal internationalism," rested on the conviction that economic and political progress went hand in hand and that it was the job of the United States to promote both free markets and political democracy. He came to see World War I as a great opportunity to promote these goals.

Although Wilson declared American neutrality when the war began in Europe in 1914 and ran for reelection in 1916 pledging to keep the United States out of the war, Germany's resumption of unrestricted submarine warfare early in 1917, including the targeting of American ships transporting goods to England, convinced Wilson that the United States must enter the war. On April 2, 1917, he called on Congress for a declaration of war against Germany. His speech promised that victory would lead to a new world order based on "peace and justice" among the "free and self-governing peoples of the world." In his most celebrated sentence, he declared, "The world must-be made safe for democracy."

───────────

OUR OBJECT ... is to vindicate the principles of peace and justice in the life of the world as against selfish and autocratic power and to set up among the really free and self-governed peoples of the world such a concert of purpose and of action as will henceforth ensure the observance of those principles. Neutrality is no longer feasible or desirable where the peace of the world is involved and the freedom of its peoples, and the menace to that peace and freedom lies in the existence of autocratic governments backed by organized force which is controlled wholly by their will, not by the will of their people. We have seen the last of neutrality in such circumstances. We are at the beginning of an age in which it will be insisted that the same standards of conduct and of responsibility for wrong done shall be observed among nations and their governments that are observed among the individual citizens of civilized states.

We have no quarrel with the German people. We have no feeling toward them but one of sympathy and friendship. It was not upon their impulse that their government acted in entering this war. It was not with their previous knowledge or approval. It was a war determined upon as wars used to be determined upon in the old, unhappy days when peoples were nowhere consulted by their rulers and wars were provoked and waged in the interest of dynasties or of little groups of ambitious men who were accustomed to use their fellow men as pawns and tools.

Self-governed nations do not fill their neighbor states with spies or set the course of intrigue to bring about some critical posture of affairs which will give them an opportunity to strike and make conquest. Such designs can be successfully worked out only under cover and where no one has the right to ask questions. Cunningly contrived plans of deception or aggression, carried, it may be, from generation to generation, can be worked out and kept from the light only within the privacy of courts or behind the carefully guarded confidences of a

narrow and privileged class. They are happily impossible where public opinion commands and insists upon full information concerning all the nation's affairs.

A steadfast concert for peace can never be maintained except by a
partnership of democratic nations. No autocratic government could
be trusted to keep faith within it or observe its covenants. It must be
a league of honor, a partnership of opinion.... Only free peoples can
hold their purpose and their honor steady to a common end and prefer the interests of mankind to any narrow interest of their own....

The world must be made safe for democracy. Its peace must be
planted upon the tested foundations of political liberty. We have no
selfish ends to serve. We desire no conquest, no dominion. We seek no
indemnities for ourselves, no material compensation for the sacrifices
we shall freely make. We are but one of the champions of the rights
of mankind. We shall be satisfied when those rights have been made
as secure as the faith and the freedom of nations can make them.

Questions

1. What changes in the relationship between the United States and the
rest of the world does Wilson foresee emerging from World War I?

2. Why does Wilson believe that autocratic governments, not democratic
ones, are the cause of wars?

---

127. Randolph Bourne, "Trans-National America" (1916)

Source: **The Atlantic** *(July 1916), pp. 86–97.*

American entry into World War I inspired a massive campaign demanding that immigrants from Europe prove their loyalty to the United
States, not only by enlisting in the army but also by sloughing off their

Old World cultures in favor of Americanization into the Anglo-Saxon mainstream. Probably the most penetrating rejection of the Americanization model issued from the pen of the young social critic Randolph Bourne. In an article in *The Atlantic*, Bourne envisioned a democratic, cosmopolitan society in which immigrants and natives alike retained their group identities while at the same time embracing a new "trans-national" culture. Bourne died in the influenza epidemic of 1918. At the time he had been working on an essay about the consequences of the war for American life.

———

NO REVERBERATORY EFFECT of the great war has caused American public opinion more solicitude than the failure of the "melting-pot." The discovery of diverse nationalistic feelings among our great alien population has come to most people as an intense shock. It has brought out the unpleasant inconsistencies of our traditional beliefs. We have had to watch hard-hearted old Brahmins virtuously indignant at the spectacle of the immigrant refusing to be melted, while they jeer at patriots like Mary Antin who write about "our forefathers." We have had to listen to publicists who express themselves as stunned by the evidence of vigorous nationalistic and cultural movements in this country among Germans, Scandinavians, Bohemians, and Poles, while in the same breath they insist that the mien shall be forcibly assimilated to that Anglo-Saxon tradition which they unquestioningly label "American."

As the unpleasant truth has come upon us that assimilation in this country was proceeding on lines very different from those we had marked out for it, we found ourselves inclined to blame those who were thwarting our prophecies. The truth became culpable. We blamed the war, we blamed the Germans. And then we discovered with a moral shock that these movements had been making great headway before the war even began. We found that the tendency, reprehensible and paradoxical as it might be, has been for the national clusters of immigrants, as they became more and more firmly established and more and more prosperous, to cultivate more and more assiduously the literatures and cultural traditions of their homelands. Assimilation, in other words, instead of washing out the memories of Europe, made them more and more intensely real. Just as these clusters became more and more objectively American, did they become more and more German or Scandinavian or Bohemian or Polish.

To face the fact that our aliens are already strong enough to take a share in the direction of their own destiny, and that the strong cultural movements represented by the foreign press, schools, and colonies are a challenge to our facile attempts, is not, however, to admit the failure of Americanization. It is not to fear the failure of democracy. It is rather to urge us to an investigation of what Americanism may rightly mean. It is to ask ourselves whether our ideal has been broad or narrow—whether perhaps the time has not come to assert a higher ideal than the "melting-pot." Surely we cannot be certain of our spiritual democracy when, claiming to melt the nations within us to a comprehension of our free and democratic institutions, we fly into panic at the first sign of their own will and tendency. We act as if we wanted Americanization to take place only on our own terms, and not by the consent of the governed. All our elaborate machinery of settlement and school and union, of social and political naturalization, however, will move with friction just in so far as it neglects to take into account this strong and virile insistence that America shall be what the immigrant will have a hand in making it, and not what a ruling class, descendant of those British stocks which were the first permanent immigrants, decide that America shall be made. This is the condition which confronts us, and which demands a clear and general readjustment of our attitude and our ideal....

We are all foreign-born or the descendants of foreign-born, and if distinctions are to be made between us, they should rightly be on some other ground than indigenousness. The early colonists came over with motives no less colonial than the later. They did not come to be assimilated in an American melting pot. They did not come to adopt the culture of the American Indian. They had not the smallest intention of "giving themselves without reservation" to the new country. They came to get freedom to live as they wanted to. They came to escape from the stifling air and chaos of the old world; they came to make their fortune in a new land. They invented no new social framework. Rather they brought over bodily the old ways to which they had been accustomed. Tightly concentrated on a hostile frontier, they were conservative beyond belief. Their pioneer daring was reserved for the objective conquest of material resources. In their folkways, in their social and political institutions, they were, like every colonial people, slavishly imitative of the mother country. So that, in spite of the "Revolution," our whole legal and political system remained more English than the English, petrified and unchanging, while in England law developed to meet the needs of the changing times....

The non-English American can scarcely be blamed if he sometimes thinks of the Anglo-Saxon predominance in America as little more than a predominance of priority. The Anglo-Saxon was merely the first immigrant.... Colonials from the other nations have come and settled down beside him. They found no definite native culture... and consequently they looked back to their mother-country, as the earlier Anglo-Saxon immigrant was looking back to his....

There is no distinctively American culture. It is apparently our lot rather to be a federation of cultures. This we have been for half a century, and the war has made it ever more evident that this is what we are destined to remain.... What we have achieved has been rather a cosmopolitan federation of national colonies, of foreign cultures, from whom the sting of devastating competition has been removed. America is already the world-federation in miniature, the continent where for the first time in history has been achieved that miracle of hope, the peaceful living side by side, with character substantially preserved, of the most heterogeneous peoples under the sun.... America is coming to be, not a nationality but a transnationality, a weaving back and forth, with the other lands, of many threads of all sizes and colors. Any movement which attempts to thwart this weaving, or to dye the fabric any one color, or disentangle the threads of the strands, is false to this cosmopolitan vision.

Questions

1. Why does Bourne believe that the "melting-pot" had failed?

2. What does he mean by describing America as a "trans-nationality"?

128. A Critique of the Versailles Peace Conference (1919)

Source: Mao Zedong, republished with permission of Taylor & Francis Group LLC Books, from "So Much for National Self-Determination!" and "Poor Wilson" in Mao's Road to Power: Revolutionary Writings 1912–1949, Mao Zedong, ed. by Stuart R. Schram, 1992; permission conveyed through Copyright Clearance Center, Inc.

In early 1918, nine months after the United States entered World War I, President Wilson issued the Fourteen Points, a blueprint for the postwar world. Among the key principles were national self-determination, freedom of the seas, worldwide free trade, redrawing of the map of the colonial world with colonized people being given "equal weight" in deciding their own futures, and the establishment of a League of Nations to preserve peace. After the war ended with the victory of the United States and its allies, Wilson traveled to Versailles, France, to take part in drafting the peace treaty.

Unfortunately, the final result violated many of the principles Wilson had enunciated. He was outmaneuvered by his Allied counterparts—David Lloyd George of England, Georges Clemenceau of France, Vittorio Orlando of Italy, and Makino Nobuaki of Japan—all of whom coveted former German colonies and spheres of influence. In the end, the principle of self-determination was applied to eastern Europe, where new nations were carved out of the remnants of the Austro-Hungarian empire, but not Asia or Africa. Asian and African nationalists, who had taken Wilson's rhetoric seriously, were bitterly disappointed. Mao Zedong—then a young student activist and later the leader of the revolution that would bring communists to power in China—penned two short pieces that reflected the widespread disappointment in the Treaty of Versailles.

So Much for National Self-Determination!

Poland and Czechoslovakia, in reestablishing their national existence, have presided over the death of Germany. The Allies did their utmost to help them in this, in the name of "national self-determination." The Arabs benefit from the splitting up of Turkey, and therefore were allowed to become semi-independent. The desire of the Jews to restore their nation in Palestine will not succeed because it is of no great concern to the Allied powers.... Korea bewails the loss of its independence; so many of its people have died, and so much of its land has been devastated, but it was simply ignored by the Peace Conference. So much for national self-determination! I think it is really shameless!

Poor Wilson

Wilson in Paris was like an ant on a hot skillet. He didn't know what to do. He was surrounded by thieves like Clemenceau, Lloyd George, Makino, and Orlando. He heard nothing except accounts of receiving certain amounts of territory and of reparations worth so much in gold. He did nothing except to attend various kinds of meetings where he could not speak his mind. One day a ... telegram read, "President Wilson has finally agreed with Clemenceau's view that Germany not be admitted to the League of Nations." When I saw the words "finally agreed," I felt very sorry for him for a long time. Poor Wilson!

Questions

1. According to Mao, in what parts of the world was the principle of national self-determination adhered to, and where was it violated?

2. Why does Mao feel sorry for President Wilson?

129. Carrie Chapman Catt, Address to Congress on Woman's Suffrage (1917)

Source: Carrie Chapman Catt, An Address to the Congress of the United States (New York, 1917).

Carrie Chapman Catt, a longtime campaigner for votes for women, served as president of the National American Women Suffrage Association from 1900 to 1904 and again from 1915 to 1920. Many women activists had been associated with the pacifist movement and opposed American entry into World War I. In 1917, Catt shocked them by announcing the association's support for the Wilson administration and American participation in World War I. Catt reasoned that by taking part in the war effort, women would finally win the right to vote.

In the winter of 1917, Catt addressed Congress urging support for a constitutional amendment to enfranchise women. To bolster her argument, she invoked the nation's founding principles, and Wilson's claim that the United States was the leader in the worldwide struggle for democracy. Catt's strategy bore fruit when Congress in 1918 approved the Nineteenth Amendment, which became part of the Constitution two years later.

———

WOMAN SUFFRAGE IS INEVITABLE. . . .

First, the history of our country. Ours is a nation born of revolution, of rebellion against a system of government so securely entrenched in the customs and traditions of human society that in 1776 it seemed impregnable. From the beginning of things, nations had been ruled by kings and for kings, while the people served and paid the cost. The American Revolutionists boldly proclaimed the heresies: "Taxation without representation is tyranny." "Governments derive their just powers from the consent of the governed." The colonists won, and the nation which was established as a result of their victory has held unfailingly that these two fundamental principles of democratic government are not only the spiritual source of our national existence but have been our chief historic pride and at all times the sheet anchor of our liberties.

Eighty years after the Revolution, Abraham Lincoln welded those two maxims into a new one: "Ours is a government of the people, by the people, and for the people." Fifty years more passed and the president of the United States, Woodrow Wilson, in a mighty crisis of the nation, proclaimed to the world: "We are fighting for the things which we have always carried nearest to our hearts: for democracy, for the right of those who submit to authority to have a voice in their own government."

All the way between these immortal aphorisms political leaders have declared unabated faith in their truth. Not one American has arisen to question their logic in the 141 years of our national existence. However stupidly our country may have evaded the logical application at times, it has never swerved from its devotion to the theory of democracy as expressed by those two axioms....

With such a history behind it, how can our nation escape the logic it has never failed to follow, when its last unenfranchised class calls for the vote? Behold our Uncle Sam floating the banner with one hand, "Taxation without representation is tyranny," and with the other seizing the billions of dollars paid in taxes by women to whom he refuses "representation." Behold him again, welcoming the boys of twenty-one and the newly made immigrant citizen to "a voice in their own government" while he denies that fundamental right of democracy to thousands of women public school teachers from whom many of these men learn all they know of citizenship and patriotism, to women college presidents, to women who preach in our pulpits, interpret law in our courts, preside over our hospitals, write books and magazines, and serve in every uplifting moral and social enterprise. Is there a single man who can justify such inequality of treatment, such outrageous discrimination? Not one....

Second, the suffrage for women already established in the United States makes women suffrage for the nation inevitable. When Elihu

Root, as president of the American Society of International Law, at the eleventh annual meeting in Washington, April 26, 1917, said, "The world cannot be half democratic and half autocratic. It must be all democratic or all Prussian. There can be no compromise," he voiced a general truth. Precisely the same intuition has already taught the blindest and most hostile foe of woman suffrage that our nation cannot long continue a condition under which government in half its territory rests upon the consent of half of the people and in the other half upon the consent of all the people; a condition which grants representation to the taxed in half of its territory and denies it in the other half; a condition which permits women in some states to share in the election of the president, senators, and representatives and denies them that privilege in others. It is too obvious to require demonstration that woman suffrage, now covering half our territory, will eventually be ordained in all the nation. No one will deny it. The only question left is when and how will it be completely established.

Third, the leadership of the United States in world democracy compels the enfranchisement of its own women. The maxims of the Declaration were once called "fundamental principles of government." They are now called "American principles" or even "Americanisms." They have become the slogans of every movement toward political liberty the world around, of every effort to widen the suffrage for men or women in any land. Not a people, race, or class striving for freedom is there anywhere in the world that has not made our axioms the chief weapon of the struggle. More, all men and women the world around, with farsighted vision into the verities of things, know that the world tragedy of our day is not now being waged over the assassination of an archduke, nor commercial competition, nor national ambitions, nor the freedom of the seas. It is a death grapple between the forces which deny and those which uphold the truths of the Declaration of Independence....

Do you realize that in no other country in the world with democratic tendencies is suffrage so completely denied as in a considerable number of our own states? There are thirteen black states where no suffrage for women exists, and fourteen others where suffrage for women is more limited than in many foreign countries.

Do you realize that when you ask women to take their cause to state referendum you compel them to do this: that you drive women of education, refinement, achievement, to beg men who cannot read for their political freedom?

Do you realize that such anomalies as a college president asking her janitor to give her a vote are overstraining the patience and driving women to desperation?

Do you realize that women in increasing numbers indignantly resent the long delay in their enfranchisement?

Your party platforms have pledged women suffrage. Then why not be honest, frank friends of our cause, adopt it in reality as your own, make it a party program, and "fight with us"? As a party measure—a measure of all parties—why not put the amendment through Congress and the legislatures? We shall all be better friends, we shall have a happier nation, we women will be free to support loyally the party of our choice, and we shall be far prouder of our history.

"There is one thing mightier than kings and armies"—aye, than Congresses and political parties—"the power of an idea when its time has come to move." The time for woman suffrage has come. The woman's hour has struck. If parties prefer to postpone action longer and thus do battle with this idea, they challenge the inevitable. The idea will not perish; the party which opposes it may. Every delay, every trick, every political dishonesty from now on will antagonize the women of the land more and more, and when the party or parties which have so delayed women suffrage finally let it come, their sincerity will be doubted and their appeal to the new voters will be met with suspicion. This is the psychology of the situation. Can you afford the risk? Think it over.

We know you will meet opposition. There are a few "women haters" left, a few "old males of the tribe," ... who know better than women what is good for them. There are women, too, with "slave souls" and "clinging vines" for backbones. There are female dolls and male dandies. But the world does not wait for such as these, nor does liberty pause to heed the plaint of men and women with a grouch. She does not wait for those who have a special interest to serve, nor a selfish reason for depriving other people of freedom. Holding her torch aloft, liberty is pointing the way onward and upward and saying to America, "Come."

To you and the supporters of our cause in Senate and House, and the number is large, the suffragists of the nation express their grateful thanks. This address is not meant for you. We are more truly appreciative of all you have done than any words can express. We ask you to make a last, hard fight for the amendment during the present session. Since last we asked a vote on this amendment, your position has been fortified by the addition to suffrage territory of Great Britain, Canada, and New York.

Some of you have been too indifferent to give more than casual attention to this question. It is worthy of your immediate consideration. A question big enough to engage the attention of our allies in wartime is too big a question for you to neglect.

Some of you have grown old in party service. Are you willing that those who take your places by and by shall blame you for having failed to keep pace with the world and thus having lost for them a party advantage? Is there any real gain for you, for your party, for your nation by delay? Do you want to drive the progressive men and women out of your party?

Some of you hold to the doctrine of states' rights as applying to woman suffrage. Adherence to that theory will keep the United States far behind all other democratic nations upon this question. A theory which prevents a nation from keeping up with the trend of world progress cannot be justified.

Gentlemen, we hereby petition you, our only designated representatives, to redress our grievances by the immediate passage of the Federal Suffrage Amendment and to use your influence to secure its ratification in your own state, in order that the women of our nation may be endowed with political freedom before the next presidential election, and that our nation may resume its world leadership in democracy.

Woman suffrage is coming—you know it. Will you, Honorable Senators and Members of the House of Representatives, help or hinder it?

Questions

1. Why does Catt claim that denying women the right to vote violates the principle of democracy?

2. How does Catt characterize women who do not support the campaign for suffrage?

---

130. Eugene V. Debs, Speech to the Jury (1918)

Source: **The Debs White Book** *(Girard, Kans. 1920), pp. 37–57.*

Despite President Wilson's claim that the United States entered World War I in 1917 to "make the world safe for democracy," American intervention was followed at home by the most massive suppression of freedom of expression in the country's history. The Espionage Act of 1917 prohibited not only spying and interfering with the draft but also "false statements" that might impede military success. In 1918, the Sedition Act made it a crime to make spoken or printed statements intended to cast "contempt, scorn, or disrepute" on the "form of government" or that advocated interference with the war effort.

The government charged more than 2,000 individuals with violating these laws. The most prominent victim was Eugene V. Debs, the leader of the Socialist Party, convicted in 1918 under the Espionage Act for delivering an antiwar speech. Before his sentencing, Debs gave the court a lesson in the history of American freedom, tracing the tradition of dissent from Tom Paine to the abolitionists and pointing out that the nation had never engaged in a war without internal opposition. Sentenced to ten years in prison, Debs was released in 1921 by Woodrow Wilson's successor, Warren G. Harding.

———

MAY IT PLEASE the court, and gentlemen of the jury:

For the first time in my life I appear before a jury in a court of law to answer to an indictment for crime. I am not a lawyer. I know little about court procedure, about the rules of evidence or legal practice. I know only that you gentlemen are to hear the evidence brought against me, that the court is to instruct you in the law, and that you are then to determine by your verdict whether I shall be branded with criminal guilt and be consigned, perhaps to the end of my life, in a felon's cell.

• • •

I wish to admit the truth of all that has been testified to in this proceeding. I have no disposition to deny anything that is true. I would not, if I could, escape the results of an adverse verdict. I would not retract a word that I have uttered that I believe to be true to save myself from going to the penitentiary for the rest of my days.

Gentlemen, you have heard the report of my speech at Canton on June 16, and I submit that there is not a word in that speech to warrant the charges set out in the indictment. I admit having delivered the speech. I admit the accuracy of the speech in all of its main features as reported in this proceeding.

In what I had to say there my purpose was to have the people understand something about the social system in which we live and to prepare them to change this system by perfectly peaceable and orderly means into what I, as a Socialist, conceive to be a real democracy.

From what you heard in the address of the counsel for the prosecution, you might naturally infer that I am an advocate of force and violence. It is not true. I have never advocated violence in any form.

I have always believed in education, in intelligence, in enlighten-ment; and I have always made my appeal to the reason and to the conscience of the people.

I admit being opposed to the present social system. I am doing what little I can, and have been for many years, to bring about a change that shall do away with the rule of the great body of the peo-ple by a relatively small class and establish in this country an indus-trial and social democracy.

• • •

Washington, Jefferson, Franklin, Paine and their compeers were the rebels of their day. When they began to chafe under the rule of a foreign king and to sow the seed of resistance among the colonists they were opposed by the people and denounced by the press.... But they had the moral courage to be true to their convictions, to stand erect and defy all the forces of reaction and detraction; and that is why their names shine in history, and why the great respectable majority of their day sleep in forgotten graves.

• • •

William Lloyd Garrison, Wendell Phillips, Elizabeth Cady Stan-ton, Susan B. Anthony, Gerrit Smith, Thaddeus Stevens and other leaders of the abolition movement who were regarded as public ene-mies and treated accordingly, were true to their faith and stood their ground. They are all in history. You are now teaching your children to revere their memories, while all of their detractors are in oblivion.

• • •

From the beginning of the war to this day I have never by word or act been guilty of the charges embraced in this indictment. If I have criticized, if I have condemned, it is because I believed it to be my duty, and that it was my right to do so under the laws of the land. I have had ample precedents for my attitude. This country has been engaged in a number of wars and every one of them has been condemned by some of the people, among them some of the most eminent men of their time. The war of the American Revolution was violently opposed. The Tory press representing the "upper classes" denounced its leaders as criminals and outlaws.

The war of 1812 was opposed and condemned by some of the most influential citizens; the Mexican war was vehemently opposed and bitterly denounced, even after the war had been declared and was in progress, by Abraham Lincoln, Charles Sumner, Daniel Webster, Henry Clay and many other well-known and influential citizens. These men denounced the President, they condemned his administration while the war was being waged, and they charged in substance that the war was a crime against humanity. They were not indicted; they were not charged with treason nor tried for crime. They are honored today by all of their countrymen.

The Civil War between the states met with violent resistance and passionate condemnation. In the year 1864 the Democratic Party met in national convention at Chicago and passed a resolution condemning the war as a failure. What would you say if the Socialist Party were to meet in convention today and condemn the present war as a failure? You charge us with being disloyalists and traitors. Were the Democrats of 1864 disloyalists and traitors because they condemned the war as a failure?

And if so, why were they not indicted and prosecuted accordingly? I believe in the Constitution. Isn't it strange that we Socialists stand almost alone today in upholding and defending the Constitution of the United States? The revolutionary fathers who had been oppressed under king rule understood that free speech, a free press and the right of free assemblage by the people were fundamental principles in democratic government.

● ● ●

That is the right I exercised at Canton on the sixteenth day of last June; and for the exercise of that right, I now have to answer to this indictment. I believe in the right of free speech, in war as well as in peace. I would not, under any circumstances suppress free speech. It is far more dangerous to attempt to gag the people than to allow them to speak freely what is in their hearts.

I have told you that I am no lawyer, but it seems to me that I know enough to know that if Congress enacts any law that conflicts with this provision in the Constitution, that law is void. If the Espionage

Law finally stands, then the Constitution of the United States is dead. If that law is not the negation of every fundamental principle established by the Constitution, then certainly I am unable to read or to understand the English language.

• • •

I am not on trial here. There is an infinitely greater issue that is being tried today in this court, though you may not be conscious of it. American institutions are on trial here before a court of American citizens. The future will render the final verdict.

Questions

1. Why does Debs insist that the Espionage Act represents "the negation of every fundamental principle established by the Constitution"?

2. Why does Debs recount the history of political dissent and opposition to previous American wars?

131. Rubie Bond, "The Great Migration" (1917)

Source: Rubie Bond, "The Great Migration" (1917). Reprinted by permission of the Beloit College Archives.

World War I redrew the racial map of the United States. With immigration from Europe suspended, northern employers for the first time offered industrial jobs to southern blacks. The result was the Great Migration, in which tens of thousands of African-Americans left the rural South in the hope of finding greater opportunities in cities like New York and Chicago. In 1917, when she was ten years old, Rubie Bond moved with her parents from Mississippi to Beloit, Wisconsin, where her father found work in a factory. Over half a century later, in 1976, Bond related her experiences as part of an oral history project documenting the migration of African-Americans to Beloit throughout the twentieth century.

INTERVIEW WITH RUBIE BOND

I'm wondering why your family decided to leave Mississippi. How was that decision made and why was it made?

Well, the North offered better opportunities for blacks. John McCord, who was a distant cousin, came and explained about conditions, here and so my father and mother decided to come....

I've heard that recruiters were often in danger in Mississippi if they came down to get workers for northern companies. Do you recall him ever expressing any fear about this job that he was doing?

Yes. I know that many of the blacks would leave the farms at night and walk for miles. Many of them caught the train to come North, come to Beloit at a little place called Ecru, Mississippi. Usually they would leave with just the clothes on their backs. Maybe the day before they would be in the field working and the plantation owner wouldn't even know that they planned to go and the next day he would go and the little shanty would be empty. These people would have taken off and come up here.

Was there a fear that the plantation owner wouldn't let them go or that they couldn't leave?

That's very true. They wouldn't. Plantation owners had much to lose. These people were illiterate and they had to depend on the plantation owner. He would give them so much flour for use during the year, cornmeal or sugar or that sort of thing and then at the end of the year you would go to settle up with him and you would always be deeply in debt to him. That was his way of keeping people. You never got out of debt with him. And that's the way it was with my dad and this fellow, Mr. Stiggel.

So, many of the people who left were legally in debt and could have been forced to stay in Mississippi? Did you know of any instances where that happened?

No, because they would leave at night. They would leave when the plantation owner wasn't around. Of course, they needed these workers to work the cotton fields, that sort of thing. But many of them left under those circumstances. . . .

Now, as a young girl, did you agree with this decision to move North? Did you think it was a good idea?

Yes. I think I did. Because even as a child I think I was pretty sensitive to a lot of the inequalities that existed between blacks and whites, and I know that after we came here my mother and dad used to tell me that if I went back to Mississippi, they would hang me to the first tree. . . .

What role did the church play in your early life in Mississippi?

Well, I think the church played a very important part in the life of all blacks in Mississippi because it was a religious center as well as social. That was one place that they could go and meet and discuss their problems. Relax. So just the—their big picnics and big church meetings they used to have.

I might tell about the type of house we lived in. We lived in a little three-room house. There were two big rooms with a fireplace in between . . . the fireplace on each side of the partition, and one was where we lived and the other my mother kept for company, and I remember the embroidered bedspreads and pillow shams and that sort of thing that she had in there. And the third little room was the kitchen, where we had the old wood stove, and my sister and I would gather up the wood for cooking. Whenever they would have one of these big church meetings, usually, some minister or some delegate or somebody from the church would come to our house and they would have this one room that we were permitted to peep in once a week. But the church did, it served as a gathering place for people and they had many union meetings for example between mostly Methodist and Baptist faiths. . . .

Given the opportunities that were available in the North, why did anyone decide to stay in Mississippi?

Well, I think that it was a lack of knowledge of about what the North had to offer until these agents came there to get them to come up here to work.

You were leaving at least a few of your relatives and friends behind. How did you feel about those people that you left behind and weren't ever going to see again?

Well, I think it comes back to a matter of trying to exist, really, and trying to improve your own lot.

Were there any differences that you noticed between those people who left and those people who stayed?

No. Not really.

Were the people who left more ambitious or anything like that?

No. I think not, because many of those who stayed had either begun to acquire a small plot of land or something like that and there were black tradesmen, like I say, the carpenters and the masons and that sort of thing, who had been able to improve their own lot in Mississippi. And many of those stayed and some came North. Most of these people, I think, that came North at first were people who hadn't been able to acquire anything.

Questions

1. What are the most important reasons for the family's decisions to move to Beloit?

2. What do these recollections tell us about limitations on the freedom blacks enjoyed in the early twentieth-century South?

132. Marcus Garvey on Africa for the Africans (1921)

Source: "Speech Delivered at Liberty Hall, New York City, August 21, 1921,"
in Amy Jacques-Garvey, ed., Philosophy and Opinions of Marcus Garvey
(New York, 1923–25), *vol. 2, pp. 93–97.*

In the new, densely populated black ghettos created in the wake of the Great Migration, disappointment with conditions in the North inspired widespread support for a separatist movement launched by Marcus Garvey, a recent immigrant from Jamaica. Throughout the world, Garvey pointed out, the war had inspired movements for national self-determination—in Ireland, eastern Europe, and Europe's Asian and African colonies. Blacks, he insisted, should enjoy the same internationally recognized identity enjoyed by other peoples. The government soon deported Garvey after convicting him of mail fraud. But the massive following his movement achieved testified to the sense of both racial pride and betrayal kindled in black communities during and after the war.

⸻

FOUR YEARS AGO, realizing the oppression and the hardships from which we suffered, we organized ourselves into an organization for the purpose of bettering our condition, and founding a government of our own. The four years of organization have brought good results, in that from an obscure, despised race we have grown into a mighty power, a mighty force whose influence is being felt throughout the length and breadth of the world. The Universal Negro Improvement Association existed but in name four years ago, today it is known as the greatest moving force among Negroes. We have accomplished this through unity of effort and unity of purpose, it is a fair demonstration of what we will be able to accomplish in the very near future, when the millions who are outside the pale of the Universal Negro Improvement Association will have linked themselves up with us.

By our success of the last four years we will be able to estimate the grander success of a free and redeemed Africa. In climbing the heights to where we are today, we have had to surmount difficulties, we have had to climb over obstacles, but the obstacles were stepping stones to the future greatness of this Cause we represent. Day by day we are writing a new history, recording new deeds of valor performed by this race of ours. It is true that the world has not yet valued us at our true worth but we are climbing up so fast and with such force that every day the world is changing its attitude towards us. Wheresoever you turn your eyes today you will find the moving influence of the Universal Negro Improvement Association among Negroes from all corners of the globe. We hear among Negroes the cry of "Africa for the Africans." This cry has become a positive, determined one. It is a cry that is raised simultaneously the world over because of the universal oppression that affects the Negro. You who are congregated here tonight as Delegates representing the hundreds of branches of the Universal Negro Improvement Association in different parts of the world will realize that we in New York are positive in this great desire of a free and redeemed Africa. We have established this Liberty Hall as the centre from which we send out the sparks of liberty to the four corners of the globe, and if you have caught the spark in your section, we want you to keep it a-burning for the great Cause we represent.

There is a mad rush among races everywhere towards national independence. Everywhere we hear the cry of liberty, of freedom, and a demand for democracy. In our corner of the world we are raising the cry for liberty, freedom and democracy. Men who have raised the cry for freedom and liberty in ages past have always made up their minds to die for the realization of the dream. We who are assembled in this Convention as Delegates representing the Negroes of the world give out the same spirit that the fathers of liberty in this country gave out over one hundred years ago. We give out a spirit that knows no compromise, a spirit that refuses to turn back, a spirit that says "Liberty or Death", and in prosecution of this great ideal—the ideal of a free and redeemed Africa, men may scorn, men may spurn us, and may say that we are on the wrong side of life, but let me tell you that way in which you are travelling is just the way all peoples who are free have travelled in the past. If you want liberty you yourselves must strike the blow. If you must be free you must become so through your own effort, through your own initiative. Those who have discouraged you in the past are those who have enslaved you for centuries and it is not expected that they will admit that you have a right to strike out at this late hour for freedom, liberty and democracy.

• • •

It falls to our lot to tear off the shackles that bind Mother Africa. Can you do it? You did it in the Revolutionary War. You did it in the Civil War; You did it at the Battles of the Marne and Verdun; You did it in Mesopotamia. You can do it marching up the battle heights of Africa. Let the world know that 400,000,000 Negroes are prepared to die or live as free men. Despise us as much as you care. Ignore us as much as you care. We are coming 400,000,000 strong. We are coming with our woes behind us, with the memory of suffering behind us—woes and suffering of three hundred years—they shall be our inspiration. My bulwark of strength in the conflict for freedom in Africa, will be the three hundred years of persecution and hardship left behind in this Western Hemisphere. The more I remember the suffering of my fore-fathers, the more I remember the lynchings and burnings in the Southern States of America, the more I will fight on even though the battle seems doubtful. Tell me that I must turn back, and I laugh you to scorn. Go on! Go on! Climb ye the heights of liberty and cease not in well doing until you have planted the banner of the Red, the Black and the Green on the hilltops of Africa.

Questions

1. How does Garvey define black freedom?

2. How do you think Garvey felt that African independence would benefit black Americans?

133. John A. Fitch on the Great Steel Strike (1919)

Source: John A. Fitch, "The Closed Shop," The Survey (November 8, 1919), pp. 53–56, 86, 91.

Among American workers, wartime language linking patriotism with democracy and freedom inspired hopes that an era of social justice was at hand. In 1919, over 4 million workers engaged in strikes—the greatest wave of labor unrest in American history. The strike wave reached its peak in the era's greatest labor uprising, the steel strike. Centered in Pittsburgh and Chicago, it united some 365,000 mostly immigrant workers in demands for union recognition, higher wages, and an eight-hour workday. Before 1917, the steel mills were little autocracies, where managers arbitrarily established wages and working conditions and suppressed all efforts at union organizing. "For why this war?" asked a Polish immigrant steel worker at a union meeting attended by the writer John Fitch, who visited Pittsburgh to report on the strike. "For why we buy Liberty bonds? For the mills? No, for freedom and America—for everybody. No more [work like a] horse and wagon. For eight-hour day." By 1920, with middle-class opinion having turned against the labor movement and native-born workers abandoning their immigrant counterparts, the strike collapsed.

WHAT ARE THE chief issues in the steel strike? Is the strike revolution in disguise or is it a bona fide trade union struggle? Is the issue the closed union shop or the closed anti-union shop? Is the strike an effort of a minority to dominate, led by rank outsiders who came into the steel district as professional agitators? Or is it the expression of long pent-up desires held by large numbers of genuine steel workers, under a welcomed leadership? Is it a fight of Americans against foreigners? Or is it an old-fashioned dispute of anti-union employers against organized labor in any form, such as has long since been threshed out and settled in other major American industries in favor of collective bargaining?

It was to obtain the latest evidence bearing on these questions at the point of greatest interest and of greatest friction that I went to Pittsburgh in mid-October at the time that the Senate committee under the chairmanship of Senator Kenyon went there for a similar reason. I attended the committee hearings and then went out to the mill towns to meet the strikers, the citizens, the police and everyone else whom I could reach. I got some evidence and herewith I pass it on just as it came to me:

• • •

It has been alleged that the strike is one of foreigners alone and that there is some sort of issue between them and the Americans. That is certainly not the case in Johnstown, Pa., where the Cambria Steel Company plant is completely tied up—Americans and foreigners standing firm together. It is not true in Cleveland where thousands of skilled Americans have joined the unions nor is it true in Youngstown and Steubenville, O., or in Gary or South Chicago. At all of those points Americans in large numbers are in the unions and are out on strike.

In the Pittsburgh mill towns, however, it is apparent that the strikers are largely foreign-born and that the Americans are at work. Everywhere you encounter irritation. "These organizers didn't appeal to the Americans," you are told; "they just went among the foreigners." This is what you are told everywhere by business and professional men.

The cleavage between native American stock and foreigners, long a marked feature of life in Pittsburgh mill towns, has been accentuated during this strike. Among the strikers I found naturalized citizens and native-born citizens, but they were all Hunkies because they or their fathers were born in Europe. One young fellow was of the third generation in this country. His grandfather came from Hungary in 1848, about the time America was going wild over Louis Kossuth, the Hungarian patriot. But he is a Hunky. I was especially interested when I learned that his father also is a steel worker and on strike. "Your father must have been working in '92," I remarked, wondering if he were in the famous Homestead strike of that year. "Working in '92?" he demanded, growing red in the face. "The hell he was! He was on strike. Let me tell you scabbing doesn't run in our family." I hastened to explain that I had no intention of accusing his father of being a strike breaker.

In the Pittsburgh district the Americans are mostly at work. Whether this is due to their superior economic condition—the best jobs all belong to the Americans—or whether it is their distrust of the Hunky or their fear of discharge and blacklist, it is difficult to say. It is certain that they have had experience with the reprisals that follow organizing campaigns. It is plain also that forces opposed to the strike are making the most of the traditional antagonism between Americans and Hunkies. But the foreigners represent two-thirds of the employees in most steel mills. In any strike, therefore, a majority of the strikers would probably be foreigners.

• • •

Since 1909 unionism has not been permitted at any steel corporation mill and in most of them there is no collective bargaining of any sort. There has even been refusal to receive petitions—as in the case of groups of workmen in McKeesport and Braddock, who wanted the eight-hour day.

And these policies of ten years are still the policies of the United States Steel Corporation. During my recent trip to Pittsburgh, L. H. Burnett, assistant to the president of the Carnegie Steel Company, told me that committees of men might confer over grievances, but that if a committee wanted to negotiate with the officials over wages and hours, it would not be met. He stated that it was the policy of the company to discharge union men who were active or who were organizing within the plant.

Out in the mill towns the strikers told me of being discharged for joining the union. In half an hour at Homestead I talked with a half dozen men who claimed to have been disciplined in that way. I talked with three or four at Braddock and with two at Clairton, all of whom happened to be in strike headquarters when I called. Strikers are not permitted to gather in McKeesport, and I talked with no discharged men there, but business and professional men of that city who are opposed to the strike told me it had always been the policy of the National Tube Company to discharge men who were trying to organize a union. It was a McKeesport paper that remarked, in connection with Judge Gary's testimony at Washington that the United States Steel Corporation does not discharge men for joining unions, that Judge Gary "ought to know better than to make such a statement."

• • •

These open-hearth men work six days in the week in normal times, but during the war they worked seven days a week, working a long shift of twenty-four hours every second week. Blast furnace men spoke up and said they worked twelve hours a day and on a seven-day basis, all the time—twenty-four hours on at one weekend and twenty-four hours off at the next. Men on the rolls were twelve-hour, six-day men. Shop men, machinists, blacksmiths, mill wrights and repair men have a ten-hour day and a six-day week in theory, but when needed they must jump in and work until a breakdown is repaired. Twenty-four hours' continuous work is common, and thirty-six and forty-eight hours' by no means unknown.

• • •

I came away from Pittsburgh more than ever convinced that the issues of the strike are hours and the right of collective bargaining. Until there is such a reduction in hours of labor in the steel industry as will permit men to recuperate after a day's work, to mingle with their fellows and to play, there can be no opportunity for the development of good citizenship in the mill towns. So long as 50 per cent of the men work twelve hours a day, thousands of them seven days a week with a long shift of eighteen or twenty-four hours every second week, no one can claim for the steel industry the maintenance of an "American" standard of living.

• • •

In this strike the foreigners of Pittsburgh are shaking off that old reproach that they are undermining American standards of living.

They are standing up and fighting for American standards and are doing it lawfully and with amazing patience while the constituted authorities are harassing them on every side. They are fighting for the restoration of constitutional guarantees, torn down by public officials of western Pennsylvania who have sworn to uphold the Constitution. Revolutionists? I went into a strikers' meeting in Homestead, and Joseph Cannon, an organizer and one of the orators of the American labor movement, was speaking. "Men," he was saying,

> we want you to have eight hours so you can learn English. And then you must study American history. Read the Declaration of Independence. Read the history of the American Revolution of George Washington at Valley Forge, his soldiers without shoes in the dead of winter. Read of the hardships they endured and how they fought for liberty. And read of what the foreigners have done to build America. Why, men, did you know that 75 per cent of Washington's soldiers were foreigners? That 50 per cent of the men who fought to end the slavery of the black man in 1861 were foreign born? In every war America has ever had, the foreigner has played his part and has kept Old Glory flying.

You should have heard the thunder of applause. I stood where I could see the men's faces. Foreign-born they were for the most part, Slavic in origin almost altogether, and as they heard this appeal to American tradition every man stood the straighter, and the expression on every face was that of men who felt a kinship with the soldiers of Valley Forge.

These are the men whom it is proposed to "Americanize" as a remedy for industrial unrest. The best way to do that, I think, will be to Americanize their working conditions and their local government, so that they may have time for thinking and time and opportunity to hold such meetings as those they are holding now. Not since 1892 had there been such meetings in Homestead.

While in Pittsburgh, I heard about a great speech made at a strikers' meeting by a Pole. Someone who was there wrote it down for me. It was probably this immigrant's first public speech in the English language and it was something of a struggle; but he had something which had to be said.

"Mr. Chairman," he said. "Mr. Chairman—just like horse and wagon. Put horse in wagon, work all day. Take horse out of wagon—put in stable. Take horse out of stable, put in wagon. Same way like mills. Work all day. Come home—go sleep. Get up—go work in mills—come home. Wife say, 'John, children sick. You help with children.' You say, 'Oh, go to hell'—go sleep. Wife say, 'John, you go town.' You say, 'No'—go sleep. No know what the hell you do. For why this war? For why we buy Liberty bonds? For mills? No, for freedom and America—for everybody. No more horse and wagon. For eight-hour day."

Questions

1. How do the striking workers understand economic freedom?

2. Why do you think that in some instances, native-born and immigrant workers adopted different attitudes toward the strike?

CHAPTER 20

From Business Culture to Great Depression: The Twenties, 1920–1932

134. Immigration Quotas under the Johnson-Reed Act (1924)

Source: **Statistical Abstract of the United States** *(Washington, D.C., 1929),* **p. 100.**

In 1921, Congress imposed temporary country-by-country immigration quotas based on the number of persons from each nation living in the country according to the 1910 census. Three years later it revised the quotas to further limit the number of immigrants allowed to enter the country, and changed the base date to 1890, before the arrival of most of the "new immigrants" from southern and eastern Europe. Countries in the Western Hemisphere, including Canada and Mexico, were not subject to quota limitations. The largest reductions applied to Italy (from which 283,000 immigrants had arrived in 1914) and Russia (255,000 in that year). The quotas in the 1924 law added up to 164,667 immigrants from the entire world.

Country or Area of Birth	Immigration Quota
Africa (total of various countries)	1,100
Albania	100
Arabian Peninsula	100
Asia (total of various countries)	0
Bulgaria	100
Denmark	2,789
Germany	51,227
Great Britain	34,007
Greece	100
Hungary	473
Ireland	28,567
Italy	3,845
Latvia	142
Norway	6,453
Poland	5,982
Russia	2,248
San Marino	100
Spain	131
Sweden	9,561
Turkey	100

Questions

1. What do the numbers tell us about which immigrants Congress considered most and least desirable?

2. Why do you think no quotas were established for countries in the Western Hemisphere?

135. Mrs. W. C. Lathrop, New Freedom in the Home (1921)

Source: Library of Congress, American Memory Collection.

The 1920s marked an important moment in the transition to a society in which freedom involved individual fulfillment through consumption and entertainment. The idea promoted by advertisers that the availability of household appliances represented an expansion of freedom was embraced by many American women. Mrs. W. C. Lathrop, the wife of a Kansas physician and mother of four children, was inspired to write to the inventor Thomas Edison and thank him for how such items, powered by electricity, had changed her life.

Norton, Kansas
March 5, 1921

Dear Sir:

It is not always the privilege of a woman to thank personally the inventor of articles which make life livable for her sex. I feel that it is my duty as well as privilege to tell you how much we women of the small town are indebted to you for our pleasures as well as our utmost needs. I am a college graduate and probably my husband is one of the best known surgeons between Topeka and Denver. I am an officer in the District of Women's Clubs as well as President of our Town Organization.

We have four children. The oldest lad expects to have a telegraph station in the summer on the U. P. [Union Pacific Railroad]. We have a large house so you see when doing practically all my work my duties are many and my activities most varied, yet I enjoy my labors and do not feel that I entirely neglect to get pleasure out of life. Positively as I hear my wash machine chugging along, down in the laundry, as I write this it does seem as though I am entirely dependent on the fertile brain of one thousand miles away for every pleasure and labor saving device I have. The house is lighted by electricity. I cook on a Westinghouse range, wash dishes in an electric dish washer. An electric fan even helps to distribute the heat over part of the house. At our private hospital electricity helps to heat some of the rooms. I wash clothes with an electric machine and iron . . . with an electric iron. I clean house with electric cleaners. I rest, take an electric massage and curl my hair on an electric iron. Dress in a gown sewed on a machine run by a motor. Then start the Victrola [phonograph] and either study Spanish for a while or listen to Kreisler and Gluck and Galli-Curci [a violinist and classical singers] in almost heavenly strains, forgetting I'm living in a tiny town of two thousand where nothing much ever happens. . . . The doctor comes home, tired with a day's work wherein electricity has played almost as much part as it has at home, to find a wife not tired and dissatisfied but a woman . . . who is now rested and ready to serve the tired man and discuss affairs of the day. To play him a beautiful piece on the Victrola and possibly see a masterpiece at the "Movies." Possibly he brings in a guest without warning but electricity and a pressure cooker save the day for the hostess.

Please accept the thanks, Mr. Edison of one most truly appreciative woman.

Sincerely,

Mrs. W. C. Lathrop

Questions

1. How do you think the work and family life of a Kansas housewife in the late nineteenth century differed from that described by Mrs. Lathrop?

2. Why do you think Mrs. Lathrop emphasizes how electricity helps her to "get pleasure out of life" as well as to do housework?

136. The Fight for Civil Liberties (1921)

Source: American Civil Liberties Union, The Fight for Free Speech *(New York, 1921), pp. 15–18.*

The repression of dissent under the Espionage and Sedition Acts of World War I sparked a new appreciation among some reformers of the importance of civil liberties. In 1917, a group of pacifists, Progressives shocked by wartime attacks on freedom of speech, and lawyers outraged at what they considered violations of Americans' legal rights formed the Civil Liberties Bureau. In 1920, it became the American Civil Liberties Union (ACLU). For the rest of the century, the ACLU would take part in most of the landmark legal cases that helped to bring about a "rights revolution." Its efforts helped to give meaning to traditional civil liberties, like freedom of speech, and defined new ones, like the right to privacy. When it began, however, the ACLU was a small, beleaguered organization. Its own pamphlets defending free speech were barred from the mail by postal inspectors.

One of the first documents issued by the ACLU was a general statement defining civil liberties, especially in areas where they had been violated during World War I. The group also insisted that civil liberties should apply equally to all Americans, regardless of race. Full protection of the rights outlined by the ACLU lay years in the future.

A STATEMENT DEFINING THE POSITION OF THE AMERICAN CIVIL
LIBERTIES UNION ON THE ISSUES IN THE UNITED STATES TODAY
(Adopted by the National Committee)

We stand on the general principle that all thought on matters of public concern should be freely expressed without interference. Orderly social progress is promoted by unrestricted freedom of opinion. The punishment of mere opinion, without overt acts, is never in the interest of orderly progress. Suppression of opinion makes for violence and bloodshed.

The principle of freedom of speech, press and assemblage, embodied in our constitutional law, must be reasserted in its application to American conditions today. That application must deal with various methods now used to repress new ideas and democratic movements. The following paragraphs cover the most significant of the tactics of repression in the United States today.

1. Free Speech. There should be no control whatever in advance over what any person may say. The right to meet and to speak freely without permit should be unquestioned.

There should be no prosecutions for the mere expression of opinion on matters of public concern, however radical, however violent. The expression of all opinions, however radical, should be tolerated. The fullest freedom of speech should be encouraged by setting aside special places in streets or parks and in the use of public buildings, free of charge, for public meetings of any sort.

2. Free Press. There should be no censorship over the mails by the post-office or any other agency at any time or in any way. Privacy of communication should be inviolate. Printed matter should never be subject to a political censorship. The granting or revoking of second class mailing privileges should have nothing whatever to do with a paper's opinions and policies.

If libelous, fraudulent, or other illegal matter is being circulated, it should be seized by proper warrant through the prosecuting authorities, not by the post-office department. The business of the post-office department is to carry the mails, not to investigate crime or to act as censors.

There should be no control over the distribution of literature at meetings or hand to hand in public or in private places. No system of licenses for distribution should be tolerated.

3. Freedom of Assemblage. Meetings in public places, parades and processions should be freely permitted, the only reasonable regulation being the advance notification to the police of the time and place. No discretion should be given the police to prohibit parades or processions, but merely to alter routes in accordance with the imperative demands of traffic in crowded cities. There should be no laws or regulations prohibiting the display of red flags or other political emblems.

The right of assemblage is involved in the right to picket in time of strike. Peaceful picketing, therefore, should not be prohibited, regulated by injunction, by order of court or by police edict. It is the business of the police in places where picketing is conducted merely to keep traffic free and to handle specific violations of law against persons upon complaint.

4. The Right to Strike. The right of workers to organize in organizations of their own choosing, and to strike, should never be infringed by law.

Compulsory arbitration is to be condemned not only because it destroys the workers' right to strike, but because it lays emphasis on one set of obligations alone, those of workers to society.

5. Law Enforcement. The practice of deputizing privately paid police as general police officers should be opposed. So should the attempts of private company employees to police the streets or property other than that of the company.

The efforts of private associations to take into their own hands the enforcement of law should be opposed at every point. Public officials, employees of private corporations, and leaders of mobs, who interfere with the exercise of the constitutionally established rights of free speech and free assembly, should be vigorously proceeded against.

The sending of troops into areas of industrial conflict to maintain law and order almost inevitably results in the government taking sides in an industrial conflict in behalf of the employer. The presence of troops, whether or not martial law is declared, very rarely affects the employer adversely, but it usually results in the complete denial of civil rights to the workers.

6. Search and Seizure. It is the custom of certain federal, state and city officials, particularly in cases involving civil liberty, to make arrests without warrant, to enter upon private property, and to seize papers and literature without legal process. Such practices should be contested. Officials so violating constitutional guarantees should be proceeded against.

7. The Right to a Fair Trial. Every person charged with an offense should have the fullest opportunity for a fair trial, for securing counsel and bail in a reasonable sum. In the case of a poor person, special aid should be organized to secure a fair trial, and when necessary, an appeal. The legal profession should be alert to defend cases involving civil liberty. The resolutions of various associations of lawyers against taking cases of radicals are wholly against the traditions of American liberty.

8. Immigration, Deportation and Passports. No person should be refused admission to the United States on the ground of holding objectionable opinions. The present restrictions against radicals of various beliefs is wholly opposed to our tradition of political asylum.

No alien should be deported merely for the expression of opinion or for membership in a radical or revolutionary organization. This is as un-American a practice as the prosecution of citizens for expression of opinion.

The attempt to revoke naturalization papers in order to declare a citizen an alien subject to deportation is a perversion of a law which was intended to cover only cases of fraud.

Citizenship papers should not be refused to any alien because of the expression of radical views, or activities in the cause of labor.

The granting of passports to or from the United States should not be dependent merely upon the opinions of citizens or membership in radical or labor organizations.

9. Liberty in Education. The attempts to maintain a uniform orthodox opinion among teachers should be opposed. The attempts of educational authorities to inject into public school and college instruction propaganda in the interest of any particular theory of society to the exclusion of others should be opposed.

10. **Race Equality.** Every attempt to discriminate between races in the application of all principles of civil liberty here set forth should be opposed.

How to Get Civil Liberty

We realize that these standards of civil liberty cannot be attained as abstract principles or as constitutional guarantees. Economic or political power is necessary to assert and maintain all "rights." In the midst of any conflict they are not granted by the side holding the economic and political power, except as they may be forced by the strength of the opposition. However, the mere public assertion of the principle of freedom of opinion in the words or deeds of individuals, or weak minorities, helps win recognition, and in the long run makes for tolerance and against resort to violence.

Today the organized movements of labor and of the farmers are waging the chief fight for civil liberty throughout the United States as part of their effort for increased control of industry. Publicity, demonstrations, political activities and legal aid are organized nationally and locally. Only by such an aggressive policy of insistence can rights be secured and maintained. The union of organized labor, the farmers, radical and liberal movements is the most effective means to this.

It is these forces which the American Civil Liberties Union serves in their efforts for civil liberty. The practical work of free speech demonstrations, publicity and legal defense is done primarily in the struggles of the organized labor and farmers movements.

Questions

1. In what ways can the ACLU's statement be seen as a reaction against violations of civil liberties before and during World War I?

2. Why does the ACLU identify "organized movements of labor and of the farmers" as waging the "chief fight" for civil liberties in the United States?

137. Bartolomeo Vanzetti's Last Statement in Court (1927)

Source: Robert P. Weeks, ed., Commonwealth v. Sacco and Vanzetti *(Englewood Cliffs, N.J., 1958), pp. 220–23.*

The trial and execution for murder of two Italian immigrant anarchists, Nicola Sacco and Bartolomeo Vanzetti, became one of the most controversial events of the 1920s and sparked a worldwide movement to save the condemned men. Their trial in 1921 took place in an atmosphere of anti-immigrant and anti-radical hysteria and was marked by flagrant appeals to prejudice by the prosecution and bias by the presiding judge. To many immigrants, including those who did not share Sacco and Vanzetti's political views, the pair became symbols of the excesses of the anti-immigration movement that culminated in the 1924 law closing off entry for nearly all migrants from southern and eastern Europe. Overseas, the trial led to a transformation of the image of the United States from an asylum for liberty to a land where justice was perverted by the demands of the powerful. After six years of appeals, the two men were sentenced to death in 1927. Vanzetti's last statement in court reaffirmed his innocence and suggested some of the reasons for the verdict.

━━━━━━

WHAT I SAY is that I am innocent.... That I am not only innocent of these two crimes, but in all my life I have never stolen and I have never killed and I have never spilled blood.... Everybody that knows these two arms knows very well that I did not need to go into the streets and kill a man or try to take money. I can live by my two hands and live well. But besides that, I can live even without work with my hands for other people. I have had plenty of chance to live independently and to live what the world conceives to be a higher life than to gain our bread with the sweat of our brow.

My father in Italy is in a good condition. I could have come back in Italy and he would have welcomed me every time with open arms. Even if I come back there with not a cent in my pocket, my father could have give me a position, not to work but to make business, or to oversee upon the land that he owns....

Not only have I struggled hard against crimes, but I have refused myself of what are considered the commodity and glories of life, the prides of a life of a good position, because in my consideration it is not right to exploit man. I have refused to go in business because I understand that business is a speculation on profit upon certain people that must depend upon the business man, and I do not consider that that is right and therefore I refuse to do that.

Now, I should say that I am not only innocent of all these things, not only have I never committed a real crime in my life—though some sins but not crimes—not only have I struggled all my life to eliminate crimes, the crimes that the official law and the moral law condemns, but also the crime that the moral law and the official law sanction and sanctify,—the exploitation and the oppression of the man by the man, and if there is a reason why I am here as a guilty man, if there is a reason why you in a few minutes can doom me, it is this reason and none else.

We were tried during a time whose character has now passed into history. I mean by that, a time when there was a hysteria of resentment and hate against the people of our principles, against the foreigner, against slackers, and it seems to me—rather, I am positive of it, that both you [the judge] and Mr. Katzmann [the prosecutor] have done all what it were in your power in order to work out, in order to agitate still more the passion of the juror, the prejudice of the juror, against us.... Everybody ought to understand that the first beginning of our defense has been terrible. My first lawyer did not try to defend us. He has made no attempt to collect witnesses and evidence in our favor....

My conviction is that I have suffered for things that I am guilty of. I am suffering because I am a radical and indeed I am a radical; I have suffered because I was an Italian, and indeed I am an Italian; I have suffered more for my family and for my beloved than for myself; but I am so convinced to be right that you can only kill me once but if you could execute me two times, and if I could be reborn two other times, I would live again to do what I have done already.

Questions

1. Why does Vanzetti feel that he did not receive a fair trial?

2. How do Vanzetti's political views come through in his statement?

---

138. Congress Debates Immigration (1921)

Source: **Congressional Record, *67th Congress, 1st Session, pp. 511–15.***

Fears of foreign radicalism sparked by the labor upheavals immediately following World War I and the increased concern with Americanizing immigrants greatly strengthened pressures for wholesale immigration restriction. In 1921, Congress debated a proposal to limit immigration from Europe temporarily to 357,000 per year (one-third the annual average before the war). The excerpt that follows, from April 20, 1921, pitted Congressman Lucien W. Parrish, a Democrat from Texas, an advocate of immigration restriction, against Meyer London, a Socialist from New York and himself an immigrant from Poland.

Parrish's views prevailed. And three years later, Congress permanently limited European immigration to 150,000 per year, distributed according to a series of national quotas that severely restricted the numbers from southern and eastern Europe. The law aimed to ensure that descendants of the old immigrants forever outnumbered the children of the new. The law also barred the entry of all those ineligible for naturalized citizenship—that is, the entire population of Asia, even though Japan had fought on the American side in World War I. The quota system remained in place until the immigration reform act of 1965.

MR. PARRISH: We should stop immigration entirely until such a time as we can amend our immigration laws and so write them that hereafter no one shall be admitted except he be in full sympathy with our Constitution and laws, willing to declare himself obedient to our flag, and willing to release himself from any obligations he may owe to the flag of the country from which he came.

It is time that we act now, because within a few short years the damage will have been done. The endless tide of immigration will have filled our country with a foreign and unsympathetic element. Those who are out of sympathy with our Constitution and the spirit of our Government will be here in large numbers, and the true spirit of Americanism left us by our fathers will gradually become poisoned by this uncertain element.

The time once was when we welcomed to our shores the oppressed and downtrodden people from all the world, but they came to us because of oppression at home and with the sincere purpose of making true and loyal American citizens, and in truth and in fact they did adapt themselves to our ways of thinking and contributed in a substantial sense to the progress and development that our civilization has made. But that time has passed now; new and strange conditions have arisen in the countries over there; new and strange doctrines are being taught. The Governments of the Orient are being overturned and destroyed, and anarchy and bolshevism are threatening the very foundation of many of them, and no one can foretell what the future will bring to many of those countries of the Old World now struggling with these problems.

Our country is a self-sustaining country. It has taught the principles of real democracy to all the nations of the earth; its flag has been the synonym of progress, prosperity, and the preservation of the rights of the individual, and there can be nothing so dangerous as for us to allow the undesirable foreign element to poison our civilization and thereby threaten the safety of the institutions that our forefathers have established for us.

Now is the time to throw about this country the most stringent immigration laws and keep from our shores forever those who are not in sympathy with the American ideas. It is the time now for us to act and act quickly, because every month's delay increases the difficulty in which we find ourselves and renders the problems of government more difficult of solution. We must protect ourselves from the poisonous influences that are threatening the very foundation of the Governments of Europe; we must see to it that those who come here are loyal and true to our Nation and impress upon them that it means something to have the privileges of American citizenship. We must hold this country true to the American thought and the American ideals. . . .

MR. LONDON: This bill is a continuation of the war upon humanity. It is an assertion of that exaggerated nationalism which never appeals to reason and which has for its main source the self-conceit of accumulated prejudice.

At whom are you striking in this bill? Why, at the very people whom a short while ago you announced you were going to emancipate. We sent 2,000,000 men abroad to make the world "safe for democracy," to liberate these very people. Now you shut the door to them. Yes. So far, we have made the world safe for hypocrisy and the United States incidentally unsafe for the Democratic Party, temporarily at least. [Laughter.] The supporters of the bill claim that the law will keep out radicals. The idea that by restricting immigration you will prevent the influx of radical thought is altogether untenable. . . .

Ideas can neither be shut in nor shut out. There is only one way of contending with an idea, and that is the old and safe American rule of free and untrammeled discussion. Every attempt to use any other method has always proven disastrous.

While purporting to be a temporary measure, just for a year or so, this bill is really intended to pave the way to permanent exclusion.

To prevent immigration means to cripple the United States. Our most developed industrial States are those which have had the largest immigration. Our most backward States industrially and in the point of literacy are those which have had no immigration to speak of.

The extraordinary and unprecedented growth of the United States is as much a cause as the effect of immigration.

Defenders of this bill thoughtlessly repeat the exploded theory that there have been two periods of immigration, the good period, which the chairman of the committee fixes up to the year 1900, and the bad period since. The strange thing about it is that at no time in history has any country made such rapid progress in industry, in science, and in the sphere of social legislation as this country has shown since 1900.

The new immigration is neither different nor worse, and besides that, identically the same arguments were used against the old immigration.

By this bill we, who have escaped the horrors of the war, will refuse a place of refuge to the victims of the war.

I repeat, this is an attempt at civilization. Progress is by no means a continuous or uninterrupted process. Many a civilization has been destroyed in the tortuous course of history and has been followed by hundreds or thousands of years of darkness. It is just possible that unless strong men who love liberty will everywhere assert themselves, the world will revert to a state of savagery. Just now we hear nothing but hatred, nothing but the ravings of the exaggerated I—"I am of the best stock, I do not want to be contaminated; I have produced the greatest literature; my intellect is the biggest; my heart is the noblest"—and this is repeated in every parliament, in every country, by every fool all over the world. [*Applause.*]

Questions

1. Why does Parrish consider continued immigration dangerous?

2. Why does London argue that immigration restriction is based on "prejudice" rather than "reason"?

139. Justice James Clark McReynolds, *Meyer v. Nebraska* and the Meaning of Liberty (1923)

Source: **Meyer v. Nebraska, 262 U.S. 390 (1923).**

One expression of the anti-immigrant sentiment sparked by World War I was the passage of laws by a number of states restricting teaching in foreign languages. Robert Meyer, a parochial schoolteacher in Nebraska, was found guilty of violating a 1919 law that mandated that all instruction be in English. The state supreme court upheld his conviction, and Meyer appealed to the U.S. Supreme Court, arguing that the law violated the Fourteenth Amendment's guarantee of liberty to all citizens.

By a 7–2 vote, the Court declared the Nebraska law unconstitutional. The decision expanded the freedom of all immigrant groups and helped to lay the groundwork for the Court's decisions of the 1960s affirming a constitutional right to privacy.

THE SUPREME COURT of [Nebraska] affirmed the judgment of conviction. . . . It declared the offense charged and established was "the direct and intentional teaching of the German language as a distinct subject to a child who had not passed the eighth grade," in the parochial school maintained by Zion Evangelical Lutheran Congregation, a collection of Biblical stories being used therefore. And it held that the statute forbidding this did not conflict with the Fourteenth Amendment, but was a valid exercise of the police power. The following excerpts from the opinion sufficiently indicate the reasons advanced to support the conclusion:

> The salutary purpose of the statute is clear. The Legislature had seen the beneful effects of permitting foreigners, who had taken residence in this country, to rear and educate their children in the language of their native land. The result of that condition was found to be inimical to our own safety. To allow the children of foreigners, who had emigrated here, to be taught from early childhood the language of the

country of their parents was to ... educate them so that they must always think in that language, and, as a consequence, naturally inculcate in them the ideas and sentiments foreign to the best interests of this country....

The problem for our determination is whether the statute as construed and applied unreasonably infringes the liberty guaranteed to the plaintiff in error by the Fourteenth Amendment:

No state ... shall deprive any person of life, liberty or property without due process of law.

While this court has not attempted to define with exactness the liberty thus guaranteed ... without doubt, it denotes not merely freedom from bodily restraint but also the right of the individual to contract, to engage in any of the common occupations of life, to acquire useful knowledge, to marry, establish a home and bring up children, to worship God according to the dictates of his own conscience, and generally to enjoy those privileges long recognized at common law as essential to the orderly pursuit of happiness by free men. The established doctrine is that this liberty may not be interfered with, under the guise of protecting the public interest, by legislative action which is arbitrary or without reasonable relation to some purpose within the competency of the state to effect....

The American people have always regarded education and acquisition of knowledge as matters of supreme importance which should be diligently promoted. The Ordinance of 1787 declares: "Religion, morality and knowledge being necessary to good government and the happiness of mankind, schools and the means of education shall forever be encouraged." Corresponding to the right of control, it is the natural duty of the parent to give his children education suitable to their station in life; and nearly all the states, including Nebraska, enforce this obligation by compulsory laws.

Practically, education of the young is only possible in schools conducted by especially qualified persons who devote themselves thereto. The calling always has been regarded as useful and honorable, essential, indeed, to the public welfare. Mere knowledge of the German language cannot reasonably be regarded as harmful. Heretofore it has been commonly looked upon as helpful and desirable. Plaintiff in error taught this language in school as part of his occupation. His right thus to teach and the right of parents to engage him so to instruct their children, we think, are within the liberty of the amendment.

The challenged statute forbids the teaching in school of any subject except in English; also the teaching of any other language until the pupil has attained and successfully passed the eighth grade, which is not usually accomplished before the age of twelve. The Supreme Court of the state has held that "the so-called ancient or dead languages" are not "within the spirit or the purpose of the act." Latin, Greek, Hebrew are not proscribed; but German, French, Spanish, Italian, and every other alien speech are within the ban. Evidently the Legislature has attempted materially to interfere with the calling of modern language teachers, with the opportunities of pupils to acquire knowledge, and with the power of parents to control the education of their own.

It is said the purpose of the legislation was to promote civic development by inhibiting training and education of the immature in foreign tongues and ideals before they could learn English and acquire American ideals, and "that the English language should be and become the mother tongue of all children reared in this state." It is also affirmed that the foreign born population is very large, that certain communities commonly use foreign words, follow foreign leaders, move in a foreign atmosphere, and that the children are thereby hindered from becoming citizens of the most useful type and the public safety is imperiled.

That the state may do much, go very far, indeed, in order to improve the quality of its citizens, physically, mentally and morally, is clear; but the individual has certain fundamental rights which must be respected. The protection of the Constitution extends to all, to those who speak other languages as well as to those born with English on the tongue. Perhaps it would be highly advantageous if all had ready understanding of our ordinary speech, but this cannot be coerced with methods which conflict with the Constitution—a desirable end cannot be promoted by prohibited means. . . .

The desire of the Legislature to foster a homogenous people with American ideals prepared readily to understand current discussions of civic matters is easy to appreciate. Unfortunate experiences during the late war and aversion toward every character of truculent adversaries were certainly enough to quicken that aspiration. But the means adopted, we think, exceed the limitations upon the power of the state and conflict with rights assured to plaintiff in error. The interference is plain enough and no adequate reason therefore in time of peace and domestic tranquility has been shown.

The power of the state to compel attendance at some school and to make reasonable regulations for all schools, including a requirement that they shall give instructions in English, is not questioned. Nor has challenge been made of the state's power to prescribe a curriculum for institutions which it supports. Those matters are not within the present controversy. Our concern is with the prohibition approved by the [Nebraska] Supreme Court. . . .

No emergency has arisen which renders knowledge by a child of some language other than English so clearly harmful as to justify its inhibition with the consequent infringement of rights long freely enjoyed. We are constrained to conclude that the statute as applied is arbitrary and without reasonable relation to any end within the competency of the state. As the statute undertakes to interfere only with teaching which involves a modern language, leaving complete freedom as to other matters, there seems no adequate foundation for the suggestion that the purpose was to protect the child's health by limiting his mental activities. It is well known that proficiency in a foreign language seldom comes to one not instructed at an early age, and experience shows that this is not injurious to the health, morals or understanding of the ordinary child.

Questions

1. In what ways did the Supreme Court of Nebraska justify the English-only law?

2. Why does the U.S. Supreme Court see the law as an unreasonable infringement on liberty?

---

140. Alain Locke, *The New Negro* (1925)

Source: Alain Locke, from The New Negro. *Copyright © 1925 by Albert & Charles Boni, Inc. Introduction copyright © 1992 by Macmillan Publishing Company. Reprinted with the permission of Touchstone, a division of Simon & Schuster, Inc. All rights reserved.*

The migration of blacks from South to North, begun in large numbers during World War I, continued during the 1920s. New York's Harlem became famous for "slumming," as groups of whites visited its dance halls, jazz clubs, and speakeasies in search of exotic adventure. The Harlem of the white imagination was a place of primitive passions, free from the puritanical restraints of mainstream American culture. The real Harlem was a community of widespread poverty. But it was also the center of rising racial self-consciousness, a growing awareness of the interconnections between black Americans and persons of African descent elsewhere in the world, and a vibrant black cultural community that established links with New York's artistic mainstream. The term "New Negro," associated in politics with pan-Africanism and the militancy of the Garvey movement, in art meant the rejection of established stereotypes and a search for black values to put in their place. *The New Negro*, a book of essays and literary works edited by Alain Locke, came to symbolize the "Harlem Renaissance."

IN THE LAST decade something beyond the watch and guard of statistics has happened in the life of the American Negro and the three norns who have traditionally presided over the Negro problem have a changeling in their laps. The Sociologist, the Philanthropist, the Race-leader are not unaware of the New Negro, but they are at a loss to account for him. He simply cannot be swathed in their formulæ. For the younger generation is vibrant with a new psychology; the new spirit is awake in the masses, and under the very eyes of the professional observers is transforming what has been a perennial problem into the progressive phases of contemporary Negro life.

• • •

With this renewed self-respect and self-dependence, the life of the Negro community is bound to enter a new dynamic phase, the buoyancy from within compensating for whatever pressure there may be of conditions from without. The migrant masses, shifting from countryside to city, hurdle several generations of experience at a leap, but more important, the same thing happens spiritually in the life-attitudes and self-expression of the Young Negro, in his poetry, his art, his education and his new outlook, with the additional advantage, of course, of the poise and greater certainty of knowing what it is all about. From this comes the promise and warrant of a new leadership. As one of them has discerningly put it:

> We have tomorrow
> Bright before us
> Like a flame.
>
> Yesterday, a night-gone thing
> A sun-down name.
>
> And dawn today
> Broad arch above the road we came.
> We march!

• • •

The day of "aunties," "uncles" and "mammies" is equally gone. Uncle Tom and Sambo have passed on, and even the "Colonel" and "George" play barnstorm roles from which they escape with relief when the public spotlight is off. The popular melodrama has about played itself out, and it is time to scrap the fictions, garret the bogeys and settle down to a realistic facing of facts.

First we must observe some of the changes which since the traditional lines of opinion were drawn have rendered these quite obsolete. A main change has been, of course, that shifting of the Negro population which has made the Negro problem no longer exclusively or even predominantly Southern.

• • •

Here in Manhattan is not merely the largest Negro community in the world, but the first concentration in history of so many diverse elements of Negro life. It has attracted the African, the West Indian, the Negro American; has brought together the Negro of the North and the Negro of the South; the man from the city and the man from the town and village; the peasant, the student, the business man, the professional man, artist, poet, musician, adventurer and worker, preacher and criminal, exploiter and social outcast. Each group has come with its own separate motives and for its own special ends, but their greatest experience has been the finding of one another. Proscription and prejudice have thrown these dissimilar elements into a common area of contact and interaction. Within this area, race sympathy and unity have determined a further fusing of sentiment and experience. So what began in terms of segregation becomes more and more, as its elements mix and react, the laboratory of a great race-welding. Hitherto, it must be admitted that American Negroes have been a race more in name than in fact, or to be exact, more in sentiment than in experience. The chief bond between them has been that of a common condition rather than a common consciousness; a problem in common rather than a life in common. In Harlem, Negro life is seizing upon its first chances for group expression and self-determination. It is—or promises at least to be—a race capital. That is why our comparison is taken with those nascent centers of folk-expression and self-determination which are playing a creative part in the world to-day. Without pretense to their political significance, Harlem has the same role to play for the New Negro as Dublin has had for the New Ireland or Prague for the New Czechoslovakia.

• • •

[Two new] interests are racial but in a new and enlarged way. One is the consciousness of acting as the advance-guard of the African peoples in their contact with Twentieth Century civilization; the other, the sense of a mission of rehabilitating the race in world esteem from that loss of prestige for which the fate and conditions of slavery have so largely been responsible. Harlem, as we shall see, is the center of both these movements; she is the home of the Negro's "Zionism." The pulse of the Negro world has begun to beat in Harlem. A Negro Newspaper carrying news material in English, French and Spanish, gathered from all quarters of America, the West Indies and Africa has maintained itself in Harlem for over five years. Two important magazines, both edited from New York, maintain their news and circulation consistently on a cosmopolitan scale. Under American auspices and backing, three pan-African congresses have been held abroad for the discussion of common interests, colonial questions and the future cooperative development of Africa. In terms of the race question as a world problem, the Negro mind has leapt, so to speak, upon the parapets of prejudice and extended its cramped horizons. In so doing it has linked up with the growing group consciousness of the dark peoples and is gradually learning their common interests. As one of our writers has recently put it: "It is imperative that we understand the white world in its relations to the non-white world." As with the Jew, persecution is making the Negro international.

As a world phenomenon this wider race consciousness is a different thing from the much asserted rising tide of color. Its inevitable causes are not of our making. The consequences are not necessarily damaging to the best interests of civilization. Whether it actually brings into being new Armadas of conflict or argosies of cultural exchange and enlightenment can only be decided by the attitude of the dominant races in an era of critical change. With the American Negro, his new internationalism is primarily an effort to recapture contact with the scattered peoples of African derivation. Garveyism may be a transient, if spectacular, phenomenon, but the possible role of the American Negro in the future development of Africa is one of the most constructive and universally helpful missions that any modern people can lay claim to.

• • •

Questions

1. What does Locke mean when he writes, "The day of 'aunties,' 'uncles' and 'mammies'" is gone?

2. Why does Locke consider Harlem a true "race capital" for blacks?

141. Elsie Hill and Florence Kelley Debate the Equal Rights Amendment (1922)

Source: The Nation, *April 12, 1922, p. 421.*

With the ratification of the constitutional amendment barring states from discriminating in voting qualifications because of sex, the women's movement faced a crossroads. The National Woman's Party, whose militant protests during World War I had helped secure passage of the Nineteenth Amendment, now called for a new Equal Rights Amendment (ERA) prohibiting all legal distinctions between the sexes. Only in this way, its leaders insisted, could women gain full access to the economic, educational, and other opportunities of American society. But many veterans of the movement to protect women workers feared that the ERA would wipe away their hard-won gains as well as deny women alimony and child support in the event of divorce. The result was a bitter split among feminists, illustrated in a debate in the pages of the liberal magazine *The Nation* in 1922. Elsie Hill, the daughter of a Connecticut congressman who had been arrested for picketing at the White House during Woodrow Wilson's presidency, represented the Woman's Party. Florence Kelley, the head of the National Consumers' League and an architect of legislation limiting the hours of work for women, offered the traditional view that women needed special protection by the government. The ERA failed, and the debate would be repeated in the 1970s when it once again entered national politics.

———

HILL: THE REMOVAL of all forms of the subjection of women is the purpose to which the National Woman's Party is dedicated. Its present campaign to remove the discriminations against women in the laws of the United States is but the beginning of its determined effort to secure the freedom of women, an integral part of the struggle for human liberty for which women are first of all responsible. Its interest lies in the final release of women from the class of a dependent, subservient being to which early civilization committed her.

The laws of the various states at present hold her in that class. They deny her a control of her children equal to the father's; they deny her, if married, the right to her own earnings; they punish her for offenses for which men go unpunished.... These laws are not the creation of this age, but the fact that they are still tolerated on our statute books and that in some states their removal is vigorously resisted shows the hold of old traditions upon us. Since the passage of the Suffrage Amendment the incongruity of these laws, dating back many centuries, has become more than ever marked....

An amendment to the Federal Constitution ... if adopted, would remove them at one stroke.

KELLEY: Sex is a biological fact. The political rights of citizens are not properly dependent upon sex, but social and domestic relations and industrial activities are. All modern-minded people desire that women should have full political equality and like opportunity in business and the professions.... The inescapable facts are, however, that men do not bear children, are freed from the burdens of maternity, and are not susceptible, in the same measure as women, to poisons now increasingly characteristic of certain industries, and to the universal poison of fatigue. These are differences so far-reaching, so fundamental, that it is grotesque to ignore them. Women cannot be made men by act of the legislature or by amendment of the Federal Constitution.... The inherent differences are permanent. Women will always need many laws different from those needed by men.

The effort to enact the blanket bill in defiance of all biological differences recklessly imperils the special laws for women as such, for wives, for mothers, and for wage-earners.... Is the National Woman's Party for or against protective measures for wage-earning women? Will it publicly state whether it is for or against the eight-hour day and minimum-wage commissions for women? Yes or no?

Questions

1. How do the arguments of Hill and Kelley reflect different definitions of women's freedom and their role in society?

2. Why does Kelley think that the Equal Rights Amendment will do a disservice to women?

CHAPTER 21

The New Deal, 1932–1940

142. Letter to Secretary of Labor Frances Perkins (1937)

Source: Gerald Markowitz and David Rosner, eds., "Slaves of the Depression": Workers' Letters about Life on the Job (Ithaca, N.Y., 1987), pp. 103–4.

The election of Franklin D. Roosevelt as president in 1932 did much to rekindle hope among the victims of the Great Depression, the worst economic disaster in American history. Throughout the 1930s, ordinary Americans, one of whom referred to the downtrodden as "slaves of the depression," wrote poignant letters to federal officials describing the oppressive working conditions of those who retained their jobs and the difficulty of finding work for the unemployed. They wrote of the threat of starvation, the impossibility of obtaining medical care when ill, and the abuses of dictatorial employers and supervisors. One such letter, addressed to Secretary of Labor Frances Perkins, described the "terrible and inhuman condition" of workers in the sugar fields of Louisiana.

━━━━━

PLAQUEMINE, LOUISIANA, JULY 27, 1937

Dear Miss Perkins:

I am writing to you because I think you are pretty square to the average laboring man. but I am wondering if anyone has told you of the cruel and terrible condition that exist in this part of the country or the so called sugar cane belt in Louisiana. I am sure that it hasn't made any progress or improvement since slavery days and to many people here that toil the soil or saw mills as laboring men I am sure slavery days were much better for the black slaves had their meals for sure three times a day and medical attention at that. but if an American nowadays had that much he is a communist I am speaking of the labor not the ones that the government give a sugar bounty too but the real forgotten people for the ones the government give the sugar bounty too are the ones that really don't need it for those same people that has drawn the sugar bonus for two years has never gave an extra penny to their white and black slaves labor. I will now make an effort to give you an idea of the terrible inhuman condition.

I will first give you the idea of the sugar cane tenants and plantations poor laboring people. The bell rings at 2 a.m. in the morning when all should really be sleeping at rest. they work in the summer until 9 or 10 a.m. the reason they knock them off from the heat is not because of killing the labor from heat but they are afraid it kills the mule not the slave. Their wages runs from 90¢ to $1.10 per day. Their average days per week runs from three to four days a week in other words people that are living in so called United States have to live on the about $4.00 per week standing of living in a so called American Community which is way below the Chinese standard of living for the Chinese at least have a cheaper food and clothing living but here one has to pay dear for food and clothing because these sugar cane slave owners *not* only give inhuman wages but the ones that work for them have to buy to their stores, which sells from 50 per cent to 60 per cent higher than the stores in town still these same people that are worst than the old time slave owners or yelling and hollering for more sugar protection, why should they get more when they don't pay their white and black slaves more. It is true they give the white and black slaves a place to live on. But Miss Perkins if you were to see these places they live on you'd swear that this is not our so call rich America with it high standing of living for I am sure that the lowest places in China or Mexico or Africa has better places to live in. These Southern Senators which are backed by the big shots will tell you it is cheaper to live in the South but have you investigated their living condition. Sometimes I don't wonder why some of these people don't be really communism but they are true Americans only they are living in such a low standing of living that one wouldn't believe they are living in the good old U.S.A.

Now regarding the saw mills of this town and other towns in this section but most particular this town they pay slightly more than the plantation but they get it back by charging more for food & clothing which they have to buy in their stores.

I am writing you this hoping that you will try to read it and understand the situation which if you think is not true you can send an investigator in this section of Louisiana that has American freedom of speech for some hasn't that speech in our so called free America and if you can get in touch with people who are not concern about it I am sure you will see that I am right and I do hope that you are kind enough to give this your carefully attention and I am sure that President Roosevelt nor Mrs. Roosevelt nor you would like to see this terrible and inhuman condition go on worst now then old slavery days for I know you people believe in the real American standing of living.

Again I will call your attention if you don't believe of the slave wages condition in this lost part of U.S. investigate and you will find out. Thanking you for humanity sake.

R.J.

Questions

1. Why does the writer feel that Secretary of Labor Perkins will give the letter a sympathetic reading?

2. Why does the writer refer to "our so called free America"?

143. John Steinbeck, *The Harvest Gypsies* (1936)

Source: *John Steinbeck, excerpt from* The Harvest Gypsies *by John Steinbeck. Copyright © 1936 by* The San Francisco News. *Reprinted by permission of Heyday Books, Berkeley, California.*

The 1930s had a devastating impact on American agriculture. The Great Depression coupled with a prolonged drought and dust storms in the nation's heartland spurred an exodus of displaced farmers to nearby cities or to the promised land of California. John Steinbeck's novel *The Grapes of Wrath* (1939) and a popular film based on the book captured their plight, tracing a dispossessed family's trek from Oklahoma to California. Before the book appeared, Steinbeck had written a series of newspaper articles based on interviews with the migrants, later gathered in a book, *The Harvest Gypsies.*

THUS, IN CALIFORNIA we find a curious attitude toward a group that makes our agriculture successful. The migrants are needed, and they are hated. Arriving in a district they find the dislike always meted out by the resident to the foreigner, the outlander. This hatred of the stranger occurs in the whole range of human history, from the most primitive village form to our own highly organized industrial farming. The migrants are hated for the following reasons, that they are ignorant and dirty people, that they are carriers of disease, that they increase the necessity for police and the tax bill for schooling in a community, and that if they are allowed to organize they can, simply by refusing to work, wipe out the season's crops. They are never received into a community nor into the life of a community. Wanderers in fact, they are never allowed to feel at home in the communities that demand their services.

Let us see what kind of people they are, where they come from, and the routes of their wanderings. In the past they have been of several races, encouraged to come and often imported as cheap labor;

Chinese in the early period, then Filipinos, Japanese and Mexicans. These were foreigners, and as such they were ostracized and segregated and herded about.

If they attempted to organize they were deported or arrested, and having no advocates they were never able to get a hearing for their problems. But in recent years the foreign migrants have begun to organize, and at this danger signal they have been deported in great numbers, for there was a new reservoir from which a great quantity of cheap labor could be obtained.

The drought in the middle west has driven the agricultural populations of Oklahoma, Nebraska and parts of Kansas and Texas westward. Their lands are destroyed and they can never go back to them. Thousands of them are crossing the borders in ancient rattling automobiles, destitute and hungry and homeless, ready to accept any pay so that they may eat and feed their children. And this is a new thing in migrant labor, for the foreign workers were usually imported without their children and everything that remains of their old life with them.

They arrive in California usually having used up every resource to get here, even to the selling of the poor blankets and utensils and tools on the way to buy gasoline. They arrive bewildered and beaten and usually in a state of semi-starvation, with only one necessity to face immediately, and that is to find work at any wage in order that the family may eat.

And there is only one field in California that can receive them. Ineligible for relief, they must become migratory field workers....

The earlier foreign migrants have invariably been drawn from a peon class. This is not the case with the new migrants. They are small farmers who have lost their farms, or farm hands who have lived with the family in the old American way. They are men who have worked hard on their own farms and have felt the pride of possessing and living in close touch with the land. They are resourceful and intelligent Americans who have gone through the hell of the drought, have seen their lands wither and die and the top soil blow away; and this, to a man who has owned his land, is a curious and terrible pain....

And there is another difference between their old life and the new. They have come from the little farm districts where democracy was not only possible but inevitable, where popular government, whether practiced in the Grange, in church organization or in local government, was the responsibility of every man. And they have come into the country where, because of the movement necessary to make a living, they are not allowed any vote whatever, but are rather considered a properly unprivileged class.

... As one little boy in a squatters' camp said, "When they need us they call us migrants, and when we've picked their crop, we're bums and we got to get out."

Questions

1. How do the migrants of the 1930s differ from previous waves of migrant laborers who emigrated to California?

2. What does Steinbeck see as the impact of the farm migration on American democracy?

---

144. John L. Lewis on Labor's Great Upheaval (1937)

Source: John L. Lewis, "Guests at Labor's Table," speech by John L. Lewis, September 15, 1937. Reprinted by permission of the United Mineworkers of America.

The most striking development of the mid-1930s was the mobilization of millions of workers in mass production industries that had successfully resisted unionization. "Labor's great upheaval," as this era was called, came as a great surprise. Previous depressions had devastated the labor movement. Unlike in the past, however, the federal government now seemed to be on the side of labor, as reflected in the Wagner Act of 1935, which granted workers the legal right to form unions.

In 1935, labor leaders dissatisfied with the American Federation of Labor's policy of organizing workers along traditional craft lines called for the creation of unions that united all workers in a specific industry. They formed the Committee for Industrial Organization, which set out to create unions in the main bastions of the American economy. In September 1937, John L. Lewis, the head of the United Mine Workers of America, delivered a radio address refuting charges that the labor movement was controlled by communists and explaining in militant language labor's vision.

———

THE UNITED STATES Chamber of Commerce, the National Association of Manufacturers and similar groups representing industry and financial interests are rendering a disservice to the American people in their attempts to frustrate the organization of labor and in their refusal to accept collective bargaining as one of our economic institutions. These groups are encouraging a systematic organization under the sham pretext of local interests. They equip these vigilantes with tin hats, wooden clubs, gas masks and lethal weapons and train them in the arts of brutality and oppression.

No tin hat brigade of goose-stepping vigilantes or bible-babbling mob of blackguarding and corporation-paid scoundrels will prevent the onward march of labor, or divert its purpose to play its natural and rational part in the development of the economic, political and social life of our nation.

Unionization, as opposed to communism, presupposes the relation of employment; it is based upon the wage system and it recognizes fully and unreservedly the institution of private property and the right to investment profit. It is upon the fuller development of collective bargaining, the wider expansion of the labor movement, the increased influence of labor in our national councils, that the perpetuity of our democratic institutions must largely depend.

The organized workers of America, free in their industrial life, conscious partners in production, secure in their homes and enjoying a decent standard of living, will prove the finest bulwark against the intrusion of alien doctrines of government. Do those who have hatched this foolish cry of communism in the C.I.O. fear the increased influence of labor in our democracy? Do they fear its influence will be cast on the side of shorter hours, a better system of distributed employment, better homes for the underprivileged, social security for the aged, a fairer distribution of the national income?

Certainly the workers that are being organized want a voice in the determination of these objectives of social justice. Certainly labor wants a fairer share in the national income. Assuredly labor wants a larger participation in increased productive efficiency. Obviously the population is entitled to participate in the fruits of the genius of our men of achievement in the field of the material sciences. Labor has suffered just as our farm population has suffered from a viciously unequal distribution of the national income. In the exploitation of both classes of workers has been the source of panic and depression, and upon the economic welfare of both rests the best assurance of a sound and permanent prosperity.

Under the banner of the Committee for Industrial Organization American labor is on the march. Its objectives today are those it had in the beginning: to strive for the unionization of our unorganized millions of workers and for the acceptance of collective bargaining as a recognized American institution. It seeks peace with the industrial world. It seeks cooperation and mutuality of effort with the agricultural population. It would avoid strikes. It would have its rights determined under the law by the peaceful negotiations and contract relationships that are supposed to characterize American commercial life. Until an aroused public opinion demands that employers accept that rule, labor has no recourse but to surrender its rights or struggle for their realization with its own economic power.

The objectives of this movement are not political in a partisan sense. Yet it is true that a political party which seeks the support of labor and makes pledges of good faith to labor must, in equity and good conscience, keep that faith and redeem those pledges. The spectacle of august and dignified members of Congress, servants of the people and agents of the Republic, skulking in hallways and closets, hiding their faces in a party caucus to prevent a quorum from acting upon a larger measure, is one that emphasizes the perfidy of politicians and blasts the confidence of labor's millions in politicians' promises and statesmen's vows.

Labor next year cannot avoid the necessity of a political assay of the work and deeds of its so-called friends and its political beneficiaries. It must determine who are its friends in the arena of politics as elsewhere. It feels that its cause is just and that its friends should not view its struggle with neutral detachment or intone constant criticism of its activities. Those who chant their praises of democracy, but who lose no chance to drive their knives into labor's defenseless back, must feel the weight of labor's woe, even as its open adversaries must ever feel the thrust of labor's power.

Labor, like Israel, has many sorrows. Its women weep for their fallen and they lament for the future of the children of the race. It ill behooves one who has supped at labor's table and who has been sheltered in labor's house to curse with equal fervor and fine impartiality both labor and its adversaries when they become locked in deadly embrace.

I repeat that labor seeks peace and guarantees its own loyalty, but the voice of labor, insistent upon its rights, should not be annoying to the ears of justice nor offensive to the conscience of the American people.

Questions

1. In what ways does Lewis contrast the values represented by the labor movement with those of the its opponents?

2. What does Lewis mean by enabling workers to become "free in their industrial life"?

145. Franklin D. Roosevelt, "Greater Security for the Average Man" (1934)

Source: **Franklin D. Roosevelt Presidential Library and Museum, Hyde Park, New York.**

Along with being a superb politician, Franklin D. Roosevelt was a master of political communication. Through his fireside chats, he used the new medium of radio to bring his message directly into Americans' living rooms, bypassing the mostly pro-Republican press. Roosevelt worked to reclaim the word "freedom" from conservatives, and made it a rallying cry for the New Deal. Throughout the 1930s, he consistently linked freedom with economic security and identified economic inequality as its greatest enemy. In this excerpt from one of the fireside chats of 1934, Roosevelt directly challenges the idea that governmental intervention in the economy threatens American freedom. The older view of liberty, he insists, served the needs only of "the privileged few." He would continue this argument during his campaign for reelection in 1936, when he triumphed with over 60 percent of the popular vote.

─────────────

TO THOSE WHO say that our expenditures for public works and other means for recovery are a waste that we cannot afford, I answer that no country, however rich, can afford the waste of its human resources. Demoralization caused by vast unemployment is our greatest extravagance. Morally, it is the greatest menace to our social order. Some people try to tell me that we must make up our minds that for the future we shall permanently have millions of unemployed just as other countries have had them for over a decade. What may be necessary for those countries is not my responsibility to determine. But as for this country, I stand or fall by my refusal to accept as a necessary condition of our future a permanent army of unemployed. On the contrary, we must make it a national principle that we will not tolerate a large army of unemployed and that we will arrange our national economy to end our present unemployment.... I do not want to think that it is the destiny of any American to remain permanently on relief rolls.

. . .

In our efforts for recovery we have avoided, on the one hand, the theory that business should and must be taken over into an all-embracing Government. We have avoided, on the other hand, the equally untenable theory that it is an interference with liberty to offer reasonable help when private enterprise is in need of help. The course we have followed fits the American practice of Government—a practice of taking action step by step, of regulating only to meet concrete needs—a practice of courageous recognition of change. I believe with Abraham Lincoln, that "The legitimate object of Government is to do for a community of people whatever they need to have done but cannot do at all or cannot do so well for themselves in their separate and individual capacities."

I still believe in ideals. I am not for a return to that definition of liberty under which for many years a free people were being gradually regimented into the service of the privileged few. I prefer and I am sure you prefer that broader definition of Liberty under which we are moving forward to greater freedom, to greater security for the average man than he has ever known before in the history of America.

Questions

1. How does Roosevelt feel that American understandings of freedom should change?

2. Why does Roosevelt feel that mass unemployment is a threat to American freedom?

146. Herbert Hoover on the New Deal and Liberty (1936)

Source: Herbert Hoover, "On the New Deal and Liberty," Official Report of the Proceedings of the 21st Republican National Convention, 1936, pp. 115–19, 122–24. Reprinted by permission of the Republican National Committee.

Even as Roosevelt invoked the word to uphold the New Deal, "liberty"—in the sense of freedom from powerful government—became the fighting slogan of his opponents. As the 1930s progressed, opponents of the New Deal invoked the language of liberty with greater and greater passion. Freedom, they claimed, meant unrestrained economic opportunity for the enterprising individual. In a speech at the Republican national convention of 1936, former president Hoover accused his successor of endangering "fundamental American liberties." Roosevelt, he charged, either was operating out of sheer opportunism, with no coherent purpose of policy, or was conspiring to impose "European ideas" on the United States. The election, he continued, in strident language that reflected how wide the gap between the parties had become, was a "holy crusade for liberty" that would "determine the future" of freedom in the United States.

———

In this room rests the greatest responsibility that has come to a body of Americans in three generations. In the lesser sense this is a convention of a great political party. But in the larger sense it is a convention of Americans to determine the fate of those ideals for which this nation was founded. That far transcends all partisanship.

There are elemental currents which make or break the fate of nations. There is a moral purpose in the universe. Those forces which affect the vitality and the soul of a people will control its destinies. The sum of years of public service in these currents is the overwhelming conviction of their transcendent importance over the more transitory, even though difficult, issues of national life.

I have given about four years to research into the New Deal, trying to determine what its ultimate objectives were, what sort of a system it is imposing on this country.

To some people it appears to be a strange interlude in American history in that it has no philosophy, that it is sheer opportunism, that it is a muddle of a spoils system, of emotional economics, of reckless adventure, of unctuous claims to a monopoly of human sympathy, of greed for power, of a desire for popular acclaim and an aspiration to make the front pages of the newspapers. That is the most charitable view.

To other people it appears to be a cold-blooded attempt by starry-eyed boys to infect the American people by a mixture of European ideas, flavored with our native predilection to get something for nothing.

You can choose either one you like best. But the first is the road of chaos which leads to the second. Both of these roads lead over the same grim precipice that is the crippling and possibly the destruction of the freedom of men.

• • •

We have seen these gigantic expenditures and this torrent of waste pile up a national debt which two generations cannot repay. One time I told a Democratic Congress that "you cannot spend yourselves into prosperity." You recall that advice did not take then. It hasn't taken yet. Billions have been spent to prime the economic pump. It did employ a horde of paid officials upon the pump handle. We have seen the frantic attempts to find new taxes on the rich. Yet three-quarters of the bill will be sent to the average man and the poor. He and his wife and his grandchildren will be giving a quarter of all their working days to pay taxes. Freedom to work for himself is changed into a slavery of work for the follies of government.

We have seen an explosive inflation of bank credits by this government borrowing. We have seen varied steps toward currency inflation that have already enriched the speculator and deprived the poor. If this is to continue the end result is the tears and anguish of universal bankruptcy and distress. No democracy in history has survived its final stages.

We have seen the building up of a horde of political officials, we have seen the pressures upon the helpless and destitute to trade political support for relief. Both are a pollution of the very fountains of liberty.

We have seen the most elemental violation of economic law and experience. The New Deal forgets it is solely by production of more goods and more varieties of goods and services that we advance the living and security of men. If we constantly decrease costs and prices and keep up earnings the production of plenty will be more and more widely distributed. These laws may be restitched in new phrases so that they are the very shoes of human progress. We had so triumphed in this long climb of mankind toward plenty that we had reached Mount Pisgah where we looked over the promised land of abolished poverty. Then men began to quarrel over the division of the goods. The depression produced by war destruction temporarily checked our march toward the promised land.

• • •

Great calamities have come to the whole world. These forces have reached into every calling and every cottage. They have brought tragedy and suffering to millions of firesides. I have great sympathy for those who honestly reach for short cuts to the immensity of our problems. While design of the structure of betterment for the common man must be inspired by the human heart, it can only be achieved by the intellect. It can only be builded by using the mould of justice, by laying brick upon brick from the materials of scientific research; by the painstaking sifting of truth from the collection of fact and experience. Any other mould is distorted; any other bricks are without straw; any other foundations are sand. That great structure of human progress can be built only by free men and women.

The gravest task which confronts the party is to regenerate these freedoms.

• • •

Fundamental American liberties are at stake. Is the Republican party ready for the issue? Are you willing to cast your all upon the issue, or would you falter and look back? Will you, for expediency's sake, also offer will-o'-the-wisps which beguile the people? Or have you determined to enter in a holy crusade for liberty which shall determine the future and the perpetuity for a nation of free men? That star shell fired today over the no man's land of world despair would illuminate the world with hope.

Questions

1. Why does Hoover believe that the future of freedom is at stake in the election of 1936?

2. How does his definition of freedom differ from that of Roosevelt?

147. Norman Cousins, "Will Women Lose Their Jobs?" (1939)

Source: Norman Cousins, "Will Women Lose Their Jobs?" from The Depression and New Deal: A History in Documents, *ed. Robert S. McElvaine (Oxford University Press, 2000). Copyright © 2000 by Robert S. McElvaine. Reproduced with permission of the Licensor through PLSclear.*

Mass unemployment during the 1930s persuaded many Americans that women were taking jobs that would otherwise go to men. The federal government prohibited both members of a married couple from holding government jobs, and many states and localities prohibited the hiring of women whose husbands earned a "living wage." In the excerpt that follows, the writer Norman Cousins commented on the movement to reduce or eliminate women's presence in the workforce and the various arguments, economic and moral, that lay behind it.

HERE IS THE latest depression cure-all, results guaranteed by its supporters:

"There are approximately 10,000,000 people out of work in the United States today. There are also 10,000,000 or more women, married and single, who are job-holders. Simply fire the women, who shouldn't be working anyway, and hire the men. Presto! No unemployment. No relief rolls. No depression."

This is the general idea behind the greatest assault on women's rights in two decades. Its supporters include not only the something-for-nothing groups which can always be depended upon to support chain-letter movements and share-the-wealth plans, but a large section of public opinion—as yet unacquainted with all the facts—which finds it hard to resist the supposed logic of millions of unemployed men replacing millions of employed women. Impetus to the drive—at least psychologically—is lent by the fact that the payrolls of many communities and private organizations are open only to males.

The first move toward the complete defeminizing of public and private jobs is discrimination against the married woman. Having thus inserted its foot in the door, the oust-women campaign seeks eventually to enter and hang up the verboten [German for "forbidden"] sign to all women, married or single, employed or seeking employment....

Of such concern is this trend to the nation's women leaders that it has been called the greatest issue to affect women since their victorious fight for suffrage. In its recent convention at Kansas City, the National Federation of Business and Professional Women's Clubs announced a frontal attack on what it considers the most serious problem it has faced in twenty years. In the eyes of Federation leaders the legislation already introduced is a portent of even more widespread attacks to come....

There are, of course, many familiar "moral" arguments against the working wife: woman's place is in the home, the management of which is enough work for any person; her first allegiance is to the bearing and raising of children; there is a direct relationship between the increase of women in business and the declining birth rate....

The Women's Bureau of the Department of Labor reports that in recent years the majority of married women at work have been working not because of a desire for a career or for economic independence but because of the need to provide or supplement the family income....

Analysis of these figures prompts the Department of Labor to point out that competition in industry is between one man and another, rather than between men and women. At most, not more than 1,000,000 jobs now held by women could pass to men. And of the 3,000,000-odd jobs held by women who admittedly are married, probably no more than 300,000 could be satisfactorily or willingly filled by males. This would "create" new jobs for only 3 per cent of the men now out of work.

Fundamentally, the unemployment of men is not caused by women who hold jobs but by the infirmities of the economic structure itself. Nor is the depression an affliction visited exclusively upon the male; the woman must bear her part of the burden, as more than 2,000,000 unemployed women can attest....

In answer to all of which the oust-women-from-jobs group may say that, yes, we are living in changing times and that, indeed, this is an emergency. And that, they may add, is precisely why extreme measures are needed and justified. Millions of men, many of them with families, are out of work. Most of them would be satisfied with salaries now paid to women. The ouster should begin with the working married woman because she should be dependent upon the man. After that, single women should be withdrawn from jobs. And who will look after them? Well, someone will; someone always does. Besides, unemployment with women is a matter of relative hardship at worst. But with men—especially family men—the hardship is absolute and complete. The state should have the right to step in and, for the greater benefit of all, say who shall work and who shall not.

An intriguing but hardly a practical thought. Because the more you study the figures of the various occupations which would be involved in the taking over of women's jobs by men, the more preposterous the scheme becomes. Imagine an average day in an America without working women:

John Citizen arrives at his office to be greeted by a male receptionist, a male switchboard operator and a male private secretary who opens his mail, arranges his appointments and takes dictation. At lunch his favorite waitress is missing, her place taken by a young man. At three o'clock he visits his dentist and is greeted by a male nurse. At four-thirty Mrs. Citizen calls to complain about Harry, who has taken the place of the part-time maid, and who refuses to wash the baby's clothes.

At the dinner table, Mary, who has just entered kindergarten, complains about Mr. Mann, the new teacher. Mrs. Citizen resents the personal questions asked by the new male salesclerk when she went shopping for underwear. She also resents the husky baritone voice that moans "Number, please," every time she picks up the phone.

Ridiculous? Certainly. But this is what a general purge of all women in industry would mean. It is impossible to carry through a large-scale replacement of one large bloc of labor for another unless there is an identity of functions all along the line. Approximately 3,500,000 men out of work are manual laborers. Which places vacated by women can they take? Approximately 3,100,000 women are employed as domestics. Which men want to take their places? There are about 920,000 salesgirls, whose replacement by men in most cases would be ludicrous. . . .

But even outside the economic sphere, arguments against the working wife reveal weakness. There is much talk about the mother's place in the home, very little about the fact that the home has changed. Housekeeping for the average family today is no longer a full-time job. We are no longer living in the days when families numbered a dozen or more, and, what with cooking, baking, canning, washing, spinning, sewing and mending, woman's work was never done. The average American family today numbers three children or less, who are away from home at least five hours a day. Inexpensive, modern gadgets simplify what were once long, tedious household tasks. In short, the home has changed from a producing to a consuming unit.

This change is reflected not only in employment of married women but in the growth of social and church work, and in the spread of adult education, of culture and entertainment groups. In these circumstances, it is difficult to blame the married woman who is not content to remain a semi-idle dependent, but who seeks in business an outlet for her talents and energies. Dr. Richard Cabot, of Boston, recently noted that many of his nervous patients were women suffering for want of serious occupational interest.

Nazi Germany thought it could casually disregard these important questions when it decided to oust its 900,000 women workers from industrial and governmental life. For years Germany had been looked upon as the foremost example of a nation in which, to the benefit of the state, equal rights for women were scrupulously upheld. The Nazi regime waved the women out of their jobs and herded them back to the home, where they were told to bear children.

However as Clifford Kirkpatrick revealed in *Nazi Germany: Its Women and Family Life*, the Nazi conception of woman as a biological instrument soon changed when it was realized that no such large bloc of labor could be displaced—or even replaced—without severely upsetting the national economy. "The 'sacred' mothers went back to the machine," observed Dr. Kirkpatrick, "and the employment of women even increased." ...

... [I]n the final analysis this question of women and jobs will be fought out on the issue of equal rights and opportunities for men and women alike.

Questions

1. Why does Cousins consider the effort to replace employed women with men "the greatest assault on women's rights in two decades"?

2. Why does he consider the proposal impractical?

---

148. Frank H. Hill on the Indian New Deal (1935)

Source: Frank H. Hill, "A New Pattern of Life for the Indian" from The Depression and New Deal: A History in Documents, *ed. Robert S. McElvaine (Oxford University Press, 2000). Copyright © 2000 by Robert S. McElvaine. Reproduced with permission of the Licensor through PLSclear.*

The New Deal marked the most radical shift in Indian policy in the nation's history. Under Commissioner of Indian Affairs John Collier, the administration launched an "Indian New Deal," which ended the policy of forced assimilation and allowed Indians unprecedented cultural autonomy. It replaced boarding schools meant to eradicate the tribal heritage of Indian children with schools on reservations and dramatically increased spending on Indian health. Federal authorities once again recognized Indians' right to govern their own affairs.

In 1935, the journalist Frank E. Hill presented a glowing description of the Indian New Deal among the Navajo, the nation's largest tribe. He stressed the benefits of the new policy for Indians but did not mention that the Navajo strongly protested against a federal soil conservation program that required them to reduce their herds of livestock—an indication that their sovereignty was far from absolute.

MORE THAN A mile above the sea level, on a plateau of the American Southwest, two hundred and fifty men are building a new capitol. It is not the capitol of a State. Its stone walls rise in shapes that are strange to most Americans; its name—Nee Alneeng—falls with a strange accent. Nee Alneeng belongs to a world far from Manhattan and Main Street. It is an Indian world, and the capitol belongs to the Navajo, now the largest of the North American tribes.

This little centre is symbolic of a new way of life among the Navajo: in fact, a new way of life for the 340,000 Indians of the United States. A year ago the Wheeler-Howard Act gave to the tribes the right to decide whether they would accept important privileges in education, self-determination and self-government. A popular vote was asked; the essential question was: "Do you want to help save yourselves?" . . .

Thus the Wheeler-Howard Act embodies an Indian policy far different from that pursued in the past. The Federal Government could have conferred self-government upon the American Indian without asking him if he wanted it. To understand why he was asked, one must take a brief but discriminating glance at American history as it has affected the Red man. . . .

The third stage may be said to have begun with the growing conviction among thoughtful Americans that Indian life had latent strength and important cultural values and that the Indian if given the right opportunities could do what the government had failed to do: he could arrange a place for himself and his customs in this modern America. The appointment of John Collier as Commissioner of Indian Affairs in April, 1933, brought into power a leader of this trend of opinion. . . .

Mr. Collier, slight, almost scholarly in appearance, at his desk in Washington describes what the administration is trying to do for the Indian and why he believes the new policy to be enlightened.

"In the past," he says, "the government tried to encourage economic independence and initiative by the allotment system, giving each Indian a portion of land and the right to dispose of it. As a result, of the 138,000,000 acres which Indians possessed in 1887 they have lost all but 47,000,000 acres, and the lost area includes the land that was the most valuable. Further, the government sought to give the Indian the schooling of the whites, teaching him to despise his old customs and habits as barbaric. Through this experiment the Indian lost much of his understanding of his own culture and received no usable substitute. In many areas such efforts to change the Indian have broken him economically and spiritually.

"We have proposed in opposition to such a policy to recognize and respect the Indian as he is. We think he must be so accepted before he can be assisted to become something else, if that is desirable. It is objected that we are proposing to make a 'blanket Indian' of him again. That is nonsense. But if he happens to be a blanket Indian we think he should not be ashamed of it. We believe further that while he needs protection and assistance in important ways, these aids should be extended with the idea of enabling him to help himself. We are sure that he can and will do this. But he must have the opportunity to do it in his own way. This is what we have been trying to extend to him. It is an opportunity that he has not had since he entered the reservations, where he has been discouraged from thinking and acting for himself.

"... Our design is to plow up the Indian soul, to make the Indian again the master of his own mind. If this fails, everything fails; if it succeeds, we believe the Indian will do the rest."...

The people whom the commissioner is trying to reanimate, and to incite to this crusade for self-survival, are in one sense heterogeneous. There is no typical Indian but rather a hundred different types. These are scattered. The 230 tribes that comprise the race are to be found here and there in twenty-two States. They are of many different stocks physically and they speak dozens of different languages.

Their cultures vary, and so does the degree to which they have adopted the white man's ways....

Underneath all their differences lie identical, unifying instincts, habits, aptitudes and spiritual feelings. Fine qualities are to be observed in almost any Indian group: artistic cleverness, tenacity, courage, dignity, and a decent pride. Under the parochial control of the past, with its effort to make the Indian a white man, these qualities have shown but little. They have come out best where the Indian, as in the Southwest, has lived his own life. . . .

The new policy has already started a renaissance in Indian arts. Young Indians are painting murals on the walls of school houses and government buildings. They are studying the ancient pottery of their tribes in museums, and devising new designs and textures in their workshops. The young people are flocking to the ceremonial dances, which for a time they had avoided. This cultural revival goes hand in hand with an interest in self-government and economic independence. In Mr. Collier's opinion, it is equally valuable.

"The Indian," he says, "can use white technologies and remain an Indian. Modernity and white Americanism are not identical. If the Indian life is a good life, then we should be proud and glad to have this different and native culture going on by the side of ours. Anything less than to let Indian culture live on would be a crime against the earth itself. The destruction of a pueblo is a barbarous thing. America is coming to understand this, and to know that in helping the Indian to save himself we are helping to save something that is precious to us as well as to him."

Questions

1. How does Hill describe the motivations for the Indian New Deal?

2. What benefits does he believe the new federal policy brings to the Indians?

---

149. W. E. B. Du Bois, "A Negro Nation within a Nation" (1935)

Source: W. E. B. Du Bois, "A Negro Nation within a Nation." Reprinted with permission from Current History *magazine (June 1935). Copyright © 2019 Current History, Inc.*

As the "last hired and first fired," African-Americans were hit hardest by the Depression. Half of the families in Harlem received public assistance during the 1930s. But many New Deal programs either were administered in an extremely discriminatory manner or, like Social Security, excluded most blacks from benefits at the insistence of white supremacist southern representatives who controlled key committees in Congress.

During the 1930s, W. E. B. Du Bois abandoned his earlier goal of racial integration as unrealistic for the foreseeable future. He now concluded that blacks must recognize themselves as "a nation within a nation." He called on blacks to organize for economic survival by building an independent, cooperative economy within their segregated communities, and gain control of their own separate schools. Du Bois's shifting position illustrated how the Depression had propelled economic survival to the top of the black agenda and how, despite the social changes of the 1930s, the goal of racial integration remained as remote as ever.

IN THIS BROADER and more intelligent democracy we can hope for progressive softening of the asperities and anomalies of race prejudice, but we cannot hope for its early and complete disappearance. Above all, the doubt, deep-planted in the American mind, as to the Negro's ability and efficiency as worker, artisan and administrator will fade but slowly. Thus, with increased democratic control of industry and capital, the place of the Negro will be increasingly a matter of human choice, of willingness to recognize ability across the barriers of race, of putting fit Negroes in places of power and authority by public opinion. At present, on the railroads, in manufacturing, in the telephone, telegraph and radio business, and in the larger divisions of trade, it is only under exceptional circumstances that any Negro no matter what his ability, gets an opportunity for position and power. Only in those lines where individual enterprise still counts, as in some of the professions, in a few of the trades, in a few branches of retail business and in artistic careers, can the Negro expect a narrow opening.

Negroes and other colored folk nevertheless, exist in larger and growing numbers. Slavery, prostitution to white men, theft of their labor and goods have not killed them and cannot kill them. They are growing in intelligence and dissatisfaction. They occupy strategic positions, within nations and beside nations, amid valuable raw material and on the highways of future expansion. They will survive, but on what terms and conditions? On this point a new school of Negro thought is arising. It believes in the ultimate uniting of mankind and in a unified American nation, with economic classes and racial barriers leveled, but it believes this is an ideal and is to be realized only by such intensified class and race consciousness as will bring irresistible force rather than mere humanitarian appeals to bear on the motives and actions of men.

The peculiar position of Negroes in America offers an opportunity. Negroes today cast probably 2,000,000 votes in a total of 40,000,000, and their vote will increase. This gives them, particularly in northern cities, and at critical times, a chance to hold a very considerable balance of power, and the mere threat of this being used intelligently and with determination may often mean much. The consuming power of 2,800,000 Negro families has recently been estimated at $166,000,000 a month—a tremendous power when intelligently directed. Their manpower as laborers probably equals that of Mexico or Yugoslavia. Their illiteracy is much lower than that of Spain or Italy. Their estimated per capita wealth about equals that of Japan.

For a nation with this start in culture and efficiency to sit down and await the salvation of a white God is idiotic. With the use of their political power, their power as consumers, and their brainpower, added to that chance of personal appeal which proximity and neighborhood always give to human beings, Negroes can develop in the United States an economic nation within a nation, able to work through inner cooperation, to found its own institutions, to educate its genius, and at the same time, without mob violence or extremes of race hatred, to keep in helpful touch and cooperate with the mass

of the nation. This has happened more often than most people realize, in the case of groups not so obviously separated from the mass
of people as are American Negroes. It must happen in our case, or
there is no hope for the Negro in America.

Any movement toward such a program is today hindered by the
absurd Negro philosophy of Scatter, Suppress, Wait, Escape. There
are even many of our educated young leaders who think that
because the Negro problem is not in evidence where there are few or
no Negroes, this indicates a way out! They think that the problem of
race can be settled by ignoring it and suppressing all reference to it.
They think that we have only to wait in silence for the white people
to settle the problem for us; and finally and predominantly, they
think that the problem of twelve million Negro people, mostly poor,
ignorant workers, is going to be settled by having their more educated and wealthy classes gradually and continually escape from
their race into the mass of the American people, leaving the rest to
sink, suffer and die.

Proponents of this program claim, with much reason, that the
plight of the masses is not the fault of the emerging classes. For the
slavery and exploitation that reduced Negroes to their present level
or at any rate hindered them from rising, the white world is to blame.
Since the age-long process of raising a group is through the escape of
its upper class into welcome fellowship with risen peoples, the
Negro intelligentsia would submerge itself if it bent its back to the
task of lifting the mass of people. There is logic in this answer, but
futile logic.

If the leading Negro classes cannot assume and bear the uplift
of their own proletariat, they are doomed for all time. It is not a case
of ethics; it is a plain case of necessity. The method by which this
may be done is, first, for the American Negro to achieve a new economic solidarity.

There exists today a chance for the Negroes to organize a cooperative state within their own group. By letting Negro farmers feed
Negro artisans, and Negro technicians guide Negro home industries,

and Negro thinkers plan this integration of cooperation, while Negro artists dramatize and beautify the struggle, economic independence can be achieved. To doubt that this is possible is to doubt the essential humanity and the quality of brains of the American Negro.

No sooner is this proposed than a great fear sweeps over older Negroes. They cry "No segregation"—no further yielding to prejudice and race separation. Yet any planning for the benefit of American Negroes on the part of a Negro intelligentsia is going to involve organized and deliberate self-segregation. There are plenty of people in the United States who would be only too willing to use such a plan as a way to increase existing legal and customary segregation between the races. This threat which many Negroes see is no mere mirage. What of it? It must be faced.

If the economic and cultural salvation of the American Negro calls for an increase in segregation and prejudice, then that must come. American Negroes must plan for their economic future and the social survival of their fellows in the firm belief that this means in a real sense the survival of colored folk in the world and the building of a full humanity instead of a petty white tyranny. Control of their own education, which is the logical and inevitable end of separate schools, would not be an unmixed ill; it might prove a supreme good. Negro schools once meant poor schools. They need not today; they must not tomorrow. Separate Negro sections will increase race antagonism, but they will also increase economic cooperation, organized self-defense and necessary self-confidence.

Questions

1. Why does Du Bois believe that the situation of American blacks was as "critical" in the 1930s as at any previous point in the nation's past?

2. Why does he feel that economic "self-segregation" offers a more viable strategy for blacks than continued pressure for racial integration?

CHAPTER 22

Fighting for the Four Freedoms: World War II, 1941–1945

150. Franklin D. Roosevelt on the Four Freedoms (1941)

Source: Annual Message to Congress, January 6, 1941, in Samuel I. Rosenman, ed., The Public Papers and Addresses of Franklin Delano Roosevelt *(New York, 1938–50), vol. 9, p. 672.*

As in other American wars, freedom became a rallying cry and the foundation of the language of national unity during World War II. Even before the United States entered the war, President Roosevelt outlined to Congress his vision of a future world order founded on the "essential human freedoms": freedom of speech, freedom of worship, freedom from want, and freedom from fear. The Four Freedoms became Roosevelt's favorite statement of Allied aims. Freedom from fear meant not only a longing for peace but a more general desire for security in a world that appeared to be out of control. Freedom of speech and religion scarcely required detailed explanation. Freedom from want was the most controversial of the four. To Roosevelt, it meant economic security; to his critics, the phrase conjured up images of socialism or of Americans living off the largesse of the government.

IN THE FUTURE days, which we seek to make secure, we look forward to a world founded upon four essential human freedoms.

The first is freedom of speech and expression—everywhere in the world.

The second is freedom of every person to worship God in his own way—everywhere in the world.

The third is freedom from want—which, translated into world terms, means economic understandings which will secure to every nation a healthy peacetime life for its inhabitants—everywhere in the world.

The fourth is freedom from fear—which, translated into world terms, means a world-wide reduction of armaments to such a point and in such a thorough fashion that no nation will be in a position to commit an act of physical aggression against any neighbor—anywhere in the world.

That is no vision of a distant millennium. It is a definite basis for a kind of world attainable in our own time and generation. That kind of world is the very antithesis of the so-called new order of tyranny which the dictators seek to create with the crash of a bomb.

To that new order we oppose the greater conception—the moral order. A good society is able to face schemes of world domination and foreign revolutions alike without fear.

Since the beginning of our American history, we have been engaged in change—in a perpetual peaceful revolution—a revolution which goes on steadily, quietly adjusting itself to changing conditions—without the concentration camp or the quick-lime in the ditch. The world order which we seek is the cooperation of free countries, working together in a friendly, civilized society.

This nation has placed its destiny in the hands and heads and hearts of its millions of free men and women; and its faith in freedom under the guidance of God. Freedom means the supremacy of human rights everywhere. Our support goes to those who struggle to gain those rights or keep them. Our strength is our unity of purpose.

To that high concept there can be no end save victory.

Questions

1. How do the Four Freedoms reflect Americans' experiences during the 1930s?

2. Roosevelt himself added the phrase "everywhere in the world" to the first draft of this speech. Why do you think he did so?

---

151. Will Durant, "Freedom of Worship" (1943)

Source: Will Durant, Freedom of Worship *essay © SEPS licensed by Curtis Licensing. Indianapolis, IN. Reprinted by permission of Curtis Licensing.*

Norman Rockwell's paintings representing the Four Freedoms are some of the most iconic images from World War II. In 1943, they were published in successive issues of the popular magazine the *Saturday Evening Post*, each accompanied by a short essay by a prominent writer. For "Freedom of Worship," the editors chose Will Durant, author, with his wife, Ariel, of an eleven-volume *History of Civilization*, published between 1935 and 1975, which adorned the bookshelves of thousands of middle-class readers. In this essay, Durant ruminated on the centrality of freedom of religion to American society and to the struggle against Nazi tyranny.

Down in the valley below the hill where I spend my summers is a little white church whose steeple has been my guiding goal in many a pleasant walk.

Often, as I passed the door on weekdays when all was silent there, I wished that I might enter, sit quietly in one of the empty pews, and feel more deeply the wonder and the longing that had built such chapels—temples and mosques and great cathedrals—everywhere on the earth....

This little church is the first and final symbol of America. For men came across the sea not merely to find new soil for their plows but to win freedom for their souls, to think and speak and worship as they would. This is the freedom men value most of all; for this they have borne countless persecutions and fought more bravely than for food or gold. These men coming out of their chapel—what is the finest thing about them, next to their undiscourageable life? It is that they do not demand that others should worship as they do, or even that others should worship at all. In that waving valley are some who have not come to this service. It is not held against them; mutely these worshipers understand that faith takes many forms, and that men name with diverse words the hope that in their hearts is one.

It is astonishing and inspiring that after all the bloodshed of history this land should house in fellowship a hundred religions and a hundred doubts. This is with us an already ancient heritage; and because we knew such freedom of worship from our birth, we took it for granted and expected it of all mature men. Until yesterday the whole civilized world seemed secure in that liberty.

But now suddenly, through some paranoiac mania of racial superiority, or some obscene sadism of political strategy, persecution is renewed, and men are commanded to render unto Caesar the things that are Caesar's, and unto Caesar the things that are God's. The Japanese, who once made all things beautiful, begin to exclude from their realm every faith but the childish belief in the divinity of their emperor. The Italians, who twice littered their peninsula with genius, are compelled to oppress a handful of hunted men. The French, once honored in every land for civilization and courtesy, hand over desolate refugees to the coldest murderers that history has ever known. The Germans, who once made the world their debtors in science, scholarship, philosophy and music, are prodded into one of the bitterest persecutions in all the annals of savagery by men who seem to delight in human misery, who openly pledge themselves to destroy Christianity, who seem resolved to leave their people no religion but war, and no God but the state.

It is incredible that such reactionary madness can express the mind and heart of an adult nation. A man's dealings with his God should be a sacred thing, inviolable by any potentate. No ruler has yet existed who was wise enough to instruct a saint; and a good man who is not great is a hundred times more precious than a great man who is not good.... When we yield our sons to war, it is in the trust that their sacrifice will bring to us and our allies no inch of alien soil, no selfish monopoly of the world's resources or trade, but only the privilege of winning for all peoples the most precious gifts in the orbit of life—freedom of body and soul, of movement and enterprise, of thought and utterance, of faith and worship, of hope and charity, of a humane fellowship with all men.

Questions

1. What does Durant believe is the most important feature of American religion?

2. Why does he think that freedom of religion differentiates Americans from the country's wartime foes?

―――――――――

152. Henry R. Luce, "The American Century" (1941)

Source: Henry R. Luce, "The American Century," Life, February 17, 1941. © 1941 The Picture Collection Inc. All rights reserved. Reprinted from Life and published with permission of The Picture Collection Inc. Reproduction in any manner in any language in whole or in part without written permission is prohibited.

Even before the United States entered World War II, it had become clear that the nation would play a far more active role in international affairs than in the past. One of the most celebrated blueprints for the postwar world was written in 1941 by Henry Luce, the publisher of *Life* and *Time* magazines. In "The American Century," Luce sought to mobilize the American people for both the coming war and an era of postwar world leadership. Americans, Luce's book insisted, must embrace the role history had thrust upon them as the world's most powerful nation. After the war, American power and American values would underpin a previously unimaginable prosperity—"the abundant life," Luce called it—produced by free economic enterprise.

Luce's essay anticipated important aspects of the postwar world. But some saw the term "American Century" as a call not for future international cooperation but for an American empire.

━━━━━

IN THE FIELD of national policy, the fundamental trouble with America has been, and is, that whereas their nation became in the Twentieth Century the most powerful and the most vital nation in the world, nevertheless Americans were unable to accommodate themselves spiritually and practically to that fact. Hence they have failed to play their part as a world power—a failure which has had disastrous consequences for themselves and for all mankind. And the cure is this: to accept wholeheartedly our duty and our opportunity as the most powerful and vital nation in the world and in consequence to exert upon the world the full impact of our influence, for such purposes as we see fit and by such means as we see fit.

• • •

This Twentieth Century is baffling, difficult, paradoxical, revolutionary. But by now, at the cost of much pain and many hopes deferred, we know a good deal about it. And we ought to accommodate our outlook to this knowledge so dearly bought. For example, any true conception of our world of the Twentieth Century must surely include a vivid awareness of at least these four propositions.

First: our world of 2,000,000,000 human beings is for the first time in history one world, fundamentally indivisible. Second: modern man hates war and feels intuitively that, in its present scale and frequency, it may even be fatal to his species. Third: our world, again for the first time in human history, is capable of producing all the material needs of the entire human family. Fourth: the world of the Twentieth Century, if it is to come to life in any nobility of health and vigor, must be to a significant degree an American Century.

As to the first and second: in postulating the indivisibility of the contemporary world, one does not necessarily imagine that anything like a world state—a parliament of men—must be brought about in this century. Nor need we assume that war can be abolished. All that it is necessary to feel—and to feel deeply—is that terrific forces of magnetic attraction and repulsion will operate as between every large group of human beings on this planet. Large sections of the human family may be effectively organized into opposition to each other. Tyrannies may require a large amount of living space. But Freedom requires and will require far greater living space than Tyranny. Peace cannot endure unless it prevails over a very large part of the world. Justice will come near to losing all meaning in the minds of men unless Justice can have approximately the same fundamental meanings in many lands and among many peoples.

As to the third point—the promise of adequate production for all mankind, the "more abundant life"—be it noted that this is characteristically an American promise. It is a promise easily made, here and elsewhere, by demagogues and proponents of all manner of slick schemes and "planned economies." What we must insist on is that the abundant life is predicated on Freedom—on the Freedom which has created its possibility—on a vision of Freedom under Law. Without Freedom, there will be no abundant life. With Freedom, there can be.

And finally there is the belief—shared let us remember by most men living—that the Twentieth Century must be to a significant degree an American Century. This knowledge calls us to action now.

• • •

As America enters dynamically upon the world scene, we need most of all to seek and to bring forth a vision of America as a world power which is authentically American and which can inspire us to live and work and fight with vigor and enthusiasm. And as we come now to the great test, it may yet turn out that in all our trials and tribulations of spirit during the first part of this century we as a people have been painfully apprehending the meaning of our time and now in this moment of testing there may come clear at last the vision which will guide us to the authentic creation of the Twentieth Century—our Century.

Questions

1. What does Luce mean when he writes, "Freedom requires and will require far greater living space than Tyranny"?

2. How do you interpret the phrase "an American Century"?

153. Henry A. Wallace on "The Century of the Common Man" (1942)

Source: "Speech at the Free World Association, May 8, 1942," in Henry A. Wallace, The Price of Free World Victory, ed. Russell Lord (New York, 1942), pp. 11–17.

Many Americans who deplored the bombastic tone of Luce's call for an American Century welcomed the response offered by Vice President Henry Wallace. In a 1942 speech, Wallace outlined a different postwar vision. In contrast to Luce's American Century, a world of business dominance no less than American power, Wallace predicted that the war would usher in a "century of the common man." The "march of freedom," said Wallace, would continue in the postwar world. That world, however, would be marked by international cooperation, not any single power's rule. Governments acting to "humanize" capitalism and redistribute economic resources would eliminate hunger, illiteracy, and poverty.

Luce and Wallace both invoked the idea of freedom. Luce offered a confident vision of worldwide free enterprise, while Wallace anticipated a global New Deal. But they had one thing in common—a new conception of America's role in the world, tied to continued international involvement, the promise of economic abundance, and the idea that the American experience should serve as a model for all other nations.

THE MARCH OF freedom of the past 150 years has been a long-drawn-out people's revolution. In this Great Revolution of the people, there were the American Revolution of 1775, the French Revolution of 1792, the Latin-American revolutions of the Bolivarian era, the German Revolution of 1848, and the Russian Revolution of 1918. Each spoke for the common man in terms of blood on the battlefield. Some went to excess. But the significant thing is that the people groped their way to the light. More of them learned to think and work together.

• • •

The people are on the march toward even fuller freedom than the most fortunate peoples of the earth have hitherto enjoyed. No Nazi counter-revolution will stop it. The common man will smoke the Hitler stooges out into the open in the United States, in Latin America, and in India. He will destroy their influence. No Lavals, no Musolinis will be tolerated in a Free World.

The people in their millennial and revolutionary march toward manifesting here on earth the dignity that is in every human soul, holds as its credo the Four Freedoms enunciated by President Roosevelt in his message to Congress on January 6, 1941. These Four Freedoms are the very core of the revolution for which the United States have taken their stand. We who live in the United States may think there is nothing very revolutionary about freedom of religion, freedom of expression, and freedom from the fear of secret police. But when we begin to think about the significance of freedom from want for the average man, then we know that the revolution of the past 150 years has not been completed, either here in the United States or in any other nation in the world. We know that this revolution can not stop until freedom from want has actually been attained.

• • •

Some have spoken of the "American Century." I say that the century on which we are entering—the century which will come of this war—can be and must be the century of the common man. Perhaps it will be America's opportunity to suggest the freedoms and duties by which the common man must live. Everywhere the common man must learn to build his own industries with his own hands in a practical fashion. Everywhere the common man must learn to increase his productivity so that he and his children can eventually pay to the world community all that they have received. No nation will have the God-given right to exploit other nations. Older nations will have the privilege to help younger nations get started on the path to industrialization, but there must be neither military nor economic imperialism. The methods of the nineteenth century will not work in the people's century which is now about to begin. India, China, and Latin America have a tremendous stake in the people's century. As their masses learn to read and write, and as they become productive mechanics, their standard of living will double and treble. Modern science, when devoted whole-heartedly to the general welfare, has in it potentialities of which we do not yet dream.

• • •

When the time of peace comes, the citizen will again have a duty, the supreme duty of sacrificing the lesser interest for the greater interest of the general welfare. Those who write the peace must think of the whole world. There can be no privileged peoples. We ourselves in the United States are no more a master race than the Nazis. And we can not perpetuate economic warfare without planting the seeds of military warfare. We must use our power at the peace table to build an economic peace that is just, charitable and enduring.

Questions

1. How does Wallace's vision of the postwar world differ from Henry Luce's?

2. To what does Wallace seem to refer when he declares that there will be "no privileged peoples" in the postwar world?

154. Judge Learned Hand, The Spirit of Liberty (1944)

Source: Learned Hand, from The Spirit of Liberty: Papers and Addresses of Learned Hand, *ed. Irving Dillard. New York: Knopf, 1952. Pp. 189–91. Reprinted by permission of the President and Fellows of Harvard College.*

In 1944, over 1 million persons gathered in New York's Central Park to celebrate "I Am an American Day." Learned Hand, one of the best-known federal judges (sometimes called the greatest judge who never sat on the Supreme Court), delivered a short speech. He particularly addressed 150,000 recently naturalized citizens who were present. Liberty, he explained, was what had brought them to the United States. Unusually for a judge, he went on to say that the "spirit of liberty" lay not in laws and constitutions but in the "hearts of men and women." Hand rejected the idea that freedom meant simply doing what one wished; instead, it meant open-mindedness, respect for the opinions and rights of others, a willingness to set aside unconscious biases and to accept limits on individual action in order to promote the public good. He defended freedom of expression, even for unpopular opinions, as essential to liberty.

―――――――――

WE HAVE GATHERED here to affirm a faith, a faith in a common purpose, a common conviction, a common devotion. Some of us have chosen America as the land of our adoption; the rest have come from those who did the same. For this reason we have some right to consider ourselves a picked group, a group of those who had the courage to break from the past and brave the dangers and the loneliness of a strange land. What was the object that nerved us, or those who went before us, to this choice? We sought liberty; freedom from oppression, freedom from want, freedom to be ourselves. This we then sought; this we now believe that we are by way of winning. What do we mean when we say that first of all we seek liberty? I often wonder whether we do not rest our hopes too much upon constitutions, upon laws and upon courts. These are false hopes; believe me, these are false hopes. Liberty lies in the hearts of men and women; when it dies there, no constitution, no law, no court ... can even do much to help it. While it lies there it needs no constitution, no law, no court to save it. And what is this liberty which must lie in the hearts of men and women? It is not the ruthless, the unbridled will; it is not freedom to do as one likes. That is the denial of liberty, and leads straight to its overthrow. A society in which men recognize no check upon their freedom soon becomes a society where freedom is the possession of only a savage few; as we have learned to our sorrow.

What then is the spirit of liberty? I cannot define it; I can only tell you my own faith. The spirit of liberty is the spirit which is not too sure that it is right; the spirit of liberty is the spirit which seeks to understand the minds of other men and women; the spirit of liberty is the spirit which weighs their interests alongside its own without bias; the spirit of liberty remembers that not even a sparrow falls to earth unheeded; the spirit of liberty is the spirit of Him who, near two thousand years ago, taught mankind that lesson it has never learned, but never quite forgotten; that there may be a kingdom where the least shall be heard and considered side by side with the greatest. And now in that spirit, that spirit of an America which has never been, and which may never be; nay, which never will be except as the conscience and courage of Americans create it; yet in the spirit of that America which lies hidden in some form in the aspirations of us all; in the spirit of that America for which our young men are at this moment fighting and dying; in that spirit of liberty and of America I ask you to rise and with me pledge our faith in the glorious destiny of our beloved country.

Questions

1. What does Hand mean when he says that liberty lives in people's hearts, not in laws?

2. Why do you think that during World War II, he emphasizes respect for differences of opinion as the essence of liberty?

155. World War II and Mexican-Americans (1945)

Source: LULAC, editorial, "World War II and Mexican Americans,"
LULAC News, *Vol. 12, October 1945, pp. 5–6. Reprinted by permission of LULAC.*

Founded in 1929, the League of United Latin American Citizens (LULAC) campaigned for equal treatment for Americans of Latino descent and their full integration into American life. Some half a million Mexican-Americans served in the armed forces during World War II, but Latinos continued to face widespread discrimination. An editorial in the LULAC newsletter soon after the war ended drew upon military service to condemn anti-Latino prejudice. Its aggressive language reflected the rising demand for equal rights sparked by the war experience among many minority groups.

———————

"WE DO NOT serve Mexicans here." "You will have to get out as no Mexicans are allowed." "Your uniform and service ribbons mean nothing here. We still do not allow Mexicans."

These, and many other stronger-worded ones, are the embarrassing and humiliating retorts given our returning veterans of Latin American descent and their families. They may all be worded differently, and whereas some are toned with hate and loathness while others are toned with sympathy and remorse, still the implication remains that these so-called "Mexicans" are considered unworthy of equality, regardless of birthright or service. This situation is ironic indeed, in view of the fact that these same "Mexicans" have just finished helping this country to defeat countries to the east and west who would impose upon the world a superior people, a superior culture.

Why this hate, this prejudice, this tendency to discriminate against a people whose only fault seems to be that they are heirs of a culture older than any known "American Culture," to find themselves a part of a land and people they have helped to build and to defend, to find themselves a part of a minority group whose acquired passive nature keeps them from boldly demanding those rights and privileges which are rightfully theirs? Can it be the result of difference in race, nationality, language, loyalty, intelligence or ability?

There is no difference in race. Latin Americans, or so-called "Mexicans," are Caucasian or white. There are only three races: the Caucasian, the Negroid, and the Mongoloid. Racial characteristics place the Latin American among the white. Who dares contradict nature? There is no difference in nationality. These "Mexicans" were born and bred in this country and are just as American as Jones or Smith. In fact, the ancestors of these "Mexicans" were here before those of Jones or Smith decided to take up abode. Difference in language? No. These "Mexicans" speak English. Accented, perhaps, in some cases, but English all over the United States seems to be accented. That these "Mexicans" can speak Spanish is not a detriment, it is an asset. After all, there are not too many people in this country who can boast a knowledge of the most widely spoken languages in the world. Difference in loyalty? How can that be when all revere the same stars and stripes, when they don the same service uniforms for the same principles? Difference in intelligence and ability? Impossible. . . .

We could go on and on naming erroneously imagined differences to be used as a basis for this hate and find each one false. This condition is not a case of difference; it is a case of ignorance. Yes, ignorance. Odd indeed to find this banal state of mind in a country of such enlightment and progress. But then, ignorance is like a disease that is contagious, but contagious only for those who wish to suffer from it. Ignorance, bigotry, prejudice, and intolerance all down through the centuries have tried to crush intelligence with cruelty, reason with brutality, and spirituality with madness. This quartet of banalities constitutes the curse of the world. Ignorance is the parent of the other three.

Yes, ignorance broods hate and all its resultant actions of jealousy, misunderstandings, erroneous opinions, and premeditated feelings of discord and confusion. In this particular case of unjustified failure to foment a fraternal feeling between two groups of Americans, it is an ignorance of facts that poisons the atmosphere. An ignorance of the cultural contributions of Americans of Latin American descent to the still young American Culture; an ignorance of the blood, sweat, and efforts given to this country for its betterment; an ignorance of the sufferings withstood and the lives given to preserve this country free and independent through its various periods of strife and conflict; and finally, an ignorance of a sense of appreciation for a long, profitable, and loyal association with a group of Americans whose voice cries out in desperate supplication:

> We have proved ourselves true and loyal Americans by every trial and test that has confronted us; now give us social, political, and economic equality and the opportunity to practice and enjoy that equality. We ask for it not as a favor, but as a delegated right guaranteed by our Constitution, and as a reward for faithful service.

Questions

1. What are the implications of explaining prejudice and discrimination as arising from ignorance rather than economic self-interest?

2. Why does the editorial insist on identifying Latinos as white?

156. Charles H. Wesley on African-Americans and the Four Freedoms (1944)

Source: Charles H. Wesley, from What the Negro Wants *ed. Rayford W. Logan. Copyright © 1944 by the University of North Carolina Press, renewed 1972 by Rayford W. Logan. Used by permission of the publisher. www.uncpress.org*

World War II reinvigorated the black struggle for equality in America. In 1944, the University of North Carolina Press published *What the Negro Wants*, a book of essays by fourteen prominent black leaders. Virtually every contributor called for the right to vote in the South, the dismantling of segregation, and access to the "American standard of living." Several essays also linked the black movement for racial justice with movements against European imperialism in Africa and Asia. Many whites could not accept these demands. When he read the manuscript, W. T. Couch, the director of the press, was stunned. "If this is what the Negro wants," he told the book's editor, "nothing could be clearer than what he needs, and needs most urgently, is to revise his wants." In this excerpt, the historian Charles H. Wesley explains that blacks are denied each of the Four Freedoms and also illustrates how the war strengthened black internationalism.

━━━━━━

[NEGROES] HAVE WANTED what other citizens of the United States have wanted. They have wanted freedom and opportunity. They have wanted the pursuit of the life vouchsafed to all citizens of the United States by our own liberty documents. They have wanted freedom of speech, [but] they were supposed to be silently acquiescent in all aspects of their life.... They have wanted freedom of religion, for they had been compelled to "steal away to Jesus"...in order to worship God as they desired.... They have wanted freedom from want.... However, the Negro has remained a marginal worker and the competition with white workers has left him in want in many localities of an economically sufficient nation. They have wanted freedom from fear. They have been cowed, brow-beaten or beaten, as they have marched through the years of American life....

The Negro wants ultimately the abolition of segregation in education and the equalization of educational opportunity as an immediate step. The segregated Negro school is usually an inferior school and a disparity in the bi-racial system continues to develop.... This inequality is represented by inequalities in school terms, salaries, training of teachers, buildings and equipment. The inequalities extend from the elementary schools through the graduate school....

The Negro wants democracy to begin at home. As one was heard to say ... "I would rather die for democracy here than in Germany." ... Some are already beginning to doubt that this war is a war for freedom or democracy.... They are beginning to be disillusioned when they think of the result of the first world war to save the world for democracy. The future of our democratic life is insecure so long as the hatred, disdain and disparagement of Americans of African ancestry exist....

The Negro wants not only to win the war but also to win the peace.... He wants the peace to be free of race and color restrictions, of imperialism and exploitation, and inclusive of the participation of minorities all over the world in their own governments. When it is said that we are fighting for freedom, the Negro asks, "Whose freedom?" Is it the freedom of a peace to exploit, suppress, exclude, debase and restrict colored peoples in India, China, Africa, Malaya in the usual ways? ... Will Great Britain and the United States specifically omit from the Four Freedoms their minorities and subject peoples? The Negro does not want such a peace.

Questions

1. How does this document reflect black Americans' growing sense of identification with nonwhite peoples in other parts of the world?

2. In what ways, according to Wesley, are blacks denied the Four Freedoms?

157. Justice Robert A. Jackson, Dissent in *Korematsu v. United States* (1944)

Source: **Korematsu v. United States, *323 U.S. 214 (1944).***

Unlike in World War I, the federal government during World War II actively promoted a pluralist vision of the United States as a place where persons of all races, religions, and national origins could enjoy freedom equally. The great exception to this new emphasis on tolerance was the experience of Japanese-Americans. In February 1942, the military persuaded FDR to order the expulsion of all persons of Japanese descent from the West Coast. Authorities removed over 110,000 men, women, and children, nearly two-thirds of them American citizens, to internment camps far from their homes.

In 1944, the Supreme Court denied the appeal of Fred Korematsu, who had been arrested for refusing to present himself for internment. Speaking for a 6–3 majority, Justice Hugo Black upheld the constitutionality of the internment policy, insisting that an order applying only to persons of Japanese descent was not based on race. As Justice Robert Jackson pointed out in his dissent, Korematsu was not accused of any crime. He condemned the majority for justifying a massive violation of civil liberties. In 1988, Congress apologized for internment and provided compensation to surviving victims.

━━━━━━━━

KOREMATSU WAS BORN on our soil, of parents born in Japan. The Constitution makes him a citizen of the United States by nativity and a citizen of California by residence. No claim is made that he is not loyal to this country. There is no suggestion that apart from the matter involved here he is not law-abiding and well disposed. Korematsu, however, has been convicted of an act not commonly a crime. It consists merely of being present in the state whereof he is a citizen, near the place where he was born, and where all his life he has lived.

Even more unusual is the series of military orders which made this conduct a crime. They forbid such a one to remain, and they also forbid him to leave. They were so drawn that the only way Korematsu could avoid violation was to give himself up to the military authority. This meant submission to custody, examination, and transportation out of the territory, to be followed by indeterminate confinement in detention camps.

A citizen's presence in the locality, however, was made a crime only if his parents were of Japanese birth. Had Korematsu been one of four—the others being, say, a German alien enemy, an Italian alien enemy, and a citizen of American-born ancestors convicted of treason but out on parole—only Korematsu's presence would have violated the order. The difference between their innocence and his crime would result, not from anything he did, said, or thought different than they but only in that he was born of different racial stock.

Now, if any fundamental assumption underlies our system, it is that guilt is personal and not inheritable. Even if all of one's antecedents had been convicted of treason, the Constitution forbids its penalties to be visited upon him, for it provides that "no attainder of treason shall work corruption of blood or forfeiture except during the life of the person attained." But here is an attempt to make an otherwise innocent act a crime merely because this prisoner is the son of parents as to whom he had no choice and belongs to a race from which there is no way to resign. If Congress in peacetime legislation should enact such a criminal law, I should suppose this Court would refuse to enforce it.

But the "law" which this prisoner is convicted of disregarding is not found in an act of Congress but in a military order. Neither the act of Congress nor the executive order of the President, nor both together, would afford a basis for this conviction. It rests on the orders of General DeWitt. And it is said that if the military commander had reasonable military grounds for promulgating the orders, they are constitutional and become law, and the Court is required to enforce them. There are several reasons why I cannot subscribe to this doctrine.

It would be impracticable and dangerous idealism to expect or insist that each specific military command in an area of probable operations will conform to conventional tests of constitutionality. When an area is so beset that it must be put under military control at all, the paramount consideration is that its measures be successful rather than legal. The armed services must protect a society, not merely its Constitution. The very essence of the military job is to marshal physical force, to remove every obstacle to its effectiveness, to give it every strategic advantage. Defense measures will not, and often should not, be held within the limits that bind civil authority in peace. No court can require such a commander in such circumstances to act as a reasonable man; he may be unreasonably cautious and exacting. Perhaps he should be. But a commander in temporarily focusing the life of a community on defense is carrying out a military program; he is not making law in the sense the courts know the term. He issues orders, and they may have a certain authority as military commands, although they may be very bad as constitutional law.

But if we cannot confine military expedients by the Constitution, neither would I distort the Constitution to approve all that the military may deem expedient. That is what the Court appears to be doing, whether consciously or not. I cannot say, from any evidence before me, that the orders of General DeWitt were not reasonably expedient military precautions, nor could I say that they were. But even if they were permissible military procedures, I deny that it follows that they are constitutional. If, as the Court holds, it does follow, then we may as well say that any military order will be constitutional and have done with it.

• • •

A military order, however unconstitutional, is not apt to last longer than the military emergency. Even during that period a succeeding commander may revoke it all. But once a judicial opinion rationalizes such an order to show that it conforms to the Constitution, or rather rationalizes the Constitution to show that the Constitution sanctions such an order, the Court for all time has validated the principle of racial discrimination in criminal procedure and of transplanting American citizens. The principle then lies about like a loaded weapon ready for the hand of any authority that can bring forward a plausible claim of an urgent need. Every repetition imbeds that principle more deeply in our law and thinking and expands it to new purposes. All who observe the work of courts are familiar with what Judge Cardozo described as "the tendency of a principle to expand itself to the limit of its logic." A military commander may overstep the bounds of constitutionality and it is an incident. But if we review and approve, that passing incident becomes the doctrine of the Constitution. There it has a generative power of its own, and all that it creates will be in its own image. Nothing better illustrates this danger than does the Court's opinion in this case.

• • •

I should hold that a civil court cannot be made to enforce an order which violates constitutional limitations even if it is a reasonable exercise of military authority. The courts can exercise only the judicial power, can apply only law, and must abide by the Constitution, or they cease to be civil courts and become instruments of military policy.

Questions

1. Why does Jackson believe that even though military authorities have the power to violate constitutional protections in time of war, the courts should not approve their actions?

2. How did the experience of Japanese-Americans differ from that of Americans whose ancestors came from Germany, Italy, or other countries fighting the United States?

CHAPTER 23

The United States and the Cold War, 1945–1953

158. Declaration of Independence of the Democratic Republic of Vietnam (1945)

Source: Ho Chi Minh, "Declaration of Independence of the Democratic Republic of Vietnam," Ho Chi Minh, Selected Works: Vol. 3 (Hanoi: Foreign Languages Publishing House, 1961), pp. 17–21. Reprinted by permission of Thế Giới Publishers.

Like the end of World War I, the Allied triumph in World War II inspired hopes for national independence throughout the colonial world. The Atlantic Charter, agreed to by President Roosevelt and British prime minister Winston Churchill in 1941, had declared that all peoples had a right to self-determination. But as in World War I, the victorious governments of Britain and France had no desire to see the dismantling of their empires.

Vietnam, long a French colony in Southeast Asia, had been occupied by Japan during the war. The Viet Minh, a broad coalition of Vietnamese nationalists, had fought a guerrilla war against the Japanese and with the end of World War II, took control of local government in much of the country. The movement's leader was Ho Chi Minh, a communist from a poor colonial family who had managed to obtain an education in Paris. But when Vietnam, in September 1945, proclaimed its independence, the document drew not on communist ideology but on the American

Declaration of Independence, whose famous preamble it repeated at the outset, and the French Declaration of the Rights of Man. Ho Chi Minh hoped that Western powers would see their own ideals being acted out in the Vietnamese struggle for independence. France, however, was determined to reclaim its colony, and the United States chose to side with it, with tragic long-term consequences for both Americans and Vietnamese.

———

"ALL MEN ARE created equal. They are endowed by their Creator with certain inalienable rights, among these are Life, Liberty, and the pursuit of Happiness."

This immortal statement was made in the Declaration of Independence of the United States of America in 1776. In a broader sense, this means: All the peoples on the earth are equal from birth, all the peoples have a right to live, to be happy and free.

The Declaration of the French Revolution made in 1791 on the Rights of Man and the Citizen also states: "All men are born free and with equal rights, and must always remain free and have equal rights." Those are undeniable truths.

Nevertheless, for more than eighty years, the French imperialists, abusing the standard of Liberty, Equality, and Fraternity, have violated our Fatherland and oppressed our fellow-citizens. They have acted contrary to the ideals of humanity and justice. In the field of politics, they have deprived our people of every democratic liberty. . . . They have built more prisons than schools. They have mercilessly slain our patriots—they have drowned our uprisings in rivers of blood. They have fettered public opinion; they have practiced obscurantism against our people. To weaken our race they have forced us to use opium and alcohol.

In the fields of economics, they have fleeced us to the backbone, impoverished our people, and devastated our land. They have robbed us of our rice fields, our mines, our forests, and our raw materials. They have monopolized the issuing of bank-notes and the export trade. They have invented numerous unjustifiable taxes and reduced our people, especially our peasantry, to a state of extreme poverty....

From [1940], our people were subjected to the double yoke of the French and the Japanese. Their sufferings and miseries increased. The result was that from the end of last year to the beginning of this year, from Quang Tri province to the North of Vietnam, more than two million of our fellow-citizens died from starvation.... From the autumn of 1940, our country had in fact ceased to be a French colony and had become a Japanese possession.

After the Japanese had surrendered to the Allies, our whole people rose to regain our national sovereignty and to found the Democratic Republic of Vietnam....

For these reasons, we, members of the Provisional Government, representing the whole Vietnamese people, declare that from now on we break off all relations of a colonial character with France; we repeal all the international obligation that France has so far subscribed to on behalf of Vietnam and we abolish all the special rights the French have unlawfully acquired in our Fatherland. The whole Vietnamese people, animated by a common purpose, are determined to fight to the bitter end against any attempt by the French colonialists to reconquer their country.

We are convinced that the Allied nations which ... have acknowledged the principles of self-determination and equality of nations, will not refuse to acknowledge the independence of Vietnam. A people who have courageously opposed French domination for more than eighty years, a people who have fought side by side with the Allies against the Fascists during these last years, such a people must be free and independent.

For these reasons, we, members of the Provisional Government of the Democratic Republic of Vietnam, solemnly declare to the world that Vietnam has the right to be a free and independent country and in fact it is so already. The entire Vietnamese people are determined to mobilize all their physical and mental strength, to sacrifice their lives and property in order to safeguard their independence and liberty.

Questions

1. Why do you think the Vietnamese nationalists begin by referring to the Declaration of Independence and the French Declaration of the Rights of Man and the Citizen?

2. Why are the authors of the document confident that the victorious Allies of World War II will recognize their independence?

―――――

159. The Truman Doctrine (1947)

Source: "Special Message to the Congress on Greece and Turkey, March 12, 1947," in **Public Papers of the Presidents of the United States, Harry S. Truman, 1947 *(Washington, D.C., 1963), pp. 176–80.***

In March 1947, in a speech announcing what came to be known as the Truman Doctrine, President Harry S. Truman officially embraced the containment of Soviet communism as the foundation of American foreign policy. The immediate occasion was a request for military and financial aid from Greece, a monarchy threatened by a communist-led rebellion, and Turkey, from which the Soviets were demanding joint control of the straits linking the Black Sea and the Mediterranean. Neither were models of democracy. To rally popular backing, Truman appealed to his strongest rhetorical argument—the defense of freedom. Twenty-four times in the eighteen-minute speech, Truman used the words "free" and "freedom." The Truman Doctrine created the language through which most Americans came to understand the postwar world. The speech set a precedent for American assistance to anticommunist regimes throughout the world, no matter how undemocratic, and for the creation of a set of global military alliances directed against the Soviet Union.

―――――

THE GRAVITY OF the situation which confronts the world today necessitates my appearance before a joint session of the Congress.

The foreign policy and the national security of this country are involved.

One aspect of the present situation, which I present to you at this time for your consideration and decision, concerns Greece and Turkey.

The United States has received from the Greek Government an urgent appeal for financial and economic assistance. Preliminary reports from the American Economic Mission now in Greece and reports from the American Ambassador in Greece corroborate the statement of the Greek Government that assistance is imperative if Greece is to survive as a free nation.

I do not believe that the American people and the Congress wish to turn a deaf ear to the appeal of the Greek Government.

• • •

The very existence of the Greek state is today threatened by the terrorist activities of several thousand armed men, led by Communists, who defy the government's authority at a number of points, particularly along the northern boundaries. A Commission appointed by the United Nations Security Council is at present investigating disturbed conditions in northern Greece and alleged border violations along the frontier between Greece on the one hand and Albania, Bulgaria, and Yugoslavia on the other.

Meanwhile, the Greek Government is unable to cope with the situation. The Greek army is small and poorly equipped. It needs supplies and equipment if it is to restore authority to the government throughout Greek territory.

• • •

We have considered how the United Nations might assist in this crisis. But the situation is an urgent one requiring immediate action, and the United Nations and its related organizations are not in a position to extend help of the kind that is required.

• • •

The Greek Government has been operating in an atmosphere of chaos and extremism. It has made mistakes. The extension of aid by this country does not mean that the United States condones everything that the Greek Government has done or will do. We have condemned in the past, and we condemn now, extremist measures of the right or the left. We have in the past advised tolerance, and we advise tolerance now.

Greece's neighbor, Turkey, also deserves our attention.

The future of Turkey as an independent and economically sound state is clearly no less important to the freedom-loving peoples of the world than the future of Greece. The circumstances in which Turkey finds itself today are considerably different from those of Greece. Turkey has been spared the disasters that have beset Greece. And during the war, the United States and Great Britain furnished Turkey with material aid.

Nevertheless, Turkey now needs our support.

• • •

At the present moment in world history nearly every nation must choose between alternative ways of life. The choice is too often not a free one.

One way of life is based upon the will of the majority, and is distinguished by free institutions, representative government, free elections, guarantees of individual liberty, freedom of speech and religion, and freedom from political oppression.

The second way of life is based upon the will of a minority forcibly imposed upon the majority. It relies upon terror and oppression, a controlled press and radio, fixed elections, and the suppression of personal freedoms.

I believe that it must be the policy of the United States to support free peoples who are resisting attempted subjugation by armed minorities or by outside pressures.

I believe that we must assist free peoples to work out their own destinies in their own way.

• • •

The free peoples of the world look to us for support in maintaining their freedoms.

If we falter in our leadership, we may endanger the peace of the world—and we shall surely endanger the welfare of this Nation.

Great responsibilities have been placed upon us by the swift movement of events.

I am confident that the Congress will face these responsibilities squarely.

Questions

1. Why does Truman insist that the question of assisting Greece and Turkey involves a choice between "alternative ways of life"?

2. How does he define freedom in the postwar world?

---

160. Daniel L. Schorr, "Reconverting Mexican Americans" (1946)

For all Americans, the process of "reconversion" to a peacetime economy was a wrenching experience. This was particularly true for groups—women, African-Americans, Mexican-Americans—that had made significant gains in employment because of the wartime labor shortage, and whose horizons had widened because of service in the military. The young reporter Daniel L. Schorr reported in 1946 on efforts in Texas to force Mexican-Americans back into the subordinate status they had occupied before the war. Schorr went on to a long career as a journalist on radio and television.

"IF THERE'S ANYTHING I hate worse than a—, it's a damn Mexican," said the soldier from south Texas, speaking what he had been taught. This attitude is behind a postwar "reconversion" process in Texas, aimed at depriving Mexican Americans of the few economic and social gains they won during the war and restoring the segregated, underpaid, uneducated pool of cheap labor that south Texas has always sought to maintain. The campaign, in which the authorities, business and the newspapers all play their part, amounts to a conspiracy....

There are about one million Mexican Americans in Texas—out of a total of approximately three million, who form the third largest minority in the United States. They are most densely settled in south Texas and make up about one-third of San Antonio's 300,000 population. For years they have done the sweated work that has helped to make this district rich. During the war the manpower shortage opened a scattering of skilled, occasionally even supervisory, jobs for Mexican Americans. Children left school to go to work. Although there was never more than five percent of the group in wartime industry in Texas, the taste of better living standards brought yearnings for social equality. Now that "reconversion" has set in, these Mexican Americans may not want to return to their former status.

Therein lies a potentially explosive situation. Tension is rising and there has already been some reaction to the mounting repression. In San Antonio's slum-ridden West Side, it is possible to collect a gang of bellicose youngsters by simply promising a fight against Anglo-American kids. The process produces increased repression and threats from the authorities, further heightening the tension.

An incident that has aroused widespread indignation among Mexicans concerns a winner of the Congressional Medal of Honor, Staff Sergeant Macario Garcia. While home on furlough, Garcia stopped for a cup of coffee at the Oasis Café in Sugarland, Fort Bend County, near Houston. The proprietor, Mrs. Donna Andrews, told him no Mexicans were served there. When he insisted on being served, there was a fight between Garcia, aided by two sailors, and customers in the café. A deputy sheriff arrived, told all concerned to forget the incident and sent Garcia home. Later the story was reported in Mexico City and then picked up by the Associated Press. . . . The publicity led the county authorities to seek vindication of their honor. Garcia was belatedly arrested on a charge of "aggravated assault" against Mrs. Andrews.

This was not the first case involving a Congressional Medal winner. Some time before, Sergeant Jose Mendoza Lopez, of Browns-ville, after his return from a good-will tour of Mexico, arranged with the cooperation of the United States Army, was thrown out of a restaurant in a small town in the Rio Grande Valley. I have examined dozens of affidavits made by Mexican Americans, testifying to discrimination in south Texas towns.

Social discrimination is no new phenomenon in a state where the defense of the Alamo still gets top billing in school history books and children are taught from the cradle that Mexicans are "dirty," "lazy," "shiftless" and "dishonest." The intensification of pressure, accompanied in some cases by terrorism, makes the Mexican Americans unwilling to accept the situation.

The situation in San Antonio is a story in itself. On the surface there is less discrimination in this city of old Spanish missions than in other parts of southern Texas. Mexican Americans are not segregated in buses, and they can attend public schools with Anglo-Americans (when they are not kept out by action of individual school principals). But it is here that the campaign against the Mexicans has assumed some of its most sinister aspects.

For the past several months local papers have been trumpeting a so-called wave of crime and rape and demanding sterner repressive action. They have played up cases involving Mexicans, while giving little or no publicity to assaults against Latins by Anglo-Americans. In response to newspaper agitation, District Attorney John R. Shook recently announced that the death penalty would hereafter be demanded in "flagrant" cases of rape. . . . Some of the Mexican boys held on rape charges by the District Attorney's office were juveniles, and the County Juvenile Office had to resort to habeas-corpus proceedings to obtain custody of them. Attacks by Mexicans on Anglo-Americans have drawn some stiff sentences. Yet within a two-week period last fall four juries—three in the Criminal District Court and one in the Juvenile Court—acquitted Anglo-Americans accused of killing Latins. The papers took no notice of these cases. . . .

The Mexican American's economic frontiers, which were widened somewhat during the war, are beginning to close in on him. The regional office of the Fair Employment Practice Commission closed in December. When war industries began laying off men, Mexican Americans were among the first to go. Frequently this is justified on a basis of seniority, which is another way of saying that previous discrimination makes new discrimination unnecessary; Mexican Americans were usually the last to be hired. It is expected that Help Wanted advertisements for skilled or responsible jobs will soon be carrying the note, "No Mexicans Need Apply." An FEPC official who had dealt with anti-Mexican discrimination during the war told me: "I don't think the Latin Americans will accept this situation. They can be trodden on just so long."

One of the best indices of poverty is disease. San Antonio's festering slums have made it possible for this city of charm and gaiety to claim the highest tuberculosis rate of any city in the country, with 151.7 deaths per hundred thousand, as against 113.7 for Chattanooga, its nearest rival. The Mexican death-toll percentage is more than three times the Anglo-American.

But nothing much is being done about it by the local authorities. The Bexar County Tuberculosis Association says 1,200 hospital beds are needed to cope with the problem. The county actually has 139. A tuberculosis specialist, who was appalled at the situation he found when he returned from the Army, told me he had been informed that funds existed to provide additional facilities, but that they were mysteriously tied up in bonds and could not be pried loose.

Every attempt to check anti-Mexican discrimination has been blocked. A bill to outlaw discrimination, introduced in the legislature by Senator J. Franklin Spears of San Antonio, has been defeated

at three sessions. During the war Texan bigotry and economic discrimination fought a holding action. Now a counter-offensive is taking shape to wrest from the Mexican Americans their economic and
social gains. But bitterness at this "reconversion" is growing and will
not long be contained.

Questions

1. Why does Schorr think that views of history help to sustain prejudice
against Mexican-Americans?

2. Why does he believe that resentment among Mexican-Americans "will
not be contained"?

161. Walter Lippmann, A Critique of Containment (1947)

Source: Walter Lippmann, excerpt from pp. 21–25 from The Cold War: A Study
in U.S. Foreign Policy *by Walter Lippmann. Copyright © 1947 by Walter
Lippmann. Copyright renewed © 1975 by Walter Lippmann. Reprinted by
permission of HarperCollins Publishers. Used with permission of President
and Fellows of Harvard College.*

Not all Americans happily embraced the Cold War. As a number of contemporary critics, few of them sympathetic to Soviet communism,
pointed out, casting the Cold War in terms of a worldwide battle between
freedom and slavery made it impossible to view international crises on a
case-by-case basis or to determine which genuinely involved either freedom or American interests.

In a penetrating critique of Truman's policies, as expounded by diplomat
George Kennan in an article signed "X," Walter Lippmann, one of the nation's
most prominent journalists, objected to turning foreign policy into an ideological crusade. To view every challenge to the status quo as part of a contest
with the Soviet Union, Lippmann correctly predicted, would require the

United States to recruit and subsidize an "array of satellites, clients, dependents and puppets." It would have to intervene continuously in the affairs of nations whose political problems did not arise from Moscow and could not be easily understood in terms of the battle between freedom and slavery. It would be a serious mistake, Lippmann warned, for the United States to align itself against the movement for colonial independence in the name of anticommunism—a warning amply borne out during the Vietnam War.

THE POLICY OF containment, which Mr. X recommends, demands the employment of American economic, political, and in the last analysis, American military power at "sectors" in the interior of Europe and Asia. This requires, as I have pointed out, ground forces, that is to say reserves of infantry, which we do not possess.

The United States cannot by its own military power contain the expansive pressure of the Russians "at every point where they show signs of encroaching." The United States cannot have ready "unalterable counterforce" consisting of American troops. Therefore, the counterforces which Mr. X requires have to be composed of Chinese, Afghans, Iranians, Turks, Kurds, Arabs, Greeks, Italians, Austrians, of anti-Soviet Poles, Czechoslovaks, Bulgars, Yugoslavs, Albanians, Hungarians, Finns and Germans.

The policy can be implemented only by recruiting, subsidizing and supporting a heterogeneous array of satellites, clients, dependents and puppets. The instrument of the policy of containment is therefore a coalition of disorganized, disunited, feeble or disorderly nations, tribes and factions around the perimeter of the Soviet Union.

To organize a coalition among powerful modern states is, even in time of war and under dire necessity, an enormously difficult thing to do well. To organize a coalition of disunited, feeble and immature states, and to hold it together for a prolonged diplomatic siege, which might last for ten or fifteen years, is, I submit, impossibly difficult.

It would require, however much the real name for it were disavowed, continual and complicated intervention by the United

States in the affairs of all the members of the coalition which we were proposing to organize, to protect, to lead and to use. Our diplomatic agents abroad would have to have an almost unerring capacity to judge correctly and quickly which men and which parties were reliable containers. Here at home Congress and the people would have to stand ready to back their judgments as to who should be nominated, who should be subsidized, who should be whitewashed, who should be seen through rose-colored spectacles, who should be made our clients and our allies.

Mr. X offers us the prospect of maintaining such a coalition indefinitely until—eventually—the Soviet power breaks up or mellows because it has been frustrated. It is not a good prospect. Even if we assume, which we ought not, that our diplomatic agents will know how to intervene shrewdly and skillfully all over Asia, the Middle East, and Europe, and even if we assume, which the Department of State cannot, that the American people will back them with a drawing account of blank checks both in money and in military power, still it is not a good prospect. For we must not forget that the Soviet Union, against which this coalition will be directed, will resist and react.

In the complicated contest over this great heterogeneous array of unstable states, the odds are heavily in favor of the Soviets. For if we are to succeed, we must organize our satellites as unified, orderly and reasonably contented nations. The Russians can defeat us by disorganizing states that are already disorganized, by disuniting peoples that are torn with civil strife, and by inciting their discontent which is already very great.

As a matter of fact this borderland in Europe and Asia around the perimeter of the Soviet Union is not a place where Mr. X's "unassailable barriers" can be erected. Satellite states and puppet governments are not good material out of which to construct unassailable barriers. A diplomatic war conducted as this policy demands, that is to say conducted indirectly, means that we must stake our own security and the peace of the world upon satellites, puppets, clients, agents about whom we can know very little. Frequently they will act for their own reasons, and on their own judgments, presenting us with accomplished facts that we did not intend, and with crises for which we are unready. The "unassailable barriers" will present us with an unending series of insoluble dilemmas. We shall have either to disown our puppets, which would be tantamount to appeasement and defeat and the loss of face, or must support them at an incalculable cost on an unintended, unforeseen and perhaps undesirable issue.

Questions

1. Why does Lippmann advise the United States to concentrate its efforts on Europe, not the rest of the world?

2. Why does he feel that the Truman Doctrine's reliance on "satellites, clients, dependents and puppets" violates important American values?

---

162. The Universal Declaration of Human Rights (1948)

Source: United Nations, from "Official Records of the Third Session of the General Assembly, Part 1: Resolutions," by the United Nations General Assembly, © 1948 United Nations. Reprinted with the permission of the United Nations.

The atrocities committed during World War II as well as the global language of the Four Freedoms forcefully raised the issue of human rights in the postwar world. In 1948, the UN General Assembly approved the Universal Declaration of Human Rights, drafted by a committee chaired by Eleanor Roosevelt, the widow of the late president. The declaration identified a broad range of rights to be enjoyed by all members of the human family, everywhere, including freedom of speech, religious toleration, and protection against arbitrary government, as well as social and economic entitlements like the right to an adequate standard of living and access to housing, education, and medical care. The document had no enforcement mechanism. Some considered it an exercise in empty rhetoric. But the core principle—that a nation's treatment of its own citizens should be subject to outside evaluation—slowly became part of the language in which freedom was discussed.

THE GENERAL ASSEMBLY PROCLAIMS

This universal declaration of human rights as a common standard of achievement for all peoples and all nations, to the end that every individual and every organ of society, keeping this Declaration constantly in mind, shall strive by teaching and education to promote respect for these rights and freedoms and by progressive measures, national and international, to secure their universal and effective recognition and observance, both among the peoples of Member States themselves and among the peoples of territories under their jurisdiction.

Article 1. All human beings are born free and equal in dignity and rights. They are endowed with reason and conscience and should act towards one another in a spirit of brotherhood.

Article 2. Everyone is entitled to all the rights and freedoms set forth in this Declaration, without distinction of any kind, such as race, colour, sex, language, religion, political or other opinion, national or social origin, property, birth or other status.

Furthermore, no distinction shall be made on the basis of the political, jurisdictional or international status of the country or territory to which a person belongs, whether it be independent, trust, non-self-governing or under any other limitation of sovereignty.

Article 3. Everyone has the right to life, liberty and security of person.

Article 4. No one shall be held in slavery or servitude; slavery and the slave trade shall be prohibited in all their forms.

Article 5. No one shall be subjected to torture or to cruel, inhuman or degrading treatment or punishment.

Article 6. Everyone has the right to recognition everywhere as a person before the law.

Article 7. All are equal before the law and are entitled without any discrimination to equal protection of the law. All are entitled to equal protection against any discrimination in violation of this Declaration and against any incitement to such discrimination.

Article 8. Everyone has the right to an effective remedy by the competent national tribunals for acts violating the fundamental rights granted him by the constitution or by law.

Article 9. No one shall be subjected to arbitrary arrest, detention or exile.

Article 10. Everyone is entitled in full equality to a fair and public hearing by an independent and impartial tribunal, in the determination of his rights and obligations and of any criminal charge against him.

Article 11. (1) Everyone charged with a penal offense has the right to be presumed innocent until proved guilty according to law in a public trial at which he has had all the guarantees necessary for his defense.

(2) No one shall be held guilty of any penal offense or of any act or omission which did not constitute a penal offense, under national or international law, at the time when it was committed. Nor shall a heavier penalty be imposed than the one that was applicable at the time the penal offense was committed.

Article 12. No one shall be subject to arbitrary interference with his privacy, family, home or correspondence, nor to attacks upon his honour and reputation. Everyone has the right to the protection of the law against such interference or attacks.

Article 13. (1) Everyone has the right to freedom of movement and residence within the borders of each state.

(2) Everyone has the right to leave any country, including his own, and to return to his country.

Article 14. (1) Everyone has the right to seek and to enjoy in other countries asylum from persecution.

(2) This right may not be invoked in the case of prosecutions genuinely arising from non-political crimes or from acts contrary to the purposes and principles of the United Nations.

Article 15. (1) Everyone has the right to a nationality.

(2) No one shall be arbitrarily deprived of his nationality nor denied the right to change his nationality.

Article 16. (1) Men and women of full age, without any limitation due to race, nationality or religion, have the right to marry and to found a family. They are entitled to equal rights as to marriage, during marriage, and at its dissolution.

(2) Marriage shall be entered into only with the free and full consent of the intending spouses.

(3) The family is the natural and fundamental group unit of society and is entitled to protection by society and the State.

Article 17. (1) Everyone has the right to own property alone as well as in association with others.

(2) No one shall be arbitrarily deprived of his property.

Article 18. Everyone has the right to freedom of thought, conscience and religion; this right includes freedom to change his religion or belief, and freedom, either alone or in community with others and in public or private, to manifest his religion or belief in teaching, practice, worship and observance.

Article 19. Everyone has the right to freedom of opinion and expression; this right includes freedom to hold opinions without interference and to seek, receive and impart information and ideas through any media and regardless of frontiers.

Article 20. (1) Everyone has the right to freedom of peaceful assembly and association.

(2) No one may be compelled to belong to an association.

Article 21. (1) Everyone has the right to take part in the government of his country, directly or through freely chosen representatives.

(2) Everyone has the right of equal access to public service in his country.

(3) The will of the people shall be the basis of the authority of government; this will shall be expressed in periodic and genuine elections which shall be by universal and equal suffrage and shall be held by secret vote or by equivalent free voting procedures.

Article 22. Everyone, as a member of society, has the right to social security and is entitled to realization, through national effort and international co-operation and in accordance with the organization and resources of each State, of the economic, social and cultural rights indispensable for his dignity and the free development of his personality.

Article 23. (1) Everyone has the right to work, to free choice of employment, to just and favourable conditions of work and to protection against unemployment.

(2) Everyone, without any discrimination, has the right to equal pay for equal work.

(3) Everyone who works has the right to just and favourable remuneration ensuring for himself and his family an existence worthy of human dignity, and supplemented, if necessary, by other means of social protection.

(4) Everyone has the right to form and to join trade unions for protection of his interests.

Article 24. Everyone has the right to rest and leisure, including reasonable limitation of working hours and periodic holidays with pay.

Article 25. (1) Everyone has the right to a standard of living adequate for the health and well-being of himself and his family, including food, clothing, housing and medical care and necessary social services, and the right to security in the event of unemployment, sickness, disability, widowhood, old age or other lack of livelihood in circumstances beyond his control.

(2) Motherhood and childhood are entitled to special care and assistance. All children, whether born in or out of wedlock, shall enjoy the same social protection.

Article 26. (1) Everyone has the right to education. Education shall be free, at least in the elementary and fundamental states. Elementary education shall be compulsory. Technical and professional education shall be made generally available and higher education shall be equally accessible to all on the basis of merit.

(2) Education shall be directed to the full development of the human personality and to the strengthening of respect for human rights and fundamental freedoms. It shall promote understanding, tolerance and friendship among all nations, racial or religious groups, and shall further the activities of the United Nations for the maintenance of peace.

(3) Parents shall have a prior right to choose the kind of education that shall be given to their children.

Article 27. (1) Everyone has the right freely to participate in the cultural life of the community, to enjoy the arts and to share in scientific advancement and its benefits.

(2) Everyone has the right to the protection of the moral and material interests resulting from any scientific, literary or artistic production of which he is the author.

Article 28. Everyone is entitled to a social and international order in which the rights and freedoms set forth in this Declaration can be fully realized.

Article 29. (1) Everyone has duties to the community in which alone the free and full development of his personality is possible.

(2) In the exercise of his rights and freedoms, everyone shall be subject only to such limitations as are determined by law solely for the purpose of securing due recognition and respect for the rights and freedoms of others and of meeting the just requirements of morality, public order and the general welfare in a democratic society.

(3) These rights and freedoms may in no case be exercised contrary to the purposes and principles of the United Nations.

Article 30. Nothing in this Declaration may be interpreted as implying for any State, group or person any right to engage in any activity or to perform any act aimed at the destruction of any of the rights and freedoms set forth herein.

Questions

1. Why is a declaration with no enforcement mechanism nonetheless considered significant?

2. How fully, in your opinion, does the United States today live up to the standards set forth in the Universal Declaration of Human Rights?

---

163. President's Commission on Civil Rights, *To Secure These Rights* (1947)

Source: To Secure These Rights: The Report of the President's Commission on Civil Rights *(Washington, D.C., 1947), pp. 99–103, 139–48.*

In the years immediately following World War II, the status of black Americans enjoyed a prominence in national affairs unmatched since Reconstruction. In October 1947, a Commission on Civil Rights appointed by President Truman issued *To Secure These Rights*, one of the most devastating indictments ever published of racial inequality in America. It outlined the deprivation of rights in areas like employment, housing, and the vote and the widespread occurrence of police brutality against blacks. It called on the federal government to assume responsibility for ensuring equal civil rights for all Americans. The commission insisted that racial inequality posed a moral challenge to the nation because it conflicted with "the American heritage of freedom." The impact of racism on America's conduct of the Cold War was not far from members' minds. The treatment of black Americans, the commission noted, enabled the Soviets to claim that "our nation is a consistent oppressor of underprivileged people," a reputation that could prove disastrous in the battle for the allegiance of peoples throughout the world.

THE NATIONAL GOVERNMENT of the United States must take the lead in safeguarding the civil rights of all Americans. We believe that this is one of the most important observations that can be made about the civil rights problem in our country today. We agree with words used by the President, in an address at the Lincoln Memorial in Washington in June, 1947:

> We must make the Federal Government a friendly, vigilant defender of the rights and equalities of all Americans . . . Our National Government must show the way.

It is essential that our rights be preserved against the tyrannical actions of public officers. Our forefathers saw the need for such protection when they gave us the Bill of Rights as a safeguard against arbitrary government. But this is not enough today. We need more than protection of our rights against government; we need protection of our rights against private persons or groups, seeking to undermine them.

• • •

There are several reasons why we believe the federal government must play a leading role in our efforts as a nation to improve our civil rights record.

First, many of the most serious wrongs against individual rights are committed by private persons or by local public officers. In the most flagrant of all such wrongs—lynching—private individuals, aided upon occasion by state or local officials, are the ones who take the law into their own hands and deprive the victim of his life. The very fact that these outrages continue to occur, coupled with the fact that the states have been unable to eliminate them, points clearly to a strong need for federal safeguards.

• • •

The Committee rejects the argument that governmental controls are themselves necessarily threats to liberty. This statement overlooks the fact that freedom in a civilized society is always founded on law enforced by government. Freedom in the absence of law is anarchy.

• • •

Twice before in American history the nation has found it necessary to review the state of its civil rights. The first time was during the 15 years between 1776 and 1791, from the drafting of the Declaration of Independence through the Articles of Confederation experiment to the writing of the Constitution and the Bill of Rights. It was then that the distinctively American heritage was finally distilled from earlier views of liberty. The second time was when the Union was temporarily sundered over the question of whether it could exist "half-slave" and "half-free."

It is our profound conviction that we have come to a time for a third reexamination of the situation, and a sustained drive ahead. Our reasons for believing this are those of conscience, of self-interest, and of survival in a threatening world. Or to put it another way, we have a moral reason, an economic reason, and an international reason for believing that the time for action is now.

THE MORAL REASON

We have considered the American heritage of freedom at some length. We need no further justification for a broad and immediate program than the need to reaffirm our faith in the traditional American morality. The pervasive gap between our aims and what we actually do is creating a kind of moral dry rot which eats away at the emotional and rational bases of democratic beliefs. There are times when the difference between what we preach about civil rights and what we practice is shockingly illustrated by individual outrages. There are times when the whole structure of our ideology is made ridiculous by individual instances. And there are certain continuing, quiet, omnipresent practices which do irreparable damage to our beliefs.

As examples of "moral erosion" there are the consequences of suffrage limitations in the South. The fact that Negroes and many whites have not been allowed to vote in some states has actually sapped the morality underlying universal suffrage. Many men in public and private life do not believe that those who have been kept from voting are capable of self rule. They finally convince themselves that disfranchised people do not really have the right to vote.

Wartime segregation in the armed forces is another instance of how a social pattern may wreak moral havoc. Practically all white officers and enlisted men in all branches of service saw Negro military personnel performing only the most menial functions. They saw Negroes recruited for the common defense treated as men apart and distinct from themselves. As a result, men who might otherwise have maintained the equalitarian morality of their forebears were given reason to look down on their fellow citizens. This has been sharply illustrated by the Army study discussed previously, in which white servicemen expressed great surprise at the excellent performance of Negroes who joined them in the firing line. Even now, very few people know of the successful experiment with integrated combat units. Yet it is important in explaining why some Negro troops did not do well; it is proof that equal treatment can produce equal performance.

It is impossible to decide who suffers the greatest moral damage from our civil rights transgressions, because all of us are hurt. That is certainly true of those who are victimized. Their belief in the basic truth of the American promise is undermined. But they do have the realization, galling as it sometimes is, of being morally in the right. The damage to those who are responsible for these violations of our moral standards may well be greater. They, too, have been reared to honor the command of "free and equal." And all of us must share in the shame at the growth of hypocrisies like the "automatic" marble champion. All of us must endure the cynicism about democratic values which our failures breed.

The United States can no longer countenance these burdens on its common conscience, these inroads on its moral fiber.

• • •

THE ECONOMIC REASON

One of the principal economic problems facing us and the rest of the world is achieving maximum production and continued prosperity. The loss of a huge, potential market for goods is a direct result of the economic discrimination which is practiced against many of our minority groups. A sort of vicious circle is produced. Discrimination depresses the wages and income of minority groups. As a result, their purchasing power is curtailed and markets are reduced. Reduced markets result in reduced production. This cuts down employment, which of course means lower wages and still fewer job opportunities. Rising fear, prejudice, and insecurity aggravate the very discrimination in employment which sets the vicious circle in motion.

Minority groups are not the sole victims of this economic waste; its impact is inevitably felt by the entire population.

• • •

THE INTERNATIONAL REASON

Our position in the postwar world is so vital to the future that our smallest actions have far-reaching effects. We have come to know that our own security in a highly interdependent world is inextricably tied to the security and well-being of all people and all countries. Our foreign policy is designed to make the United States an enormous, positive influence for peace and progress throughout the world. We have tried to let nothing, not even extreme political differences between ourselves and foreign nations, stand in the way of this goal. But our domestic civil rights shortcomings are a serious obstacle.

We cannot escape the fact that our civil rights record has been an issue in world politics. The world's press and radio are full of it. This Committee has seen a multitude of samples. We and our friends have been, and are, stressing our achievements. Those with competing philosophies have stressed—and are shamelessly distorting—our shortcomings. They have not only tried to create hostility toward us among specific nations, races, and religious groups. They have tried to prove our democracy an empty fraud, and our nation a consistent oppressor of underprivileged people. This may seem ludicrous to Americans, but it is sufficiently important to worry our friends.

• • •

Our achievements in building and maintaining a state dedicated to the fundamentals of freedom have already served as a guide for those seeking the best road from chaos to liberty and prosperity. But it is not indelibly written that democracy will encompass the world. We are convinced that our way of life—the free way of life—holds a promise of hope for all people. We have what is perhaps the greatest responsibility ever placed upon a people to keep this promise alive. Only still greater achievements will do it.

The United States is not so strong, the final triumph of the democratic ideal is not so inevitable that we can ignore what the world thinks of us or our record.

Questions

1. Why does the commission believe that the federal government must take the lead in promoting civil rights?

2. Why does it consider "our domestic civil rights shortcomings" a threat to the triumph of democratic ideals in the Cold War?

━━━━

164. Joseph R. McCarthy on the Attack (1950)

Source: Congressional Record, *81st Congress, 2nd Session, pt. 2, pp. 1954–56.*

Soon after the announcement of the Truman Doctrine, the president instituted a loyalty review system in which government employees were required to demonstrate their patriotism without, in many cases, knowing the charges against them. But the individual whose name came to be most closely associated with the anticommunist crusade was Senator Joseph R. McCarthy of Wisconsin. In a speech in West Virginia in February 1950, McCarthy stated that he had a list of 205 communists working for the State Department. The charge was preposterous; and a few days later, when he entered the speech in the *Congressional Record*, McCarthy reduced the number to 57—still a wild and unsubstantiated claim. The demagogic pursuit of communists riding roughshod over civil liberties came to be known as McCarthyism.

FIVE YEARS AFTER a world war has been won, men's hearts should anticipate a long peace, and men's minds should be free from the heavy weight that comes with war. But this is not such a period—for this is not a period of peace. This is a time of the "cold war." This is a time when all the world is split into two vast, increasingly hostile armed camps—a time of a great armaments race. . . .

Today we are engaged in a final, all-out battle between communistic atheism and Christianity. The modern champions of communism have selected this as the time. And, ladies and gentlemen, the chips are down—they are truly down. . . .

Ladies, and gentlemen, can there be anyone here tonight who is so blind as to say that the war is not on? Can there be anyone who fails to realize that the Communist world has said, "The time is now"—that this is the time for the show-down between the democratic Christian world and the Communist atheist world?

Unless we face this fact, we shall pay the price that must be paid by those who wait too long.

Six years ago, at the time of the first conference to map out the peace . . . there was within the Soviet orbit 180,000,000 people. Lined up on the antitotalitarian side there were in the world at that time roughly 1,625,000,000 people. Today, only six years later, there are 800,000,000 people under the absolute domination of Soviet Russia—an increase of over 400 percent. On our side, the figure has shrunk to around 500,000,000. In other words, in less than six years the odds have changed from 9 to 1 in our favor to 8 to 5 against us. This indicates the swiftness of the tempo of Communist victories and American defeats in the cold war. . . .

The reason why we find ourselves in a position of impotency is not because our only powerful potential enemy has sent men to invade our shores, but rather because of the traitorous actions of those who have been treated so well by this Nation. It has not been the less fortunate or members of minority groups who have been selling this Nation out, but rather those who have had all the benefits that the wealthiest nation on earth has had to offer—the finest homes, the finest college education, and the finest jobs in Government we can give.

This is glaringly true in the State Department. There the bright young men who are born with silver spoons in their mouths are the ones who have been worst. . . .

In my opinion the State Department, which is one of the most important government departments, is thoroughly infested with Communists.

I have in my hand 57 cases of individuals who would appear to be either card carrying members or certainly loyal to the Communist Party, but who nevertheless are still helping to shape our foreign policy.

One thing to remember in discussing the Communists in our Government is that we are not dealing with spies who get thirty pieces of silver to steal the blueprints of a new weapon. We are dealing with a far more sinister type of activity because it permits the enemy to guide and shape our policy. . . .

Questions

1. What kind of social resentments are evident in McCarthy's speech?

2. What evidence does McCarthy offer to support his claim that communists have infiltrated the State Department?

165. Margaret Chase Smith, Declaration of Conscience (1950)

Source: **Congressional Record,** *81st Congress, 2nd Session, pp. 7894–95.*

Like other wars, the Cold War encouraged the drawing of a sharp line between patriotic Americans and those accused of being disloyal. Dividing the world between liberty and slavery automatically made those who could be linked to communism enemies of freedom and undeserving of traditional civil liberties.

By 1950, the anticommunist crusade had created a pervasive atmosphere of fear. Most of McCarthy's colleagues were cowed by his tactics. One who was not was Margaret Chase Smith of Maine, the Senate's only female member. On June 1, 1950, she delivered a brief speech, along with a Declaration of Conscience, signed by six other Republican senators, which called for a commitment to "national security based on individual freedom."

I WOULD LIKE to speak briefly and simply about a serious national condition. It is a national feeling of fear and frustration that could result in national suicide and the end of everything that we Americans hold dear. It is a condition that comes from the lack of effective leadership in either the Legislative Branch or the Executive Branch of our Government.

That leadership is so lacking that serious and responsible proposals are being made that national advisory commissions be appointed to provide such critically needed leadership.

I speak as briefly as possible because too much harm has already been done with irresponsible words of bitterness and selfish political opportunism. I speak as briefly as possible because the issue is too great to be obscured by eloquence. I speak simply and briefly in the hope that my words will be taken to heart.

I speak as a Republican. I speak as a woman. I speak as a United States Senator. I speak as an American.

The United States Senate has long enjoyed worldwide respect as the greatest deliberative body in the world. But recently that deliberative character has too often been debased to the level of a forum of hate and character assassination sheltered by the shield of congressional immunity. . . .

I think that it is high time for the United States Senate and its members to do some soul searching—for us to weigh our consciences—on the manner in which we are performing our duty to the people of America—on the manner in which we are using or abusing our individual powers and privileges. I think that it is high time that we remembered that we have sworn to uphold and defend the Constitution. I think that it is high time that we remembered; that the Constitution, as amended, speaks not only of the freedom of speech but also of trial by jury instead of trial by accusation.

Those of us who shout the loudest about Americanism in making character assassinations are all too frequently those who, by our own words and acts, ignore some of the basic principles of Americanism—

The right to criticize; The right to hold unpopular beliefs; The right to protest; The right of independent thought.

The exercise of these rights should not cost one single American citizen his reputation or his right to a livelihood nor should he be in danger of losing his reputation or livelihood merely because he happens to know some one who holds unpopular beliefs. Who of us doesn't? Otherwise none of us could call our souls our own. Otherwise thought control would have set in.

The American people are sick and tired of being afraid to speak their minds lest they be politically smeared as "Communists" or "Fascists" by their opponents. Freedom of speech is not what it used to be in America. It has been so abused by some that it is not exercised by others. The American people are sick and tired of seeing innocent people smeared and guilty people whitewashed.

The nation sorely needs a Republican victory. But I don't want to see the Republican Party ride to political victory on the Four Horsemen of Calumny—Fear, Ignorance, Bigotry and Smear. . . .

As a United States Senator, I am not proud of the way in which the Senate has been made a publicity platform for irresponsible sensationalism. I am not proud of the reckless abandon in which unproved charges have been hurled from this side of the aisle. I am not proud of the obviously staged, undignified countercharges that have been attempted in retaliation from the other side of the aisle.

I don't like the way the Senate has been made a rendezvous for vilification, for selfish political gain at the sacrifice of individual reputations and national unity. I am not proud of the way we smear outsiders from the Floor of the Senate and hide behind the cloak of congressional immunity and still place ourselves beyond criticism on the Floor of the Senate.

Questions

1. What does Smith believe is the essence of freedom of speech?

2. What does her speech suggest about how the Cold War affected discussions of freedom in the early 1950s?

---

166. Oscar Handlin, "The Immigration Fight Has Only Begun" (1952)

Source: Oscar Handlin, "The Immigration Fight Has Only Begun." Originally published in Commentary, *July 1952. Reprinted by permission of the Oscar Handlin estate.*

In the wake of World War II, existing immigration policy, which included tiny quotas for countries that were fighting as American allies, seemed increasingly indefensible. Despite efforts at reform, however, Congress in 1952 passed, over President Truman's veto, the McCarren-Walter Act. The act continued the 1924 national immigration quotas, and made it easier to deport immigrants thought to be "subversive." In this article in the magazine *Commentary*, published by the American Jewish Committee, the Harvard historian Oscar Handlin, an expert on the history of immigration, called for the fight for reform to continue. His essay became a rallying cry for those demanding a new immigration policy.

THE PASSAGE OF the McCarren-Walter Bill has frustrated five years of effort to reform our immigration laws.... The present system clashes with the democratic ideals of most Americans today. The product of an earlier troubled postwar period, it reflects the spirit of isolationism and a racist xenophobia that in those same years was also expressed through the Ku Klux Klan and in the rejection of the League of Nations, and it is clearly anachronistic at a time when the United States strives to speak for the free peoples of the world against totalitarianism. A quota system setting up a hierarchy of desirable and undesirable peoples is offensive to our allies and potential allies throughout the world, and is a slur upon millions of our own citizens.... Not since the Alien and Sedition Acts of 1798 has an act of Congress come so close to subverting the underlying assumption upon which the conception of citizenship in the United States rests: the assumption that there are no degrees of citizenship, that all Americans are completely equal in rights whatever their place of birth.

The bill perpetuates all but one of the regrettable features of the old system and, in addition, introduces a variety of new ones. It does fortunately make available quotas, albeit small ones, to the countries of Asia, and thus ends one of the worst of the old invidious discriminations. But ... it actually raises and fortifies the racist barriers. It thus deprives the Negroes of the British West Indies of the right to take advantage of the unused quotas of Great Britain. It defines as Oriental persons with even one Asiatic parent, no matter what their place of birth.... Retaining the rigid national quotas, it [also] ... curtails severely the civil liberties of immigrants and resident aliens....

The [immigration] laws are bad because they rest on the racist assumption that mankind is divided into fixed breeds, biologically and culturally separated from each other, and because, within that framework, they assume that Americans are Anglo-Saxons by origin and ought to remain so. To all other peoples, the laws say that the United States ranks them in terms of their racial proximity to our own "superior" stock; and upon the many, many millions of Americans not descended from the Anglo-Saxons, the laws cast a distinct imputation of inferiority.

More recent defenders of the quota system, unwilling to endorse the open racism that gave it birth, have urged that the differentiations it establishes be regarded as cultural rather than racial. The South Italian or the Syrian, it is argued, is culturally less capable of adjusting to American life than the Englishman or the German.... There is no evidence to support that contention.... Allowed to settle in peace, every variety of man has been able to make a place for himself in American life, to his own profit and to the enrichment of the society that has accepted him. The dreaded "riff-raff" of 1910—Greeks, Armenians, Magyars, Slovaks, Polish Jews—are the respected parents of respected citizens today....

The Americans of the 19th century had confidence enough in their own society and in their own institutions to believe any man could become an American. More than ever do we now need to reaffirm that faith.

Questions

1. Why does Handlin believe that basic premises of the immigration quota system have been disproved?

2. How does he invoke history to bolster his arguments?

CHAPTER 24

An Affluent Society, 1953–1960

167. Richard M. Nixon, "What Freedom Means to Us" (1959)

Source: **Vital Speeches of the Day** *(September 1, 1959), pp. 677–79.*

In 1958, during a "thaw" in the Cold War, the United States and the Soviet Union agreed to exchange national exhibitions in order to allow citizens of each "superpower" to become acquainted with life in the other. The American National Exhibition opened in Moscow in 1959. It was a showcase of consumer goods and leisure equipment, complete with stereo sets, a movie theater, home appliances, and twenty-two different cars. But the exhibit's message was the equating of freedom and consumerism.

Vice President Richard Nixon opened the exhibition with an address that emphasized the "extraordinarily high standard of living" in the United States, with its 56 million cars and 50 million television sets. The Moscow exhibition became the site of a classic Cold War confrontation over the meaning of freedom—the "kitchen debate" between Nixon and Soviet Premier Nikita Khrushchev. Twice during the first day, Nixon and the Soviet leader engaged in unscripted debate about the merits of capitalism and communism. Overall, Nixon's speech and the ensuing debate reflected the triumph during the 1950s of a conception of freedom centered on economic abundance and consumer choice within the context of traditional family life.

I AM HONORED on behalf of President Eisenhower to open this American Exhibition in Moscow. Mrs. Nixon and I were among the many thousands of Americans who were privileged to visit the splendid Soviet Exhibition in New York, and we want to take this opportunity to congratulate the people of the U.S.S.R. for the great achievements and progress so magnificently portrayed by your Exhibition.

We, in turn, hope that many thousands of Soviet citizens will take advantage of this opportunity to learn about life in the United States by visiting our Exhibition.

Of course, we both realize that no exhibition can portray a complete picture of all aspects of life in great nations like the U.S.S.R. and the United States.

Among the questions which some might raise with regard to our Exhibition are these: To what extent does this Exhibition accurately present life in the United States as it really is? Can only the wealthy people afford the things exhibited here? What about the inequality, the injustice, the other weaknesses which are supposed to be inevitable in a Capitalist society?

As Mr. Khrushchev often says: "You can't leave a word out of a song." Consequently, in the limited time I have, I would like to try to answer some of these questions so that you may get an accurate picture of what America is really like.

Let me start with some of the things in this Exhibit. You will see a house, a car, a television set—each the newest and most modern of its type we can produce. But can only the rich in the United States afford such things? If this were the case we would have to include in our definition of rich the millions of America's wage earners.

Let us take, for example, our 16 million factory workers. The average weekly wage of a factory worker in America is $90.54. With this income he can buy and afford to own a house, a television set, and a car in the price range of those you will see in this Exhibit. What is more, the great majority of American wage earners have done exactly that.

Putting it another way, there are 44 million families in the United States. Twenty-five million of these families live in houses or apartments that have as much or more floor space than the one you see in this Exhibit. Thirty-one million families own their own homes and the land on which they are built. America's 44 million families own a total of 56 million cars, 50 million television sets and 143 million radio sets. And they buy an average of 9 dresses and suits and 14 pairs of shoes per family per year.

Why do I cite these figures? Not because they indicate that the American people have more automobiles, TV sets, or houses than the people of the U.S.S.R.

In fairness we must recognize that our country industrialized sooner than the Soviet Union. And Americans are happy to note that Mr. Khrushchev has set a goal for the Soviet economy of catching up in the production of consumer goods.

We welcome this kind of competition because when we engage in it, no one loses—everyone wins as the living standards of people throughout the world are raised to higher levels. It also should be pointed out that while we may be ahead of you as far as these items are concerned, you are ahead of us in other fields—for example, in the size of the rockets you have developed for the exploration of outer space.

But what these statistics do dramatically demonstrate is this: That the United States, the world's largest capitalist country, has from the standpoint of distribution of wealth come closest to the ideal of prosperity for all in a classless society.

As our revered Abraham Lincoln said ". . . We do not propose any war upon capital; we do wish to allow the humblest man an equal chance to get rich with everybody else."

The 67 million American wage earners are not the downtrodden masses depicted by the critics of capitalism in the latter part of the Nineteenth and early part of the Twentieth Centuries. They hold their heads high as they proudly enjoy the highest standard of living of any people in the world's history.

The caricature of capitalism as a predatory, monopolist dominated society, is as hopelessly out of date, as far as the United States
is concerned, as a wooden plow.

This does not mean that we have solved all of our problems. Many
of you have heard about the problem of unemployment in the United
States. What is not so well known is that the average period that
these unemployed were out of work even during our recent recession was less than three months. And during that period the unemployed had an average income from unemployment insurance
funds of $131.49 per month. The day has passed in the United States
when the unemployed were left to shift for themselves.

The same can be said for the aged, the sick, and others who are
unable to earn enough to provide an adequate standard of living. An
expanded program of Social Security combined with other government and private programs provides aid and assistance for those
who are unable to care for themselves. For example, the average
retired couple on Social Security in the United States receives an
income of $116 per month apart from the additional amounts they
receive from private pensions and savings accounts.

What about the strikes which take place in our economy, the latest
example of which is the steel strike which is going on? The answer
is that here we have a firsthand example of how a free economy
works. The workers right to join with other workers in a union and to
bargain collectively with management is recognized and protected
by law. No man or woman in the United States can be forced to work
for wages he considers to be inadequate or under conditions he
believes are unsatisfactory.

Another problem which causes us concern is that of racial discrimination in our country. We are making great progress in solving this problem but we shall never be satisfied until we make the
American ideal of equality of opportunity a reality for every citizen
regardless of his race, creed or color.

We have other problems in our society but we are confident that
for us our system of government provides the best means for solving

them. But the primary reason we believe this is not because we have an economy which builds more than 1 million houses, produces 6 million cars and 6 million television sets per year.

Material progress is important but the very heart of the American ideal is that "man does not live by bread alone." To us, progress without freedom to use a common expression is like "potatoes without fat."

Let me give you some examples of what freedom means to us.

President Eisenhower is one of the most popular men ever to hold that high office in our country. Yet never an hour or a day goes by in which criticism of him and his policies cannot be read in our newspapers, heard on our radio and television, or in the Halls of Congress.

And he would not have it any other way. The fact that our people can and do say anything they want about a government official, the fact that in our elections, as this voting machine in our exhibit illustrates, every voter has a free choice between those who hold public office and those who oppose them makes ours a true peoples' government.

We trust the people. We constantly submit big decisions to the people. Our history convinces us that over the years the people have been right much more often than they have been wrong.

As an indication of the extent of this freedom and of our faith in our own system, forty hours of radio broadcasts from the Soviet Union can be heard without jamming in the United States each day, and over a million and a half copies of Soviet publications are purchased in our country each year.

Let us turn now to freedom of religion. Under our Constitution no church or religion can be supported by the State. An American can either worship in the church of his choice or choose to go to no church at all if he wishes. Acting with this complete freedom of choice, 103 million of our citizens are members of 308 American churches.

We also cherish the freedom to travel, both within our country and outside the United States. Within our country we live and travel where we please without travel permits, internal passports or police registration. We also travel freely abroad. For example, 11 million

Americans will travel to other countries during this year, including 10,000 to the Soviet Union. We look forward to the day when millions of Soviet citizens will travel to ours and other countries in this way.

Time will not permit me to tell you of all of the features of American life, but in summary I think these conclusions can objectively be stated. The great majority of Americans like our system of government. Much as we like it, however, we would not impose it on anyone else. We believe that people everywhere should have a right to choose the form of government they want.

Questions

1. Why do you think Nixon begins his speech by discussing the American standard of living rather than other manifestations of freedom?

2. What other elements of freedom does Nixon refer to in the speech?

—————

168. Clark Kerr, Freedom in Industrial Society (1960)

Source: from **Industrialism and Industrial Man: The Problems of Labor and Management in Economic Growth** *by Clark Kerr, John T. Dunlop, Frederick H. Harbison and Charles A. Myers, Cambridge, Mass.: Harvard University Press, Copyright © 1960 by the President and Fellows of Harvard College. Copyright © renewed 1988 by Clark Kerr.*

The end of World War II was followed by a period of economic expansion, low unemployment, and rising living standards. In every measurable way—diet, housing, wages, education, recreation—most Americans lived better than their parents and grandparents had. To many observers in the 1950s it seemed that the ills of American society had been solved. Scholars celebrated the "end of ideology," the triumph of a democratic, capitalist "consensus" in which all Americans, except the maladjusted and fanatics, shared the same values of individualism, respect for private property, and belief in equal opportunity. If problems remained, their solution required technical adjustments, not structural change or aggressive political intervention.

In this affluent society, consumerism increasingly replaced economic independence and democratic participation as central definitions of American freedom. A study of modern industrial society published in 1960 by Clark Kerr, the chancellor of the University of California, Berkeley, and three other scholars reflected the era's outlook. Freedom, they wrote, might have been reduced "in the workplace," where modern technology demanded disciplined effort. But society offered a far greater range of "goods and services," and therefore "a greater scope of freedom" in Americans' "personal lives." Leisure activities, not work or politics, would be "the happy hunting ground for the independent spirit" who hoped to enjoy freedom.

—————

THE INDUSTRIAL SOCIETY is necessarily characterized by a substantial range and scale of activities by the government. In a society of advanced technology there are, by virtue of this technology, a larger number of activities for government; for instance, the need for roads and highways, the provision for airports, the regulation of traffic, radio and television, a result of modern means of communication. Urban development has the same consequences. Technology also creates a more complex problem for a military establishment, extending in many directions the activities of government. The more integrated character of the world increases the activities significant to international relations and hence typically the scope of government activities. The scale of some scientific applications and the capital needs of new technologies tend to increase the scope of public agencies. As income rises, the demand of consumers may be for services largely provided by governments, such as education, parks, roads and health services.

The industrial society and individual freedom, however, are not necessarily to be regarded as antagonists. A high degree of discipline in the work place imposed by a web of rules and a large range of governmental activities is fully consistent with a larger freedom for the individual in greater leisure, a greater range of choice in occupations and place of residence, a greater range of alternatives in goods and services on which to use income, and a very wide range of subgroups or associations in which to choose participation. It is a mistake to regard the industrial society as antithetical to individual freedom by citing ways in which the scope of public and private governments has increased without also noting ways in which the industrial society expands individual freedom.

• • •

The industrial society, as any established society, develops a distinctive consensus which relates individuals and groups to each other and provides a common body of ideas, beliefs, and value judgments integrated into a whole. There must be a consensus to permit the industrial society to function. Various forms of the industrial society may create some distinctive features of an ideology, but all industrialized societies have some common values. In the pure industrial society science and technical knowledge have high values, and those engaged in advancing science and in applying it to industrial processes have high prestige and receive high rewards in the society. The pure industrial society eliminates taboos against technical change, and it places high values on being "modern," "up-to-date," and in "progress" for their own sake.

• • •

The function of making explicit a consensus and of combining discrete beliefs and convictions into a reasonably consistent body of ideas is the task of intellectuals in every society. Industrial society does not uniquely create intellectuals; they exist in all societies in some degree. There are probably more intellectuals, at least potentially, in the industrial society on account of the higher levels of general education, higher income levels, and greater leisure. There are also new patrons to the intellectuals as compared to pre-industrial society. A diversity of markets for intellectuals—the university, enterprise, labor organization, voluntary association, government, and self-employment—tends to displace the old aristocratic patrons. The function of formulating and restating the major values, premises, and consensus of a society from time to time, of sweeping away the old and adopting the new or reconciling the industrial processes with the old order, plays a significant role in industrialization. The intellectuals accordingly are an influential group in the process of the creation and molding of the new industrial society.

• • •

The individual will be in a mixed situation far removed either from that of the independent farmer organizing most aspects of his own life or from that of the Chinese in the commune under total surveillance. In his working life he will be subject to great conformity imposed not only by the enterprise manager but also by the state and by his own occupational association. For most people, any true scope for the independent spirit on the job will be missing. However, the skilled worker, while under rules, does get some control over his job, some chance to organize it as he sees fit, some possession of it. Within the narrow limits of this kind of "job control," the worker will have some freedom. But the productive process tends to regiment. People must perform as expected or it breaks down. This is now and will be increasingly accepted as an immutable fact. The state, the manager, the occupational association are all disciplinary agents. But discipline is often achieved by a measure of persuasion and incentive. The worker will be semi-independent with some choice among jobs, some control of the job, and some scope for the effects of morale; but he will also be confined by labor organizations, pensions, and seniority rules, and all sorts of rules governing the conduct of the job.

Outside his working life the individual may have more freedom under pluralistic industrialism than in most earlier forms of society. Politically he can be given some influence. Society has achieved consensus and it is perhaps less necessary for Big Brother to exercise political control. Nor in this Brave New World need genetic and chemical means be employed to avoid revolt. There will not be any revolt, anyway, except little bureaucratic revolts that can be handled piecemeal. An educated population will want political choice and can be given it. There will also be reasonable choice in the controlled labor market, subject to the confining limits of the occupation, and in the controlled product market.

The great new freedom may come in the leisure of individuals. Higher standards of living, more leisure, more education make this not only possible but almost inevitable. This will be the happy hunting ground for the independent spirit. Along with the bureaucratic conservatism of economic and political life may well go a New Bohemianism in the other aspects of life and partly as a reaction to the confining nature of the productive side of society. There may well come a new search for individuality and a new meaning to liberty. The economic system may be highly ordered and the political system barren ideologically; but the social and recreational and cultural aspects of life diverse and changing.

• • •

Utopia never arrives, but men may well settle for the benefits of a greater scope for freedom in their personal lives at the cost of considerable conformity in their working lives.

• • •

Questions

1. How much scope for individual freedom seems to exist in Kerr's description of "industrial society"?

2. What role does democratic politics seem to play in this vision of society?

169. The Southern Manifesto (1956)

Source: Congressional Record, *84th Congress, 2nd Session, pp. 4459–60.*

The Supreme Court's 1954 decision in *Brown v. Board of Education,* outlawing racial segregation in public schools, inspired widespread hopes that racial equality was finally on the horizon. It also inspired a campaign of "massive resistance" in the white South. Drawn up early in 1956 and signed by 101 southern members of the Senate and House of Representatives, the Southern Manifesto repudiated the Supreme Court decision and offered support to the campaign of resistance then gaining force throughout the South. It drew on long-standing ideas of local autonomy as the basis of individual liberty and claimed that segregation was an old southern tradition favored by both whites and blacks. The Manifesto was a prelude to a decade of sometimes violent struggles as black southerners sought to claim equal rights in American society.

———

THE UNWARRANTED DECISION of the Supreme Court in the public school cases is now bearing the fruit always produced when men substitute naked power for established law.

The Founding Fathers gave us a Constitution of checks and balances because they realized the inescapable lesson of history that no man or group of men can be safely entrusted with unlimited power.... We regard the decisions of the Supreme Court in the school cases as a clear abuse of judicial power. It climaxes a trend in the Federal Judiciary undertaking to legislate, in derogation [violation] of the authority of Congress, and to encroach upon the reserved rights of the States and the people.

The original Constitution does not mention education. Neither does the 14th Amendment nor any other amendment. The debates preceding the submission of the 14th Amendment clearly show that there was no intent that it should affect the system of education maintained by the States.

In the case of *Plessy v. Ferguson* in 1896 the Supreme Court expressly declared that under the 14th Amendment no person was denied any of his rights if the States provided separate but equal facilities. This decision ... restated time and again, became a part of the life of the people of many of the States and confirmed their habits, traditions, and way of life. It is founded on elemental humanity and common-sense, for parents should not be deprived by Government of the right to direct the lives and education of their own children.

Though there has been no constitutional amendment or act of Congress changing this established legal principle almost a century old, the Supreme Court of the United States, with no legal basis for such action, undertook to exercise their naked judicial power and substituted their personal political and social ideas for the established law of the land.

This unwarranted exercise of power by the Court, contrary to the Constitution, is creating chaos and confusion in the States principally affected. It is destroying the amicable relations between the white and Negro races that have been created through 90 years of patient effort by the good people of both races. It has planted hatred and suspicion where there has been heretofore friendship and understanding.

With the gravest concern for the explosive and dangerous condition created by this decision and inflamed by outside meddlers: ... we commend the motives of those States which have declared the intention to resist forced integration by any lawful means.

We appeal to the States and people who are not directly affected by these decisions to consider the constitutional principles involved against the time when they too, on issues vital to them may be the victims of judicial encroachment.

We pledge ourselves to use all lawful means to bring about a reversal of this decision which is contrary to the Constitution and to prevent the use of force in its implementation.

Questions

1. Why does the Southern Manifesto claim that the Supreme Court decision is a threat to constitutional government?

2. Do you think that black southerners would agree with the statement that "amicable relations" had existed between the races for the past ninety years and that the Supreme Court decision threatened to undermine them?

170. Milton Friedman, *Capitalism and Freedom* (1962)

Source: Milton Friedman, from Capitalism and Freedom, *pp. 1–4. Copyright © 1962 by The University of Chicago. Reprinted by permission of the University of Chicago Press.*

During the 1950s and early 1960s, conservative ideas seemed to have been marginalized in American politics. Nonetheless, two groups emerged in these years who, while largely ignored at the time, laid the intellectual foundations for the conservative movement's later rebirth. The "new conservatives" feared that the United States was suffering from moral decay and called for a return to traditional values grounded in the Christian tradition and in timeless notions of good and evil. If men and women did not choose to lead virtuous lives, the government must force them to do so.

A quite different group of conservative thinkers were "libertarians," to whom freedom meant individual autonomy, limited government, and unregulated capitalism. This view found powerful support in the writings of the young economist Milton Friedman. In *Capitalism and Freedom*, he identified the free market as the necessary foundation for individual liberty. He called for turning over to the private sector virtually all government functions and the repeal of minimum wage laws, the graduated income tax, and the Social Security system. Friedman extended the idea of unrestricted free choice into virtually every realm of life. Government, he insisted, should seek to regulate neither the economy nor individual conduct.

IN A MUCH quoted passage in his inaugural address, President Kennedy said, "Ask not what your country can do for you—ask what you can do for your country." It is a striking sign of the temper of our times that the controversy about this passage centered on its origin and not on its content. Neither half of the statement expresses a relation between the citizen and his government that is worthy of the ideals of free men in a free society. The paternalistic "what your country can do for you" implies that government is the patron, the citizen the ward, a view that is at odds with the free man's belief in his own responsibility for his own destiny. The organismic, "what you can do for your country" implies that government is the master or the deity, the citizen, the servant or the votary. To the free man, the country is the collection of individuals who compose it, not something over and above them. He is proud of a common heritage and loyal to common traditions. But he regards government as a means, an instrumentality, neither a grantor of favors and gifts, nor a master or god to be blindly worshipped and served. He recognizes no national goal except as it is the consensus of the goals that the citizens severally serve. He recognizes no national purpose except as it is the consensus of the purposes for which the citizens severally strive.

The free man will ask neither what his country can do for him nor what he can do for his country. He will ask rather "What can I and my compatriots do through government" to help us discharge our individual responsibilities, to achieve our several goals and purposes, and above all, to protect our freedom? And he will accompany this question with another: How can we keep the government we create from becoming a Frankenstein that will destroy the very freedom we establish it to protect? Freedom is a rare and delicate plant. Our minds tell us, and history confirms, that the great threat to freedom is the concentration of power. Government is necessary to preserve our freedom, it is an instrument through which we can exercise our freedom; yet by concentrating power in political hands, it is also a threat to freedom. Even though the men who wield this power initially be of good will and even though they be not corrupted by the power they exercise, the power will both attract and form men of a different stamp.

How can we benefit from the promise of government while avoiding the threat to freedom? Two broad principles embodied in our Constitution give an answer that has preserved our freedom so far, though they have been violated repeatedly in practice while proclaimed as precept.

First, the scope of government must be limited. Its major function must be to protect our freedom both from the enemies outside our gates and from our fellow-citizens: to preserve law and order, to enforce private contracts, to foster competitive markets. Beyond this major function, government may enable us at times to accomplish jointly what we would find it more difficult or expensive to accomplish severally. However, any such use of government is fraught with danger. We should not and cannot avoid using government in this way. But there should be a clear and large balance of advantages before we do. By relying primarily on voluntary co-operation and private enterprise, in both economic and other activities, we can insure that the private sector is a check on the powers of the governmental sector and an effective protection of freedom of speech, of religion, and of thought.

The second broad principle is that government power must be dispersed. If government is to exercise power, better in the county than in the state, better in the state than in Washington. If I do not like what my local community does, be it in sewage disposal, or zoning, or schools, I can move to another local community, and though few may take this step, the mere possibility acts as a check. If I do not like what my state does, I can move to another. If I do not like what Washington imposes, I have few alternatives in this world of jealous nations.

The very difficulty of avoiding the enactments of the federal government is of course the great attraction of centralization to many of its proponents. It will enable them more effectively, they believe, to legislate programs that—as they see it—are in the interest of the public, whether it be the transfer of income from the rich to the poor or from private to governmental purposes. They are in a sense right. But this coin has two sides. The power to do good is also the power to do harm; those who control the power today may not tomorrow; and, more important, what one man regards as good, another may regard as harm. The great tragedy of the drive to centralization, as of the drive to extend the scope of government in general, is that it is mostly led by men of good will who will be the first to rue its consequences.

Questions

1. What does Friedman mean when he refers to the United States as a "collection of individuals"?

2. How would you describe Friedman's understanding of freedom?

---

171. C. Wright Mills on "Cheerful Robots" (1959)

Source: C. Wright Mills, excerpts from The Sociological Imagination *(Oxford University Press, 2000). Copyright © 1959, 2000 by Oxford University Press, Inc. Reproduced with permission of the Licensor through PLSclear.*

With both major parties embracing the Cold War and social criticism stigmatized as "un-American," political debate in the 1950s took place within extremely narrow limits. Nonetheless, some dissenting voices could be heard. Writers criticized the monotony of modern work, the emptiness of suburban life, and the powerlessness of the individual in a world controlled by giant bureaucracies. More radical in pointing to the problem of unequal power in American society, the sociologist C. Wright Mills challenged the self-satisfied vision of democratic pluralism that dominated mainstream social science in the 1950s. Mills wrote of a "power elite"—an interlocking directorate of corporate leaders, politicians, and military men whose control of government and society had made political democracy obsolete. Such criticism helped to set the stage for the revolts of the 1960s. In the 1950s, however, it failed to dent widespread complacency about the American way of life.

FREEDOM IS NOT merely the chance to do as one pleases; neither is it merely the opportunity to choose between set alternatives. Freedom is, first of all, the chance to formulate the available choices, to argue over them—and then, the opportunity to choose. That is why freedom cannot exist without an enlarged role of human reason in human affairs. Within an individual's biography and within a society's history, the social task of reason is to formulate choices, to enlarge the scope of human decisions in the making of history. The future of human affairs is not merely some set of variables to be predicted. The future is what is to be decided—within the limits, to be sure, of historical possibility. But this possibility is not fixed; in our time the limits seem very broad indeed.

Beyond this, the problem of freedom is the problem of how decisions about the future of human affairs are to be made and who is to make them. Organizationally, it is the problem of a just machinery of decision. Morally, it is the problem of political responsibility. Intellectually, it is the problem of what are now the possible futures of human affairs. But the larger aspects of the problem of freedom today concern not only the nature of history and the structural chance for explicit decisions to make a difference in its course; they concern also the nature of man and the fact that the value of freedom cannot be based upon "man's basic nature." The ultimate problem of freedom is the problem of the cheerful robot, and it arises in this form today because today it has become evident to us that *all* men do *not* naturally *want* to be free; that all men are not willing or not able, as the case may be, to exert themselves to acquire the reason that freedom requires.

Under what conditions do men come to *want* to be free and capable of acting freely? Under what conditions are they willing and able to bear the burdens freedom does impose and to see these less as burdens than as gladly undertaken self-transformations? And on the negative side: Can men be made to want to become *cheerful* robots?

In our time, must we not face the possibility that the human mind as a social fact might be deteriorating in quality and cultural level, and yet not many would notice it because of the overwhelming accumulation of technological gadgets? Is not that one meaning of rationality without reason? Of human alienation? Of the absence of any free role for reason in human affairs? The accumulation of gadgets hides these meanings: Those who use these devices do not understand them; those who invent them do not understand much else. That is why we may *not*, without great ambiguity, use technological abundance as the index of human quality and cultural progress.

Questions

1. How does Mills's definition of freedom differ from the idea of freedom as consumer choice?

2. What does Mills mean by "cheerful robots"?

---

172. Allen Ginsberg, "Howl" (1955)

Source: Allen Ginsberg, "What sphinx of cement ... / ... American river!" (Moloch section, 34 l.) from "Howl," Allen Ginsberg, Collected Poems 1947–1980. *Copyright © 1955. Reprinted by permission of HarperCollins Publishers.*

A different kind of criticism of mainstream culture arose from a group of artists and writers of the 1950s known as the Beats, centered in New York City and San Francisco, as well as college towns like Madison, Wisconsin, and Ann Arbor, Michigan. Rejecting the work ethic, the consumer culture of the suburban middle class, and the militarization of American life by the Cold War, the Beats celebrated impulsive action, immediate pleasure (often enhanced by drugs), and sexual experimentation.

"I saw the best minds of my generation destroyed by madness, starving hysterical naked," wrote the Beat poet Allen Ginsberg in "Howl" (1955), a protest against materialism and conformism. Ginsberg wrote of American life through the image of Moloch, an idol in the Bible to whom parents sacrificed their children. In the poem, Moloch was a symbol of a militaristic, materialistic society that stifled spontaneity and human feeling. "Howl" became a kind of manifesto of the Beat Generation.

What sphinx of cement and aluminum bashed open their skulls and
ate up their brains and imagination?

Moloch! Solitude! Filth! Ugliness! Ashcans and unobtainable dollars!
Children screaming under the stairways! Boys sobbing in armies!
Old men weeping in the parks!

Moloch! Moloch! Nightmare of Moloch! Moloch the loveless! Mental
Moloch! Moloch the heavy judger of men!

Moloch the incomprehensible prison! Moloch the crossbone soul-
less jailhouse and Congress of sorrows! Moloch whose buildings
are judgment! Moloch the vast stone of war! Moloch the stunned
governments!

Moloch whose mind is pure machinery! Moloch whose blood is running money! Moloch whose fingers are ten armies! Moloch whose
breast is a cannibal dynamo! Moloch whose ear is a smoking tomb!

Moloch whose eyes are a thousand blind windows! Moloch whose
skyscrapers stand in the long streets like endless Jehovahs!
Moloch whose factories dream and croak in the fog! Moloch
whose smokestacks and antennae crown the cities!

Moloch whose love is endless oil and stone! Moloch whose soul is
electricity and banks! Moloch whose poverty is the specter of
genius! Moloch whose fate is a cloud of sexless hydrogen! Moloch
whose name is the Mind!

Moloch who entered my soul early! Moloch in whom I am a consciousness without a body! Moloch who frightened me out of my
natural ecstasy! Moloch whom I abandon! Wake up in Moloch!
Light streaming out of the sky!

Moloch! Moloch! Robot apartments! invisible suburbs! skeleton trea-
suries! blind capitals! demonic industries! spectral nations! invin-
cible mad houses! granite cocks! monstrous bombs!

They broke their backs lifting Moloch to Heaven! Pavements, trees,
   radios, tons! lifting the city to Heaven which exists and is everywhere about us!

Visions! omens! hallucinations! miracles! ecstasies! gone down the
   American river!

Questions

1. What images convey Ginsberg's critique of 1950s American life?

2. What kind of alternative, if any, does Ginsberg offer to the materialism
and conformism of American society?

---

173. Martin Luther King Jr. and the Montgomery Bus Boycott (1955)

*Source: Martin Luther King, Jr., "Meeting at Holt Street Church." Reprinted
by arrangement with The Heirs to the Estate of Martin Luther King Jr., c/o
Writers House as agent for the proprietor New York, NY. © 1955 Dr. Martin
Luther King, Jr. © renewed 1983 by Coretta Scott King.*

In December 1955, Rosa Parks, a veteran of local black politics who worked
as a tailor's assistant in a Montgomery, Alabama, department store,
refused to surrender her seat on a city bus to a white rider, as required by
local law. Her arrest sparked a year-long bus boycott. Finally, the Supreme
Court ruled segregation in public transportation unconstitutional.

The Montgomery bus boycott launched the movement for racial justice
as a nonviolent crusade based in the black churches of the South. It
marked the emergence of twenty-six-year-old Martin Luther King Jr., who
had recently arrived in the city to become pastor of a Baptist church, as
the movement's national symbol. On the night of the first protest meeting, King's speech electrified his audience. "We, the disinherited of this
land, we who have been oppressed so long, are tired of going through the

long night of captivity. And now we are reaching out for the daybreak of freedom and justice and equality."

━━━━━

MY FRIENDS, WE are certainly very happy to see each of you out this evening. We are here this evening for serious business. (*Audience: Yes*) We are here in a general sense because first and foremost we are American citizens (*That's right*) and we are determined to apply our citizenship to the fullness of its meaning. (*Yeah, That's right*) We are here also because of our love for democracy, (*Yes*) because of our deep-seated belief that democracy transformed from thin paper to thick action (*Yes*) is the greatest form of government on earth. (*That's right*).

But we are here in a specific sense, because of the bus situation in Montgomery. (*Yes*) We are here because we are to get the situation corrected. This situation is not at all new. The problem has existed over endless years. (*That's right*) For many years now Negroes in Montgomery and so many other areas have been inflicted with the paralysis of crippling fears (*Yes*) on buses in our community. (*That's right*) On so many occasions, Negroes have been intimidated and humiliated and impressed—oppressed—because of the sheer fact that they were Negroes. (*That's right*) I don't have time this evening to go into the history of these numerous cases. Many of them now are lost in the thick fog of oblivion, (*Yes*) but at least one stands before us now with glaring dimensions. (*Yes*)

Just the other day, just last Thursday to be exact, one of the finest citizens in Montgomery (*Amen*)—not one of the finest Negro citizens (*That's right*) but one of the finest citizens in Montgomery—was taken from a bus (*Yes*) and carried to jail and arrested (*Yes*) because she refused to get up to give her seat to a white person.

• • •

Mrs. Rosa Parks is a fine person. (*Well, well said*) And since it had to happen I'm happy that it happened to a person like Mrs. Parks, for nobody can doubt the boundless outreach of her integrity! (*Sure enough*) Nobody can doubt the height of her character, (*Yes*) nobody can doubt the depth of her Christian commitment and devotion to the teachings of Jesus. (*All right*) And I'm happy since it had to happen, it happened to a person that nobody can call a disturbing factor in the community. (*All right*) Mrs. Parks is a fine Christian person, unassuming, and yet there is integrity and character there. And just because she refused to get up, she was arrested.

And you know, my friends, there comes a time when people get tired of being trampled over by the iron feet of oppression. [*Thundering applause*] There comes a time, my friends, when people get tired of being plunged across the abyss of humiliation where they experience the bleakness of nagging despair. (*Keep talking*) There comes a time when people get tired of being pushed out of the glittering sunlight of life's July, and left standing amid the piercing chill of an alpine November. (*That's right*) [*Applause*] There comes a time. (*Yes sir, Teach*) [*Applause continues*]

We are here, we are here this evening because we're tired now. (*Yes*) [*Applause*] And I want to say, that we are not here advocating violence. (*No*) We have never done that. (*Repeat that, Repeat that*) [*Applause*] I want it to be known throughout Montgomery and throughout this nation (*Well*) that we are Christian people. (*Yes*) [*Applause*] We believe in the Christian religion. We believe in the teachings of Jesus. (*Well*) The only weapon that we have in our hands this evening is the weapon of protest. (*Yes*) [*Applause*] That's all.

And certainly, certainly, this is the glory of America, with all of its faults. (*Yeah*) This is the glory of our democracy. If we were incarcerated behind the iron curtains of a Communistic nation we couldn't do this. If we were dropped in the dungeon of a totalitarian regime we couldn't do this. (*All right*) But the great glory of American democracy is the right to protest for right. (*That's right*) [*Applause*] My friends, don't let anybody make us feel that we are to be compared in our actions with the Ku Klux Klan or with the White Citizens Council. [*Applause*] There will be no crosses burned at any bus stops in Montgomery. (*Well, that's right*) There will be no white persons pulled out of their homes and taken out on some distant road and lynched for not cooperating. [*Applause*] There will be nobody amid, among us who will stand up and defy the Constitution of this nation. [*Applause*] We only assemble here because of our desire to see right exist. [*Applause*] My friends, I want it to be known that we're going to work with grim and bold determination to gain justice on the buses in this city. [*Applause*]

And we are not wrong, we are not wrong in what we are doing. (*Well*) If we are wrong, the Supreme Court of this nation is wrong. (*Yes sir*) [*Applause*] If we are wrong, the Constitution of the United States is wrong. (*Yes*) [*Applause*] If we are wrong, God Almighty is wrong. (*That's right*) [*Applause*] If we are wrong, Jesus of Nazareth was merely a utopian dreamer that never came down to earth. (*Yes*) [*Applause*] If we are wrong, justice is a lie: (*Yes*) love has no meaning. [*Applause*] And we are determined here in Montgomery to work and fight until justice runs down like water (*Yes*) [*Applause*] and righteousness like a mighty stream. (*Keep talking*) [*Applause*]

We, the disinherited of this land, we who have been oppressed so long, are tired of going through the long night of captivity. And now we are reaching out for the daybreak of freedom and justice and equality. [*Applause*] May I say to you my friends, as I come to a close, and just giving some idea of why we are assembled here, that we must keep—and I want to stress this, in all of our doings, in all of our deliberations here this evening and all of the week and while—whatever we do, we must keep God in the forefront. (*Yeah*) Let us be Christian in all of our actions. (*That's right*) But I want to tell you this evening that it is not enough for us to talk about love, love is one of the pivotal points of the Christian face, faith. There is another side called justice. And justice is really love in calculation. (*All right*) Justice is love correcting that which revolts against love. (*Well*)

The Almighty God himself is not . . . only, . . . the God just standing out saying through Hosea, "I love you, Israel." He's also the God that stands up before the nations and said: "Be still and know that I'm God, (*Yeah*) that if you don't obey me I will break the backbone of your power, (*Yeah*) and slap you out of the orbits of your international and national relationships." (*That's right*) Standing beside love is always justice (*Yeah*) and we are only using the tools of justice. Not only are we using the tools of persuasion but we've come to see that we've got to use the tools of coercion. Not only is this thing a process of education but it is also a process of legislation. [*Applause*]

As we stand and sit here this evening and as we prepare ourselves for what lies ahead, let us go out with a grim and bold determination that we are going to stick together. [*Applause*] We are going to work together. [*Applause*] Right here in Montgomery, when the history books are written in the future, (*Yes*) somebody will have to say, "There lived a race of people, (*Well*) a black people, (*Yes sir*) 'fleecy locks and black complexion,' (*Yes*) a people who had the moral courage to stand up for their rights. [*Applause*] And thereby they injected a new meaning into the veins of history and of civilization." And we're gonna do that. God grant that we will do it before it is too late. (*Oh yeah*) As we proceed with our program let us think of these things. (*Yes*) [*Applause*]

Questions

1. What parts of King's speech received the most enthusiastic reception from his audience?

2. In what ways does King appeal for white support of the boycott?

CHAPTER 25

The Sixties, 1960–1968

174. John F. Kennedy, Speech on Civil Rights (1963)

Source: The White House.

On June 11, 1963, a month after the police assault on youthful demonstrators in Birmingham, Alabama, shocked the world, two black students were admitted to the University of Alabama despite the opposition of Governor George Wallace. That night, President John F. Kennedy delivered a televised address to the nation from the White House. Up to this point, Kennedy had shown little leadership on the issue of civil rights. Now, he announced his intention to ask Congress to enact legislation prohibiting discrimination in public accommodations and by private businesses throughout the country. (Congress had passed a similar law in 1875 only to see it declared unconstitutional by the Supreme Court in 1883.)

But what made Kennedy's speech a highlight of his brief presidency was the moral urgency with which he spoke, and the way he linked the black struggle for equality with the nation's rhetorical commitment to freedom. How could the United States, he asked, promote freedom around the globe while denying so many of its own citizens of their basic rights? Indeed, he praised civil rights workers as "soldiers" in the unending struggle for freedom.

Despite his eloquent plea, opposition quickly emerged in Congress to Kennedy's bill. Only after his assassination was it piloted to passage by President Lyndon B. Johnson, becoming the Civil Rights Act of 1964.

THIS AFTERNOON, FOLLOWING a series of threats and defiant statements, the presence of Alabama National Guardsmen was required on the University of Alabama to carry out the final and unequivocal order of the United States District Court of the Northern District of Alabama. This order called for the admission of two clearly qualified young Alabama residents who happen to have been born Negro. . . . I hope that every American, regardless of where he lives, will stop and examine his conscience about this and other related incidents. This nation was founded by men of many nations and backgrounds. It was founded on the principle that all men are created equal, and that the rights of every man are diminished when the rights of one man are threatened.

Today we are committed to a worldwide struggle to promote and protect the rights of all who wish to be free. When Americans are sent to Vietnam or West Berlin, we do not ask for whites only. It ought to be possible, therefore, for American students of any color to attend any public institution they select without having to be backed up by troops.

It ought to be possible for American consumers of any color to receive equal service in places of public accommodation, such as hotels and restaurants and theaters and retail stores, without being forced to resort to demonstration in the street. It ought to be possible for American citizens of any color to register and to vote in a free election without interference or fear of reprisal. It ought to be possible, in short, for every American to enjoy the privileges of being American without regard to his race or his color. In short, every American ought to have the right to be treated as he would wish to be treated, as one would wish his children to be treated. But this is not the case today.

The Negro baby born in America today, regardless of the section of the nation in which he is born, has about one-half as much chance of completing high school as a white baby born in the same place on the same day, one-third as much chance of completing college, one-third as much chance of becoming a professional man, twice as much chance of becoming unemployed, about one-seventh as much chance of earning $10,000 a year or more, a life expectancy which is seven years shorter, and the prospects of earning only half as much....

We are confronted primarily with a moral issue. It is as old as the Scriptures and is as clear as the American Constitution. The heart of the question is whether all Americans are to be afforded equal rights and equal opportunities, whether we are going to treat our fellow Americans as we want to be treated. If an American, because his skin is dark, cannot eat lunch in a restaurant open to the public, if he cannot send his children to the best public school available, if he cannot vote for the public officials who represent him, if, in short, he cannot enjoy the full and free life which all of us want, then who among us would be content to have the color of his skin changed and stand in his place? Who among us would be content with the counsels of patience and delay?

One hundred years have passed since President Lincoln freed the slaves, yet their heirs, their grandsons, are not fully free. They are not yet freed from the bonds of injustice. They are not yet freed from social and economic oppression. And this nation, for all its hopes and all its boasts, will not be fully free until all its citizens are free.

We preach freedom around the world, and we mean it, and we cherish our freedom here at home; but are we to say to the world, and, much more importantly, to each other, that this is a land of the free except for the Negroes; that we have no second-class citizens except Negroes; that we have no class or caste system, no ghettos, no master race, except with respect to Negroes?

Now the time has come for this nation to fulfill its promise. The events in Birmingham and elsewhere have so increased the cries for equality that no city or state or legislative body can prudently choose to ignore them. The fires of frustration and discord are burning in every city, North and South, where legal remedies are not at hand. Redress is sought in the streets, in demonstrations, parades, and protests which create tensions and threaten violence and threaten lives.

We face, therefore, a moral crisis as a country and as a people. It cannot be met by repressive police action. It cannot be left to increased demonstrations in the streets. It cannot be quieted by token moves or talk. It is a time to act in the Congress, in your state and local legislative bodies and, above all, in all of our daily lives. It is not enough to pin the blame on others, to say this is a problem of one section of the country or another, or deplore the facts that we face. A great change is at hand, and our task, our obligation, is to make that revolution, that change, peaceful and constructive for all. . . .

I am, therefore, asking the Congress to enact legislation giving all Americans the right to be served in facilities which are open to the public—hotels, restaurants, theaters, retail stores, and similar establishments. . . . Other features will also be requested, including greater protection for the right to vote. But legislation, I repeat, cannot solve this problem alone. It must be solved in the homes of every American in every community across our country. In this respect, I want to pay tribute to those citizens, North and South, who have been working in their communities to make life better for all. They are acting not out of a sense of legal duty but out of a sense of human decency. Like our soldiers and sailors in all parts of the world, they are meeting freedom's challenge on the firing line, and I salute them for their honor and courage.

Questions

1. Why do you think Kennedy places so much emphasis on freedom in this speech?

2. Why does Kennedy say that the crisis is essentially "moral," rather than political or legal?

175. Malcolm X, "The Ballot or the Bullet" (1964)

Source: Malcolm X, from "The Ballot or the Bullet" in Malcolm X Speaks *by Malcolm X. Copyright © 1965, 1989 by Betty Shabazz and Pathfinder Press. Reprinted by permission.*

One of the most controversial figures to emerge in the 1960s, Malcolm X was born Malcolm Little in Omaha, Nebraska, in 1925. While in prison in the 1940s, he embraced the Nation of Islam, or Black Muslims, and dropped his last name, replacing it with X to symbolize black Americans' loss of their African heritage. After his release he emerged as a fiery advocate of black nationalism and racial separation, and he rejected the civil rights movement's advocacy of integration and nonviolence. Blacks had the right, he insisted, to claim freedom by any means necessary.

By April 3, 1964, when he delivered this speech in Cleveland, Malcolm X had broken with the Nation of Islam and begun to embrace the idea of working with white allies. He still insisted that the civil rights movement was pursuing a doomed strategy. Despite the speech's inflammatory title, it was less a call for violence than a warning that if blacks did not soon obtain equality, violence was certain to follow. Malcolm X was assassinated by members of the Nation of Islam in 1965. But he became an intellectual founding father of the Black Power movement of the late 1960s.

━━━━

ALTHOUGH I'M STILL a Muslim, I'm not here tonight to discuss my religion. I'm not here to try and change your religion. I'm not here to argue or discuss anything that we differ about, because it's time for us to submerge our differences and realize that it is best for us to first see that we have the same problem, a common problem, a problem that will make you catch hell whether you're a Baptist, or a Methodist, or a Muslim, or a nationalist. Whether you're educated or illiterate, whether you live on the boulevard or in the alley, you're going to catch hell just like I am. We're all in the same boat and we all are going to catch the same hell from the same man. He just happens to be a white man. All of us have suffered here, in this country, political oppression at the hands of the white man, economic exploitation at the hands of the white man, and social degradation at the hands of the white man.

Now in speaking like this, it doesn't mean that we're anti-white, but it does mean we're anti-exploitation, we're anti-degradation, we're anti-oppression. And if the white man doesn't want us to be anti-him, let him stop oppressing and exploiting and degrading us. Whether we are Christians or Muslims or nationalists or agnostics or atheists, we must first learn to forget our differences. If we have differences, let us differ in the closet; when we come out in front, let us not have anything to argue about until we get finished arguing with the man. If the late President Kennedy could get together with Khrushchev and exchange some wheat, we certainly have more in common with each other than Kennedy and Khrushchev had with each other.

If we don't do something real soon, I think you'll have to agree that we're going to be forced either to use the ballot or the bullet. It's one or the other in 1964. It isn't that time is running out—time has run out!

1964 threatens to be the most explosive year America has ever witnessed. The most explosive year. Why? It's also a political year. It's the year when all of the white politicians will be back in the so-called Negro community jiving you and me for some votes. The year when all of the white political crooks will be right back in your and my community with their false promises, building up our hopes for a letdown, with their trickery and their treachery, with their false promises which they don't intend to keep. As they nourish these dissatisfactions, it can only lead to one thing, an explosion; and now we have the type of black man on the scene in America today . . . who just doesn't intend to turn the other cheek any longer. . . .

I'm not a politician, not even a student of politics; in fact, I'm not a student of much of anything. I'm not a Democrat. I'm not a Republican, and I don't even consider myself an American. If you and I were Americans, there'd be no problem. . . . Everything that came out of

Europe, every blue-eyed thing, is already an American. And as long as you and I have been over here, we aren't Americans yet.

Well, I am one who doesn't believe in deluding myself. I'm not going to sit at your table and watch you eat, with nothing on my plate, and call myself a diner. Sitting at the table doesn't make you a diner, unless you eat some of what's on that plate. Being here in America doesn't make you an American. Being born here in America doesn't make you an American. Why, if birth made you American, you wouldn't need any legislation; you wouldn't need any amendments to the Constitution; you wouldn't be faced with civil-rights filibustering in Washington, D.C., right now....

No, I'm not an American. I'm one of the 22 million black people who are the victims of Americanism. One of the 22 million black people who are the victims of democracy, nothing but disguised hypocrisy. So, I'm not standing here speaking to you as an American, or a patriot, or a flag-saluter, or a flag-waver—no, not I. I'm speaking as a victim of this American system. And I see America through the eyes of the victim. I don't see any American dream; I see an American nightmare....

So it's time in 1964 to wake up. And when you see them coming up with that kind of conspiracy, let them know your eyes are open. And let them know you—something else that's wide open too. It's got to be the ballot or the bullet. The ballot or the bullet. If you're afraid to use an expression like that, you should get on out of the country; you should get back in the cotton patch; you should get back in the alley. They get all the Negro vote, and after they get it, the Negro gets nothing in return....

So, where do we go from here? First, we need some friends. We need some new allies. The entire civil-rights struggle needs a new interpretation, a broader interpretation. We need to look at this civil-rights thing from another angle—from the inside as well as from the outside. To those of us whose philosophy is black nationalism, the only way you can get involved in the civil-rights struggle is give it a new interpretation. That old interpretation excluded us.... Well, we're justified in seeking civil rights, if it means equality of opportunity, because all we're doing there is trying to collect for our investment. Our mothers and fathers invested sweat and blood. Three hundred and ten years we worked in this country without a dime in return—I mean without a dime in return....

When we begin to get in this area, we need new friends, we need new allies. We need to expand the civil-rights struggle to a higher level—to the level of human rights. Whenever you are in a civil-rights struggle, whether you know it or not, you are confining yourself to the jurisdiction of Uncle Sam.... When you expand the civil-rights struggle to the level of human rights, you can then take the case of the black man in this country before the nations in the UN. You can take it before the General Assembly. You can take Uncle Sam before a world court....

Black people are fed up with the dillydallying, pussyfooting, compromising approach that we've been using toward getting our freedom. We want freedom now, but we're not going to get it saying "We Shall Overcome." We've got to fight until we overcome.... Brothers and sisters, always remember, if it doesn't take senators and congressmen and presidential proclamations to give freedom to the white man, it is not necessary for legislation or proclamation or Supreme Court decisions to give freedom to the black man. You let that white man know, if this is a country of freedom, let it be a country of freedom; and if it's not a country of freedom, change it.

Questions

1. How do Malcolm X's language and outlook differ from those of King in the previous chapter?

2. Why does Malcolm X believe the civil rights movement needs a "new interpretation"?

176. Barry Goldwater on "Extremism in the Defense of Liberty" (1964)

Source: Barry Goldwater, "Extremism in the Defense of Liberty," Official Report of the Proceedings of the 28th Republican National Convention, 1964, pp. 413–19. Reprinted by permission of the Republican National Committee.

The presidential campaign of 1964 was a milestone in the rebirth of American conservatism. Four years earlier, the Republican candidate, Senator Barry Goldwater of Arizona, had written *The Conscience of a Conservative*, which demanded a more aggressive conduct of the Cold War and warned against "internal" dangers to freedom, especially the New Deal welfare state. In the Senate, Goldwater voted against the Civil Rights Act of 1964. Attacked as an extremist by Democrats and many moderate Republicans, Goldwater used his acceptance speech at the Republican national convention to outline his conservative vision and warn against the increased power of the national government. Toward the end, he made the explosive statement, "Extremism in the defense of liberty is no vice."

Goldwater went down to a disastrous defeat. But his campaign aroused enthusiasm in the rapidly expanding suburbs of southern California and the Southwest. The funds that poured into the Goldwater campaign from the Sun Belt's oilmen and aerospace entrepreneurs established a new financial base for conservatism.

———

I ACCEPT YOUR nomination with a deep sense of humility. [*Applause*] I accept, too, the responsibility that goes with it, and I seek your continued help and your continued guidance. My fellow Republicans, our cause is too great for a man to feel worthy of it. Our task would be too great for any man, did he not have with him the hearts and the hands of this great Republican Party, and I promise you tonight that every fiber of my being is consecrated to our cause; that nothing shall be lacking from the struggle that can be brought to it by enthusiasm, by devotion and plain hard work. [*Cheers and Applause*] In this world no person, no party, can guarantee anything, but what we can do, and we shall do, is to deserve victory, and victory will be ours. [*Applause*]

The good Lord raised this mighty Republic to be a home for the brave, and to flourish as the land of the free—not to stagnate in the swampland of collectivism, not to cringe before the bullying of communism. [*Loud Applause and Cheers*]

Now, my fellow Americans, the tide has been running against freedom. Our people have followed false prophets. We must and we shall return to proven ways—not because they are old, but because they are true. [*Applause*] We must, and we shall, set the tides running again in the cause of freedom. [*Applause*] And this Party, with its every action, every word, every breath and every heartbeat has but a single resolve, and that is freedom—freedom made orderly for this Nation by our constitutional government; freedom under a government limited by the laws of nature and of nature's God; freedom—balanced so that order, lacking liberty, will not become a slave of the prison cell; balanced so that liberty, lacking order, will not become the license of the mob and the jungle. [*Applause*]

Now, we Americans understand freedom. We have earned it, lived for it, and died for it. This nation and its people are freedom's model in a searching world. We can be freedom's missionaries in a doubting world. But, ladies and gentlemen, first we must renew freedom's vision in our own hearts and in our own homes. [*Applause*]

During four futile years, the administration which we shall replace has distorted and lost that vision. [*Applause*] It has talked and talked and talked and talked the words of freedom.

• • •

Tonight there is violence in our streets, corruption in our highest offices, aimlessness among our youth, anxiety among our elders and there is a virtual despair among the many who look beyond material success for the inner meaning of their lives. Where examples of morality should be set, the opposite is seen. Small men, seeking great wealth or power, have too often and too long turned even the highest levels of public service into mere personal opportunity. [*Applause*]

Now, certainly, simple honesty is not too much to demand of men in government. We find it in most. Republicans demand it from everyone. [*Applause*] They demand it from everyone, no matter how exalted or protected his position might be. [*Applause*] The growing menace in our country tonight, to personal safety, to life, to limb and property, in homes, in churches, on the playgrounds, and places of business, particularly in our great cities, is the mounting concern, or should be, of every thoughtful citizen in the United States. [*Applause*]

Security from domestic violence, no less than from foreign aggression, is the most elementary and fundamental purpose of any government, and a government that cannot fulfill that purpose is one that cannot long command the loyalty of its citizens. [*Loud Applause*] History shows us—demonstrates that nothing—nothing prepares the way for tyranny more than the failure of public offices to keep the streets safe from bullies and marauders. [*Applause*]

Those who seek absolute power, even though they seek it to do what they regard as good, are simply demanding the right to enforce their own version of heaven on earth. [*Applause*] And let me remind you, they are the very ones who always create the most hellish tyrannies. [*Applause*] Absolute power does corrupt, and those who seek it must be suspect and must be opposed. Their mistaken course stems from false notions of equality, ladies and gentlemen. Equality, rightly understood, as our founding fathers understood it, leads to liberty and to the emancipation of creative differences. Wrongly understood, as it has been so tragically in our time, it leads first to conformity and then to despotism. [*Loud Applause and Cheers*]

We Republicans see in our constitutional form of government the great framework which assures the orderly but dynamic fulfillment of the whole man, and we see the whole man as the great reason for instituting orderly government in the first place.

We see, in private property and in economy based upon and fostering private property, the one way to make government a durable ally of the whole man, rather than his determined enemy. [*Applause*] We see, in the sanctity of private property, the only durable foundation for constitutional government in a free society. [*Applause*] And beyond that, we see, in cherished diversity of ways, diversity of thoughts, of motives and accomplishments. We do not seek to lead anyone's life for him—we seek only to secure his rights and to guarantee him opportunity to strive, with government performing only those needed and constitutionally-sanctioned tasks which cannot otherwise be performed. [*Prolonged Applause*]

We Republicans seek a government that attends to its inherent responsibilities of maintaining a stable monetary and fiscal climate, encouraging a free and a competitive economy and enforcing law and order.

• • •

The task of preserving and enlarging freedom at home and of safeguarding it from the forces of tyranny abroad is great enough to challenge all our resources and to refire all our strength. [*Cheers and Applause*] Anyone who joins us in all sincerity, we welcome. [*Applause*] Those who do not care for our cause, we don't expect to enter our ranks in any case. [*Applause*] And let our Republicanism, so focused and so dedicated, not be made fuzzy and futile by unthinking and stupid labels.

I would remind you that extremism in the defense of liberty is no vice. [*Loud Applause and Cheers*] And let me remind you also that moderation in the pursuit of justice is no virtue. [*Applause and Cheers*]

Questions

1. What evidence does Goldwater give of a decline of "morality" in American life?

2. Why does Goldwater stress the interconnection between "order" and liberty?

177. Chief Justice Earl Warren, Opinion of the Court in *Loving v. Virginia* (1967)

Source: Richard Perry Loving, Mildred Jeter Loving v. Virginia, *388 U.S. 1 (1967).*

One of the Supreme Court's most important decisions of the 1960s came in an aptly named case, *Loving v. Virginia*, in which a white man and a black woman were convicted of a crime for being married. "Anti-miscegenation" laws prohibiting marriage between individuals of different races had a long history, dating back to the colonial era. And claims that equal rights in other realms—education, employment, voting rights—would lead inevitably to what opponents called the mixing of the races were frequently raised by opponents of the civil rights revolution.

Mildred Jeer, a black woman, and Richard Loving, a white man, both residents of Virginia, were married in the District of Columbia in 1958. Shortly afterward, they returned to their home state. In 1959 they were convicted of violating Virginia's law against interracial marriage. The couple were sentenced to a year in prison, but the judge gave them the option of leaving Virginia for twenty-five years. God, the judge declared, "did not intend for the races to mix." The Lovings left the state but soon filed suit to have their conviction overturned as a violation of the clause of the Fourteenth Amendment guaranteeing to all persons the equal protection of the laws and barring states from depriving them of liberty without due process of law. The Supreme Court sided with them unanimously, in 1967. At the time of its ruling, sixteen states still had such laws on the books. The *Loving* decision marked an important step in extending personal freedom into the most intimate realms of life. Today, interracial marriages evoke little objection anywhere in the United States.

———

THIS CASE PRESENTS a constitutional question never addressed by this Court: whether a statutory scheme adopted by the State of Virginia to prevent marriages between persons solely on the basis of racial classifications violates the Equal Protection and Due Process

Clauses of the Fourteenth Amendment. For reasons which seem to us to reflect the central meaning of those constitutional commands, we conclude that these statutes cannot stand consistently with the Fourteenth Amendment....

Penalties for miscegenation arose as an incident to slavery, and have been common in Virginia since the colonial period. The present statutory scheme dates from the adoption of the Racial Integrity Act of 1924, passed during the period of extreme nativism which followed the end of the First World War. The central features of this Act, and current Virginia law, are the absolute prohibition of a "white person" marrying other than another "white person," a prohibition against issuing marriage licenses until the issuing official is satisfied that the applicants' statements as to their race are correct, certificates of "racial composition" to be kept by both local and state registrars, and the carrying forward of earlier prohibitions against racial intermarriage....

The State contends that, because its miscegenation statutes punish equally both the white and the Negro participants in an interracial marriage, these statutes, despite their reliance on racial classifications, do not constitute an invidious discrimination based upon race.... There can be no question but that Virginia's miscegenation statutes rest solely upon distinctions drawn according to race. The statutes proscribe generally accepted conduct if engaged in by members of different races. Over the years, this Court has consistently repudiated distinctions between citizens solely because of their ancestry as being odious to a free people whose institutions are founded upon the doctrine of equality.... There is patently no legitimate overriding purpose independent of invidious racial discrimination which justifies this classification. The fact that Virginia prohibits only interracial marriages involving white persons demonstrates that the racial classifications must stand on their own justification, as measures designed to maintain White Supremacy.... There can be no doubt that restricting the freedom to marry solely because of racial classifications violates the central meaning of the Equal Protection Clause.

These statutes also deprive the Lovings of liberty without due process of law in violation of the Due Process Clause of the Fourteenth Amendment. The freedom to marry has long been recognized as one of the vital personal rights essential to the orderly pursuit of happiness by free men. Marriage is one of the "basic civil rights of man," fundamental to our very existence and survival. To deny this fundamental freedom on so unsupportable a basis as the racial classifications embodied in these statutes, classifications so directly subversive of the principle of equality at the heart of the Fourteenth Amendment, is surely to deprive all the State's citizens of liberty without due process of law.... Under our Constitution, the freedom to marry, or not marry, a person of another race resides with the individual, and cannot be infringed by the State.

Questions

1. Why does the Court claim that the right to choose one's marriage partner is part of the liberty protected by the Constitution?

2. What evidence does the Court provide that the Virginia law's purpose is to bolster white supremacy?

178. The Port Huron Statement (1962)

Source: Students for a Democratic Society, The Port Huron Statement, 1964, pp. 3–8. Reprinted by permission of Tom Hayden.

One of the most influential documents of the 1960s emerged in 1962 from a meeting sponsored by the Students for a Democratic Society (SDS), then a small offshoot of the socialist League for Industrial Democracy. Meeting at Port Huron, Michigan, some sixty college students adopted a document that captured the mood and summarized the beliefs of this generation of student protesters.

But what made the document the guiding spirit of what would soon be called the New Left was its new vision of social change. It spoke of participatory democracy, an idea that suggested a rejection of the elitist strain that had marked liberal thinkers from the Progressives to postwar advocates of economic planning, in which government experts would establish national priorities in the name of the people. Although rarely defined with precision, participatory democracy became a standard by which students judged existing social arrangements—work places, schools, government—and found them wanting. By the mid-1960s, fueled by growing opposition among the young to the country's war in Vietnam, SDS would become the most important vehicle for what was rapidly becoming a full-fledged generational rebellion.

———

WE ARE PEOPLE of this generation, bred in at least modest comfort, housed now in universities, looking uncomfortably to the world we inherit.

When we were kids the United States was the wealthiest and strongest country in the world; the only one with the atom bomb, the least scarred by modern war, an initiator of the United Nations that we thought would distribute Western influence throughout the world. Freedom and equality for each individual, government of, by, and for the people—these American values we found good, principles by which we could live as men. Many of us began maturing in complacency.

As we grew, however, our comfort was penetrated by events too troubling to dismiss. First, the permeating and victimizing fact of human degradation, symbolized by the Southern struggle against racial bigotry, compelled most of us from silence to activism. Second, the enclosing fact of the Cold War, symbolized by the presence of the Bomb, brought awareness that we ourselves, and our friends, and millions of abstract "others" we knew more directly because of our common peril, might die at any time. We might deliberately ignore, or avoid, or fail to feel all other human problems, but not these two, for these were too immediate and crushing in their impact, too challenging in the demand that we as individuals take the responsibility for encounter and resolution.

While these and other problems either directly oppressed us or rankled our consciences and became our own subjective concerns, we began to see complicated and disturbing paradoxes in our surrounding America. The declaration "all men are created equal..." rang hollow before the facts of Negro life in the South and the big cities of the North. The proclaimed peaceful intentions of the United States contradicted its economic and military investments in the Cold War status quo.

We witnessed, and continue to witness, other paradoxes. With nuclear energy whole cities can easily be powered, yet the dominant nation-states seem more likely to unleash destruction greater than that incurred in all wars of human history. Although our own technology is destroying old and creating new forms of social organization, men still tolerate meaningless work and idleness. While two-thirds of mankind suffers undernourishment, our own upper classes revel amidst superfluous abundance. Although world population is expected to double in forty years, the nations still tolerate anarchy as a major principle of international conduct and uncontrolled exploitation governs the sapping of the earth's physical resources. Although mankind desperately needs revolutionary leadership, America rests in national stalemate, its goals ambiguous and tradition-bound instead of informed and clear, its democratic system apathetic and manipulated rather than "of, by, and for the people."

Not only did tarnish appear on our image of American virtue, not only did disillusion occur when the hypocrisy of American ideals was discovered, but we began to sense that what we had originally seen as the American Golden Age was actually the decline of an era. The worldwide outbreak of revolution against colonialism and imperialism, the entrenchment of totalitarian states, the menace of war, overpopulation, international disorder, supertechnology—these trends were testing the tenacity of our own commitment to democracy and freedom and our abilities to visualize their application to a world in upheaval.

Our work is guided by the sense that we may be the last generation in the experiment with living. But we are a minority—the vast majority of our people regard the temporary equilibriums of our society and world as eternally functional parts. In this is perhaps the outstanding paradox: we ourselves are imbued with urgency, yet the message of our society is that there is no viable alternative to the present. Beneath the reassuring tones of the politicians, beneath the common opinion that America will "muddle through," beneath the stagnation of those who have closed their minds to the future, is the pervading feeling that there simply are no alternatives, that our times have witnessed the exhaustion not only of Utopias, but of any new departures as well. Feeling the press of complexity upon the emptiness of life, people are fearful of the thought that at any moment things might be thrust out of control. They fear change itself, since change might smash whatever invisible framework seems to hold back chaos for them now. For most Americans, all crusades are suspect, threatening. The fact that each individual sees apathy in his fellows perpetuates the common reluctance to organize for change. The dominant institutions are complex enough to blunt the minds of their potential critics, and entrenched enough to swiftly dissipate or entirely repel the energies of protest and reform, thus limiting human expectancies. Then, too, we are a materially improved society, and by our own improvements we seem to have weakened the case for further change.

Some would have us believe that Americans feel contentment amidst prosperity—but might it not better be called a glaze above deeply felt anxieties about their role in the new world? And if these anxieties produce a developed indifference to human affairs, do they not as well produce a yearning to believe there is an alternative to the present, that something *can* be done to change circumstances in the school, the workplaces, the bureaucracies, the government? It is to this latter yearning, at once the spark and engine of change, that we direct our present appeal. The search for truly democratic alternatives to the present, and a commitment to social experimentation with them, is a worthy and fulfilling human enterprise, one which moves us and, we hope, others today. On such a basis do we offer this document of our convictions and analysis: as an effort in understanding and changing the conditions of humanity in the late twentieth century, an effort rooted in the ancient, still unfulfilled conception of man attaining determining influence over his circumstances of life.

Making values explicit—an initial task in establishing alternatives—is an activity that has been devalued and corrupted. The conventional moral terms of the age, the politician moralities—"free world," "people's democracies"—reflect realities poorly, if at all, and seem to function more as ruling myths than as descriptive principles. But neither has our experience in the universities brought us moral enlightenment. Our professors and administrators sacrifice controversy to public relations; their curriculums change more slowly than the living events of the world; their skills and silence are purchased by investors in the arms race; passion is called unscholastic. The questions we might want raised—what is really important? can we live in a different and better way? if we wanted to change society, how would we do it?—are not thought to be questions of a "fruitful, empirical nature," and thus are brushed aside.

• • •

We regard *men* as infinitely precious and possessed of unfulfilled capacities for reason, freedom, and love. In affirming these principles we are aware of countering perhaps the dominant conceptions of man in the twentieth century: that he is a thing to be manipulated, and that he is inherently incapable of directing his own affairs. We oppose the depersonalization that reduces human beings to the status of things—if anything, the brutalities of the twentieth century teach that means and ends are intimately related, that vague appeals to "posterity" cannot justify the mutilations of the present. We oppose, too, the doctrine of human incompetence because it rests essentially on the modern fact that men have been "competently" manipulated into incompetence—we see little reason why men cannot meet with increasing skill the complexities and responsibilities of their situation, if society is organized not for minority, but for majority, participation in decision-making.

Men have unrealized potential for self-cultivation, self-direction, self-understanding, and creativity. It is this potential that we regard as crucial and to which we appeal, not to the human potentiality for violence, unreason, and submission to authority. The goal of man and society should be human independence: a concern not with image or popularity but with finding a meaning in life that is personally authentic; a quality of mind not compulsively driven by a sense of powerlessness, nor one which unthinkingly adopts status values, nor one which represses all threats to its habits, but one which has full, spontaneous access to present and past experiences, one which easily unites the fragmented parts of personal history, one which openly faces problems which are troubling and unresolved; one with an intuitive awareness of possibilities, an active sense of curiosity, an ability and willingness to learn.

• • •

We would replace power rooted in possession, privilege, or circumstance by power and uniqueness rooted in love, reflectiveness, reason, and creativity. As a *social system* we seek the establishment of a democracy of individual participation, governed by two central aims: that the individual share in those social decisions determining the quality and direction of his life; that society be organized to encourage independence in men and provide the media for their common participation.

In a participatory democracy, the political life would be based in several root principles:

> that decision-making of basic social consequence be carried on by public groupings;
> that politics be seen positively, as the art of collectively creating an acceptable pattern of social relations;
> that politics has the function of bringing people out of isolation and into community, thus being a necessary, though not sufficient, means of finding meaning in personal life;

that the political order should serve to clarify problems in a way instrumental to their solution; it should provide outlets for the expression of personal grievance and aspiration; opposing views should be organized so as to illuminate choices and facilitate the attainment of goals; channels should be commonly available to relate men to knowledge and to power so that private problems—from bad recreation facilities to personal alienation—are formulated as general issues.

The economic sphere would have as its basis the principles:

that work should involve incentives worthier than money or survival: It should be educative, not stultifying; creative, not mechanical; self-directed, not manipulated, encouraging independence; a respect for others, a sense of dignity, and a willingness to accept social responsibility, since it is this experience that has crucial influence on habits, perceptions, and individual ethics;

that the economic experience is so personally decisive that the individual must share in its full determination;

that the economy itself is of such social importance that its major resources and means of production should be open to democratic participation and subject to democratic social regulation.

Like the political and economic ones, major social institutions—cultural, educational, rehabilitative, and others—should be generally organized with the well-being and dignity of man as the essential measure of success.

• • •

Questions

1. What features of American society seem most to trouble the authors of the Port Huron Statement?

2. How would you define the phrase, "a democracy of individual participation"?

179. Paul Potter on the Antiwar Movement (1965)

Source: Paul Potter, "The Incredible War" from Takin' It to the Streets:
A Sixties Reader, *eds. Alexander Bloom and Wini Breines (Oxford University
Press, 1995). Copyright © 1995 by Alexander Bloom and Wini Breines.
Reproduced with permission of the Licensor through PLSclear.*

The war in Vietnam divided American society more deeply than any
military conflict in the nation's history. Early in 1965, President Lyndon
Johnson authorized air strikes against North Vietnam and introduced
American ground troops in the south. The cause of freedom, he insisted,
was at stake. But as casualties mounted, the Cold War foreign policy
consensus began to unravel. To SDS, the war seemed the opposite of participatory democracy, since American involvement had come through secret
commitments and elite decision making, with no real public debate.

In April 1965, SDS called on opponents of American policy in Vietnam
to attend a rally in Washington. In his speech, SDS president Paul Potter
tried to reclaim the language of freedom from the administration. Potter
went on to challenge the entire basis of American foreign policy in the
Cold War. He ended by calling for the creation of a "social movement" to
demand an end to the war.

———

VIETNAM, WE MAY say, is a laboratory run by a new breed of
gamesmen who approach war as a kind of rational exercise in international power politics. It is the testing ground and staging area for
a new American response to the social revolution that is sweeping
through the impoverished downtrodden areas of the world. It is the
beginning of the American counter-revolution.

• • •

What kind of system is it that allows good men to make those
kinds of decisions? What kind of system is it that justifies the United
States or any country seizing the destinies of the Vietnamese people
and using them callously for its own purpose? What kind of system is it
that disenfranchises people in the South, leaves millions upon millions

of people throughout the country impoverished and excluded from the mainstream and promise of American society, that creates faceless and terrible bureaucracies and makes those the place where people spend their lives and do their work, that consistently puts material values before human values—and still persists in calling itself free and still persists in finding itself fit to police the world?

• • •

We must name that system. We must name it, describe it, analyze it, understand it and change it. For it is only when that system is changed and brought under control that there can be any hope for stopping the forces that create a war in Vietnam today or a murder in the South tomorrow.

• • •

If the people of this country are to end the war in Vietnam, and to change the institutions which create it; then the people of this country must create a massive social movement—and if that can be built around the issue of Vietnam then that is what we must do.

By a social movement I mean more than petitions or letters of protest, or tacit support of dissident Congressmen; I mean people who are willing to change their lives, who are willing to challenge the system, to take the problem of change seriously. By a social movement I mean an effort that is powerful enough to make the country understand that our problems are not in Vietnam, or China or Brazil or outer space or at the bottom of the ocean, but are here in the United States. What we must do is begin to build a democratic and humane society in which Vietnams are unthinkable, in which human life and initiative are precious.

Questions

1. Why does Potter challenge President Johnson's claim that the war in Vietnam is a defense of freedom?

2. What does he mean by saying, "We must name that system"?

180. The National Organization for Women (1966)

Source: National Organization for Women, "The National Organization for Women's 1966 Statement of Purpose," written by Betty Friedan. Reprinted with permission of National Organization for Women. This is a historical document and may not reflect the current language or priorities of the organization.

The civil rights revolution, soon followed by the rise of the New Left, inspired other Americans to voice their grievances and claim their rights. Most far-reaching in its impact on American society was the emergence of the "second wave" of feminism. A key catalyst in the public reawakening of feminist consciousness was the publication in 1963 of Betty Friedan's *The Feminine Mystique.* At a time when the number of women attending college was expanding rapidly, her book painted a devastating picture of talented women trapped in a world that viewed marriage and motherhood as their primary goals. Somehow, after more than a century of agitation for access to the public sphere, and half a century after women won the right to vote, women's lives still centered on the home.

   In 1966, Friedan was the leading figure in the creation of the National Organization for Women (NOW), dedicated to combating the inequalities that afflicted women in the workplace, legal system, politics, and education. Although the Statement of Purpose called for a more equitable division of labor within the family, NOW's main focus lay in the public realm. NOW was soon joined by more radical organizations that targeted inequalities in private life. Since 1966, NOW has been instrumental in winning legal gains for women. Today, it has over half a million members.

━━━━━━━━

WE, MEN AND women who hereby constitute ourselves as the National Organization for Women, believe that the time has come for a new movement toward true equality for all women in America, and toward a fully equal partnership of the sexes, as part of the world-wide revolution of human rights now taking place within and beyond our national borders....

NOW is dedicated to the proposition that women, first and foremost, are human beings, who, like all other people in our society, must have the chance to develop their fullest human potential. We believe that women can achieve such equality only by accepting to the full the challenges and responsibilities they share with all other people in our society, as part of the decision-making mainstream of American political, economic and social life.

We organize to initiate or support action, nationally, or in any part of this nation, by individuals or organizations, to break through the silken curtain of prejudice and discrimination against women in government, industry, the professions, the churches, the political parties, the judiciary, the labor unions, in education, science, medicine, law, religion and every other field of importance in American society.

Enormous changes taking place in our society make it both possible and urgently necessary to advance the unfinished revolution of women toward true equality, now. With a life span lengthened to nearly 75 years it is no longer either necessary or possible for women to devote the greater part of their lives to child-rearing; yet childbearing and -rearing which continues to be a most important part of most women's lives—still is used to justify barring women from equal professional and economic participation and advance.

Today's technology has reduced most of the productive chores which women once performed in the home and in mass-production industries based upon routine unskilled labor. This same technology has virtually eliminated the quality of muscular strength as a criterion for filling most jobs, while intensifying American industry's need for creative intelligence. In view of this new industrial revolution created by automation in the mid-twentieth century, women can and must participate in old and new fields of society in full equality—or become permanent outsiders.

Despite all the talk about the status of American women in recent years, the actual position of women in the United States has declined, and is declining, to an alarming degree throughout the 1950's and 60's. Although 46.4% of all American women between the ages of 18 and 65 now work outside the home, the overwhelming majority—75%—are in routine clerical, sales, or factory jobs, or they are household workers, cleaning women, hospital attendants. About two-thirds of Negro women workers are in the lowest paid service occupations. Working women are becoming increasingly—not less—concentrated on the bottom of the job ladder. As a consequence full-time women workers today earn on the average only 60% of what men earn, and that wage gap has been increasing over the past twenty-five years in every major industry group. In 1964, of all women with a yearly income, 89% earned under $5,000 a year; half of all full-time year round women workers earned less than $3,690; only 1.4% of full-time year round women workers had an annual income of $10,000 or more.... In all the professions considered of importance to society, and in the executive ranks of industry and government, women are losing ground. Where they are present it is only a token handful. Women comprise less than 1% of federal judges; less than 4% of all lawyers; 7% of doctors. Yet women represent 51% of the U.S. population....

Until now, too few women's organizations and official spokesmen have been willing to speak out against these dangers facing women. Too many women have been restrained by the fear of being called "feminist." There is no civil rights movement to speak for women, as there has been for Negroes and other victims of discrimination. The National Organization for Women must therefore begin to speak.

We believe that this nation has a capacity at least as great as other nations, to innovate new social institutions which will enable women to enjoy the true equality of opportunity and responsibility in society, without conflict with their responsibilities as mothers and homemakers. In such innovations, America does not lead the

Western world, but lags by decades behind many European countries. We do not accept the traditional assumption that a woman has to choose between marriage and motherhood, on the one hand, and serious participation in industry or the professions on the other.... Above all, we reject the assumption that these problems are the unique responsibility of each individual woman, rather than a basic social dilemma which society must solve. True equality of opportunity and freedom of choice for women requires such practical, and possible innovations as a nationwide network of child-care centers, which will make it unnecessary for women to retire completely from society until their children are grown, and national programs to provide retraining for women who have chosen to care for their children full-time....

We believe that a true partnership between the sexes demands a different concept of marriage, an equitable sharing of the responsibilities of home and children and of the economic burdens of their support. We believe that proper recognition should be given to the economic and social value of homemaking and child-care.

Questions

1. Why does NOW believe that the status of women is declining, not improving?

2. How does the document define freedom for women?

181. César Chavez, "Letter from Delano" (1969)

Source: César Chavez, "Letter from Delano," 1969. TM/© 2016 the César E. Chavez Foundation, www.chavezfoundation.org. Reprinted with permission.

As in the case of blacks, a movement for legal rights had long flourished among Mexican-Americans. But the mid-1960s saw the flowering of a new militancy challenging the group's second-class economic status. Like Black Power advocates, the movement emphasized pride in both the Mexican past and the new Chicano culture that had arisen in the United States. Unlike the Black Power movement and SDS, it was closely linked to labor struggles.

Beginning in 1965, César Chavez, the son of migrant farm workers and a disciple of Martin Luther King Jr., led a series of nonviolent protests including marches, fasts, and a national boycott of California grapes, to pressure growers to agree to labor contracts with the United Farm Workers Union (UFW). The boycott mobilized Latino communities throughout the Southwest and drew national attention to the pitifully low wages and oppressive working conditions of migrant laborers.

Chavez addressed a "Letter from Delano" to agricultural employers. In it he defended his own movement's aims and tactics. In 1970, the major growers agreed to contracts with the UFW.

DEAR MR. BARR [President, California Grape and Tree Fruit League]:

I am sad to hear about your accusations in the press that our union movement and table grape boycott have been successful because we have used violence and terror tactics. If what you say is true, I have been a failure and should withdraw from the struggle; but you are left with the awesome moral responsibility, before God and man, to come forward with whatever information you have so that corrective action can begin at once. If for any reason you fail to come forth to substantiate your charges, then you must be held responsible for committing violence against us, albeit violence of the tongue. I am convinced that you as a human being did not mean what you said but rather acted hastily under pressure from the public relations firm that has been hired to try to counteract the tremendous moral force of our movement. How many times we ourselves have felt the need to lash out in anger and bitterness.

Today on Good Friday 1969 we remember the life and the sacrifice of Martin Luther King, Jr., who gave himself totally to the nonviolent struggle for peace and justice. In his "Letter from Birmingham Jail" Dr. King describes better than I could our hopes for the strike and boycott: "Injustice must be exposed, with all the tension its exposure creates, to the light of human conscience and the air of national opinion before it can be cured." For our part I admit that we have seized upon every tactic and strategy consistent with the morality of our cause to expose that injustice and thus to heighten the sensitivity of the American conscience so that farm workers will have without bloodshed their own union and the dignity of bargaining with their agribusiness employers. By lying about the nature of our movement, Mr. Barr, you are working against nonviolent social change. Unwittingly perhaps, you may unleash that other force which our union by discipline and deed, censure and education has sought to avoid, that panacean shortcut: that senseless violence which honors no color, class or neighborhood.

You must understand—I must make you understand—that our membership and the hopes and aspirations of the hundreds of thousands of the poor and dispossessed that have been raised on our account are, above all, human beings, no better and no worse than any other cross-section of human society; we are not saints because we are poor, but by the same measure neither are we immoral. We are men and women who have suffered and endured much, and not only because of our abject poverty but because we have been kept poor. The colors of our skins, the languages of our cultural and native origins, the lack of formal education, the exclusion from the democratic process, the numbers of our slain in recent wars—all these burdens generation after generation have sought to demoralize us, to break our human spirit. But God knows that we are not beasts of burden, agricultural implements or rented slaves; we are men. And mark this well, Mr. Barr, we are men locked in a death struggle against man's inhumanity to man in the industry that you represent. And this struggle itself gives meaning to our life and ennobles our dying.

As your industry has experienced, our strikers here in Delano and those who represent us throughout the world are well trained for this struggle. They have been under the gun, they have been kicked and beaten and herded by dogs, they have been cursed and ridiculed, they have been stripped and chained and jailed, they have been sprayed with the poisons used in the vineyards; but they have been taught not to lie down and die nor to flee in shame, but to resist with every ounce of human endurance and spirit. To resist not with retaliation in kind but to overcome with love and compassion, with ingenuity and creativity, with hard work and longer hours, with stamina and patient tenacity, with truth and public appeal, with friends and allies, with mobility and discipline, with politics and law, and with prayer and fasting. They were not trained in a month or even a year; after all, this new harvest season will mark our fourth full year of strike and even now we continue to plan and prepare for the years to come. Time accomplishes for the poor what money does for the rich.

This is not to pretend that we have everywhere been successful enough or that we have not made mistakes. And while we do not belittle or underestimate our adversaries—for they are the rich and the powerful and they possess the land—we are not afraid nor do we cringe from the confrontation. We welcome it! We have planned for it. We know that our cause is just, that history is a story of social revolution, and that the poor shall inherit the land.

Once again, I appeal to you as the representative of your industry and as a man. I ask you to recognize and bargain with our union before the economic pressure of the boycott and strike takes an irrevocable toll; but if not, I ask you to at least sit down with us to discuss the safeguards necessary to keep our historical struggle free of violence. I make this appeal because as one of the leaders of our nonviolent movement, I know and accept my responsibility for preventing, if possible, the destruction of human life and property. For these reasons and knowing of Gandhi's admonition that fasting is the last resort in place of the sword, during a most critical time in our movement last February 1968 I undertook a 25-day fast. I repeat to you the principle enunciated to the membership at the start of the fast: if to build our union required the deliberate taking of life, either the life of a grower or his child, or the life of a farm worker or his child, then I choose not to see the union built.

Mr. Barr, let me be painfully honest with you. You must understand these things. We advocate militant nonviolence as our means for social revolution and to achieve justice for our people, but we are not blind or deaf to the desperate and moody winds of human frustration, impatience and rage that blow among us. Gandhi himself admitted that if his only choice were cowardice or violence, he would choose violence. Men are not angels, and time and tide wait for no man. Precisely because of these powerful human emotions, we have tried to involve masses of people in their own struggle. Participation and self-determination remain the best experience of freedom, and free men instinctively prefer democratic change and even protect the rights guaranteed to seek it. Only the enslaved in despair have need of violent overthrow.

This letter does not express all that is in my heart, Mr. Barr. But if it says nothing else it says that we do not hate you or rejoice to see your industry destroyed; we hate the agribusiness system that seeks to keep us enslaved, and we shall overcome and change it not by retaliation or bloodshed but by a determined nonviolent struggle carried on by those masses of farm workers who intend to be free and human.

Questions

1. Why does Chavez describe the farm workers movement as a "social revolution"?

2. What would enable the farm workers to be "free and human," the phrase with which Chavez ends his letter?

---

182. The International 1968 (1968)

Source: Barbara and John Ehrenreich, from Long March, Short Spring: The Student Uprising at Home and Abroad *by Barbara & John Ehrenreich. Copyright © 1969 by Monthly Review Foundation. Reproduced by permission of Monthly Review Foundation.*

Like 1848 and 1919, 1968 was a year of worldwide revolt. But it was not nationalists seeking independence or workers hoping to improve their conditions who took the lead, but college students. In the spring of 1968, Barbara and John Ehrenreich, two young American activists, traveled to Europe to report on events there. They were amazed to encounter in Britain, France, Italy, and Germany the same sorts of discontent that they had seen in the United States. Americans "knew a lot" about uprisings in the Third World, and especially Vietnam, they wrote, "but hardly anything about our European counterparts." Their trip led to a book in which they highlighted the fact that student rebellion had become an international phenomenon, a revolt against a political and social order young people found stultifying despite material abundance.

1968: The Year of the Revolutionary Student.

March: in Rome thousands of students fought an all-day battle with the police in the Valle Giulia.

April: in West Germany thousands of students blockaded newspaper publishing plants and burned the newspapers. In New York the Tactical Police Force battled for three hours to recapture Columbia University from its students.

May: 40,000 students and workers turned out for Berlin's biggest May Day demonstration in three decades. Paris saw the fiercest street-fighting since the Liberation [from German occupation in World War II]....

June: students in Brussels, Stockholm, Amsterdam, Tokyo, and London occupied their schools or met the police on the streets....

In September, Mexican students and police [clashed] in the heaviest fighting since the Revolution.

In the spring of 1968, revolutionary student movements emerged in almost every major country in the "Free World." No one had any reason to expect it. For twenty years European and North American governments had faced only the feeblest domestic radicalism.... Everywhere, unemployment was low. Workers were buying cars, television sets, washing machines, and camping equipment.... No social problem was too great to be solved by minor technical adjustments in the socio-political machinery....

Until the spring of 1968. When it came, no government was prepared with an answer or an excuse.... In fact it was a mass movement.... People were getting used to the sight of thousands of students marching, picketing or rallying. But in the spring of 1968 the movement wasn't only massive, it was violent. Crowds didn't march, they practiced "mobile street tactics." Demonstrations led regularly to battles with the police.... From a historical point of view, perhaps the strangest feature of the new radicalism was the new radicals themselves. They weren't underpaid or unemployed workers. They were ordinary middle-class kids....

A new specter was haunting Europe, and America. It was no longer the specter of organized communism. The Communists had settled down, content to struggle for a few percentage points per election. In 1968 it was revolutionary students.... For once, [FBI head] J. Edgar Hoover forgot about the communist threat long enough to point out the new "student threat."... But most students refused to let the threats of repression change their style. It wasn't they who were frightened.

Questions

1. What common features do the Ehrenreichs see in the unrest in the United States and western Europe in 1968?

2. What do they think is most surprising about the events of 1968?

CHAPTER 26

The Conservative Turn, 1969–1988

183. Brochure on the Equal Rights Amendment (1970s)

Source: Philadelphia Chapter of the National Organization for Women: Brochure on the Equal Rights Amendment, National Organization for Women, Philadelphia Chapter records [2054], Historical Society of Pennsylvania.

First proposed in the 1920s, the Equal Rights Amendment to the Constitution was resurrected in the 1970s as an outgrowth of the second wave of feminism. Its language was brief: "Equality of rights under the law shall not be denied or abridged by the United States or by any State on account of sex." But its implications were anything but simple. It quickly won approval by Congress, but as states debated ratification it aroused a growing storm of protest from conservatives who claimed it would undermine women's traditional roles as mothers, wives, and homemakers. The National Organization for Women, founded in the 1960s to promote women's equality, led the campaign for approval, but the amendment failed to gain ratification by the required number of states. In this brochure, the Philadelphia chapter of NOW details the gender inequalities that persisted and outlined what it hoped the ERA would accomplish.

Did You Know . . .
- Under the U.S. Constitution corporations are considered legal persons, but women are not
- Women earn on an average 41% less than men
- A man with an 8th grade education earns as much as a woman with a college degree

- Women and men do not receive the same benefits under Social Security, although they contribute the same percentage of their income
- "Equal pay for Equal Work" is based on Title VII of the Civil Rights Act which can be reversed by Congress
- If a man dies, his widow pays a large tax; if a woman dies her widower pays substantially less
- A husband controls his wife's use of "his" credit cards; a wife cannot establish credit in her name
- Insurance rates are higher for women than for men; loans for house payments, etc. are more difficult for women to obtain than men
- The military has higher entrance requirements for women, but significantly fewer benefits and opportunities
- During probate, a joint bank account is considered to be solely the property of the husband
- Women receive longer jail sentences than men for the same crime
- Unemployment is twice as high for women as for men
- There are over 1,795 laws which discriminate against women

The ERA Will . . .
- Declare women full persons under the law
- Outlaw discrimination on the basis of sex, establishing constitutionally the legal right of "equal pay for equal work"
- Provide equal Social Security benefits for women and men at the same retirement age; widowers will receive the same benefits now only received by widows
- Recognize a housewife's contribution as a financial resource to the home by not taxing her half of the estate when her husband dies
- Give married women the right to establish credit, own businesses, buy and control property, and sign contracts
- Equalize military entrance standards; make military women eligible for equal benefits and opportunities
- Extend alimony and child support responsibilities to members of either sex, depending on need and ability to pay

- Establish equal rights for both parties holding joint husband/ wife bank accounts during probate
- Mandate "equal time for equal crime"
- Strike down laws which restrict rights. If a law protects rights, it will be extended to the other sex

Questions

1. What kinds of inequality seem to concern NOW the most?

2. How does the brochure seem to define freedom for women?

---

184. Barry Commoner, *The Closing Circle* (1971)

Source: Barry Commoner, from The Closing Circle: Nature, Man, and Technology, *copyright © 1971 by Barry Commoner. Used by permission of the author's estate.*

Another movement born in the 1960s that expanded rapidly in the following decade was environmentalism, which called into question pillars of American life—the equation of progress with endless increases in consumption and the faith that science, technology, and economic growth would advance the social welfare. Concern for preserving the natural environment dated back to the creation of national parks and other conservation efforts during the Progressive era. But the new environmentalism was more activist and youth oriented. *The Closing Circle*, by the biologist Barry Commoner, did much to direct America's attention to the environmental costs of technological development. Commoner insisted that rather than focus on a particular environmental problem, Americans must view the "ecosphere"—the natural system within which people live—as a whole.

Environmentalism attracted the broadest bipartisan support of any of the new social movements. Under Republican president Richard Nixon,

Congress during the late 1960s and early 1970s passed a series of measures to protect the environment, including the Clean Air and Clean Water Acts and the Endangered Species Act. On April 22, 1970, the first Earth Day, some 20 million people, most of them under the age of thirty, participated in rallies, concerts, and teach-ins devoted to promoting awareness of dangers to the natural environment.

===

THE ENVIRONMENT HAS just been rediscovered by the people who live in it. In the United States the event was celebrated in April 1970, during Earth Week. It was a sudden, noisy awakening. School children cleaned up rubbish; college students organized huge demonstrations; determined citizens recaptured the streets from the automobile, at least for a day. Everyone seemed to be aroused to the environmental danger and eager to do something about it.

They were offered lots of advice. Almost every writer, almost every speaker, on the college campuses, in the streets and on television and radio broadcasts, was ready to fix the blame and pronounce a cure for the environmental crisis.

Some blamed pollution on the rising population.... Some blamed man's innate aggressiveness.... Earth Week and the accompanying outburst of publicity, preaching, and prognostication surprised most people, including those of us who had worked for years to generate public recognition of the environmental crisis. What surprised me most were the numerous, confident explanations of the cause and cure of the crisis. For having spent some years in the effort simply to detect and describe the growing list of environmental problems— radioactive fallout, air and water pollution, the deterioration of the soil—and in tracing some of their links to social and political processes, the identification of a single cause and cure seemed a rather bold step....

After the excitement of Earth Week, I tried to find some meaning in the welter of contradictory advice that it produced. It seemed to me that the confusion of Earth Week was a sign that the situation was so complex and ambiguous that people could read into it whatever conclusion, their own beliefs—about human nature, economics, and politics—suggested. Like a Rorschach ink blot, Earth Week mirrored personal conviction more than objective knowledge.

Earth Week convinced me of the urgency of a deeper public understanding of the origins of the environmental crisis and its possible cures. That is what this book is about. It is an effort to find out what the environmental crisis means. Such understanding must begin at the source of life itself: the earth's thin skin of air, water, and soil, and the radiant solar fire that bathes it. Here, several billion years ago, life appeared and was nourished by the earth's substance. As it grew, life evolved, its old forms transforming the earth's skin and new ones adapting to these changes. Living things multiplied in number, variety, and habitat until they formed a global network, becoming deftly enmeshed in the surroundings they had themselves created. This is the ecosphere, the home that life has built for itself on the planet's outer surface.

Any living thing that hopes to live on the earth must fit into the ecosphere or perish. The environmental crisis is a sign that the finely sculptured fit between life and its surroundings has begun to corrode. As the links between one living thing and another, and between all of them and their surroundings, begin to break down, the dynamic interactions that sustain the whole have begun to falter and, in some places, stop.

Why, after millions of years of harmonious co-existence, have the relationships between living things and their earthly surroundings begun to collapse? Where did the fabric of the ecosphere begin to unravel? How far will the process go? How can we stop it and restore the broken links?

Understanding the ecosphere comes hard because, to the modern mind, it is a curiously foreign place. We have become accustomed to think of separate, singular events, each dependent upon a unique, singular cause. But in the ecosphere every effect is also a cause: an animal's waste becomes food for soil bacteria; what bacteria excrete nourishes plants; animals eat the plants. Such ecological cycles are hard to fit into human experience in the age of technology, where machine A always yields product B, and product B, once used, is cast away, having no further meaning for the machine, the product, or the user.

Here is the first great fault in the life of man in the ecosphere. We have broken out of the circle of life, converting its endless cycles into man-made, linear events: oil is taken from the ground, distilled into fuel, burned in an engine, converted thereby into noxious fumes, which are emitted into the air. At the end of the line is smog. Other man-made breaks in the ecosphere's cycle spew out toxic chemicals, sewage, heaps of rubbish—the testimony to our power to tear the ecological fabric that has, for millions of years, sustained the planet's life.

Suddenly we have discovered what we should have known long before: that the ecosphere sustains people and everything that they do; that anything that fails to fit into the ecosphere is a threat to its finely balanced cycles; that wastes are not only unpleasant, not only toxic, but, more meaningfully, evidence that the ecosphere is being driven towards collapse.

If we are to survive, we must understand why this collapse now threatens. Here the issues become far more complex than even the ecosphere. Our assaults on the ecosystem are so powerful, so numerous, so finely interconnected, that although the damage they do is clear, it is very difficult to discover how it was done. By which weapon? In whose hand? Are we driving the ecosphere to destruction simply by our growing numbers? By our greedy accumulation of wealth? Or are the machines which we have built to gain this wealth—the magnificent technology that now feeds us out of neat packages, that clothes us in man-made fibers, that surround us with new chemical creations—at fault?

This book is concerned with these questions. It begins with the ecosphere, the setting in which civilization has done its great—and terrible—deeds. Then it moves to a description of some of the damage

we have done to the ecosphere—to the air, the water, the soil. However, by now such horror stories of environmental destruction are
familiar, even tiresome. Much less clear is what we need to learn
from them, and so I have chosen less to shed tears of our past mistakes than to try to understand them. Most of this book is an effort
to discover which human acts have broken the circle of life, and
why. I trace the environmental crisis from its overt manifestations
in the ecosphere to the ecological stresses which they reflect, to the
faults in production technology—and in its scientific background—
that generate these stresses, and finally to the economic, social, and
political forces which have driven us down this self-destructive
course. All this in the hope—and expectation—that once we understand the origins of the environmental crisis, we can begin to man-
age the huge undertaking of surviving it.

Questions

1. Why does Commoner feel that most explanations of environmental
problems are inadequate?

2. What kinds of human actions does he feel endanger the ecosphere?

185. Richard E. Blakemore on The Sagebrush Rebellion (1979)

Source: State Government News, *22 (November 1979), pp. 3–5.*

The rapid growth of the environmentalist movement in the 1970s sparked
a conservative reaction, especially in the western states. New environmental regulations led to calls for less government intervention in the
economy. These were most strident in the West. What came to be called
the Sagebrush Rebellion denounced federal control of large areas of western
land as well as new environmental regulations that, the "rebels" claimed,
threatened energy production and long-standing grazing rights. They

insisted that decision-making power on such issues should be given to the individual states. In 1979, Richard E. Blakemore, a member of the Nevada state senate, offered this explanation of the outlook of many westerners.

THE "SAGEBRUSH REBELLION" is a catchy but somewhat misleading term used to describe the western states' demands for a greater role in determining the future of the west. Unlike the dictionary definition, in this rebellion there is no armed or unlawful resistance to government. Neither is western land desolate or worthless as the term "sagebrush" connoted. Moreover, if much of the land in the west ever was considered of little worth, the need for energy has changed that.

Statistics show that much of the west is controlled by the federal government.... Over 90 percent of all federal land is from the Rockies west.... On average, the federal government controls 52.6 percent of the land in the 12 western states.... What does this large federal presence mean to westerners and why are westerners protesting?

For many years, the public domain was open to ranching, mining, and outdoor recreation. But a number of federal acts, passed to protect and conserve the environment, have closed great parts of the public domain to traditional uses. Westerners see these restrictions in the use of public lands as a portent of things to come—that eventually most of today's public lands will be locked up in wilderness or other restrictive uses....

The west today is at the confluence of two major movements—that for protection of the environment and that for production of energy. To a great extent, the success of the attempt for U.S. energy independence depends on resources of the west. In addition, the west is looked to for increased agricultural production and for its reserves of minerals necessary to modern industry.

The environmental movement prompted the passage of federal legislation aimed at protecting the environment and maintaining great portions of the country in a natural state. Among the major environmental acts of the past 15 years are the Wilderness Act, the

National Environmental Protection Act, the Federal Land Policy Management Act, the Wild and Scenic Rivers Act, and the National Forest Management Act.

The genesis of the sagebrush rebellion can be found in the conflict between the desires to protect and preserve the environment and the demands for food, minerals, and energy from the west.... Constraints on the uses of public lands and obstacles to disposal of public lands into nonfederal ownership have increased over the past 15 years....

Overregulation is bad anywhere. Imagine how much worse it is for states in which the federal government is also the landlord over most of the land in the state. Excessive regulation and heavy-handed bureaucracy are magnified where land is federally controlled.

While the particular issues on which the sagebrush rebellion are based are more common in the west, the principles behind the movement are national in scope. It is a question of the extent to which the destiny of the country is controlled by federal agencies and bureaucrats. States, local governments, and the people should make more of these determinations and the federal government less.

Because of the federal omnipresence in the west, westerners have reached the crisis first. But reversing the trend towards centralization that threatens the economy, our lands, and our freedoms is of concern to all Americans....

Questions

1. What freedoms does Blakemore see as threatened by environmental policy?

2. How do Blackmore and Barry Commoner, in the previous document, differ in their visions of the future of American society?

186. Jimmy Carter on Human Rights (1977)

Source: Address at Commencement Exercises, University of Notre Dame, May 22, 1977, **Public Papers of the Presidents of the United States,** **Jimmy Carter,** 1977 *(Washington, D.C., 1977), pp. 954–58.*

In the aftermath of the American defeat in the Vietnam War, President Jimmy Carter tried to reorient foreign policy away from Cold War assumptions. In a 1977 address at the University of Notre Dame, he insisted that foreign policy could not be separated from "questions of justice, equity, and human rights." Implicitly criticizing his predecessors' tendency to ally with Third World dictatorships in order to pursue the policy of containing communism, Carter called for a policy based on democratic principles. Combating poverty in the Third World, preventing the spread of nuclear weapons, and promoting human rights should take priority over what he called "the inordinate fear of communism." Carter sometimes found it impossible to translate rhetoric into action. Nonetheless, he helped to place human rights on the agenda of American foreign policy.

I WANT TO speak to you today about the strands that connect our actions overseas with our essential character as a nation. I believe we can have a foreign policy that is democratic, that is based on fundamental values, and that uses power and influence, which we have, for humane purposes. We can also have a foreign policy that American people both support and, for a change, know about and understand.

I have a quiet confidence in our own political system. Because we know that democracy works, we can reject the arguments of those rulers who deny human rights to their people.

We are confident that democracy's example will be compelling, and so we seek to bring that example closer to those from whom in the past few years we have been separated and who are not yet convinced about the advantages of our kind of life.

We are confident that the democratic methods are the most effective, and so we are not tempted to employ improper tactics here at home or abroad.

We are confident of our own strength, so we can seek substantial mutual reductions in the nuclear arms race.

And we are confident of the good sense of American people, and so we let them share in the process of making foreign policy decisions. We can thus speak with the voices of 215 million, and not just of an isolated handful.

Democracy's great recent successes—in India, Portugal, Spain, Greece—show that our confidence in this system is not misplaced. Being confident of our own future, we are now free of that inordinate fear of communism which once led us to embrace any dictator who joined us in that fear. I'm glad that that's being changed.

For too many years, we've been willing to adopt the flawed and erroneous principles and tactics of our adversaries, sometimes abandoning our own values for theirs. We've fought fire with fire, never thinking that fire is better quenched with water. This approach failed, with Vietnam the best example of its intellectual and moral poverty. But through failure we have now found our way back to our own principles and values, and we have regained our lost confidence.

By the measure of history, our nation's 200 years are very brief, and our rise to world eminence is briefer still. It dates from 1945, when Europe and the old international order lay in ruins. Before then, America was largely on the periphery of world affairs. But since then, we have inescapably been at the center of world affairs.

Our policy during this period was guided by two principles: a belief that Soviet expansion was almost inevitable but that it must be contained, and the corresponding belief in the importance of an almost exclusive alliance among non-Communist nations on both sides of the Atlantic. That system could not last forever unchanged. Historical trends have weakened its foundation. The unifying threat of conflict with the Soviet Union has become less intensive, even though the competition has become more extensive.

The Vietnamese war produced a profound moral crisis, sapping worldwide faith in our own policy and our system of life, a crisis of confidence made even more grave by the covert pessimism of some of our leaders.

In less than a generation, we've seen the world change dramatically. The daily lives and aspirations of most human beings have been transformed. Colonialism is nearly gone. A new sense of national identity now exists in almost 100 new countries that have been formed in the last generation. Knowledge has become more widespread. Aspirations are higher. As more people have been freed from traditional constraints, more have been determined to achieve, for the first time in their lives, social justice.

The world is still divided by ideological disputes, dominated by regional conflicts, and threatened by danger that we will not resolve the differences of race and wealth without violence or without drawing into combat the major military powers. We can no longer separate the traditional issues of war and peace from the new global questions of justice, equity, and human rights.

It is a new world, but America should not fear it. It is a new world, and we should help to shape it. It is a new world that calls for a new American foreign policy—a policy based on constant decency in its values and on optimism in our historical vision.

• • •

First, we have reaffirmed America's commitment to human rights as a fundamental tenet of our foreign policy. In ancestry, religion, color, place of origin, and cultural background, we Americans are as diverse a nation as the world has even seen. No common mystique of blood or soil unites us. What draws us together, perhaps more than anything else, is a belief in human freedom. We want the world to know that our Nation stands for more than financial prosperity.

This does not mean that we can conduct our foreign policy by rigid moral maxims. We live in a world that is imperfect and which will always be imperfect—a world that is complex and confused and which will always be complex and confused.

• • •

Throughout the world today, in free nations and in totalitarian countries as well, there is a preoccupation with the subject of human freedom, human rights. And I believe it is incumbent on us in this country to keep that discussion, that debate, that contention alive. No other country is as well-qualified as we to set an example. We have our own shortcomings and faults, and we should strive constantly and with courage to make sure that we are legitimately proud of what we have.

• • •

Questions

1. What does Carter refer to when he says that the United States has too often abandoned "democratic methods" in foreign relations in favor of adopting the "tactics of our adversaries"?

2. What are the difficulties of making respect for human rights a major consideration in conducting foreign policy?

———

187. Jerry Falwell, *Listen, America!* (1980)

Source: Jerry Falwell, excerpts from Listen, America!, *copyright © 1980 by Jerry Falwell. Used by permission of Doubleday, an imprint of the Knopf Doubleday Publishing Group, a division of Penguin Random House LLC. All rights reserved.*

The rise of religious fundamentalism during the 1970s expanded conservatism's popular base. Evangelical Christians had become more and more alienated from a culture that seemed to them to trivialize religion and promote immorality. They demanded the reversal of Supreme Court decisions banning prayer in public schools, protecting pornography as free speech, and legalizing abortion. Although it spoke of restoring traditional values, the "Religious Right" proved remarkably adept at using modern technology, including mass mailings and televised religious programming, to raise funds for their crusade and to spread their message. In 1979, Jerry Falwell, a Virginia minister, created the self-styled Moral Majority, devoted to waging a "war against sin" and electing "pro-life, pro-family, pro-America" candidates to office.

———

WE MUST REVERSE the trend America finds herself in today. Young people between the ages of twenty-five and forty have been born and reared in a different world than Americans of years past. The television set has been their primary babysitter. From the television set they have learned situation ethics and immorality—they have learned a loss of respect for human life. They have learned to disrespect the family as God has established it. They have been educated in a public-school system that is permeated with secular humanism. They have been taught that the Bible is just another book of literature. They have been taught that there are no absolutes in our world today. They have been introduced to the drug culture. They have been reared by the family and the public school in a society that is greatly void of discipline and character-building. These same young people have been reared under the influence of a government that has taught them socialism and welfarism. They have been taught to believe that the world owes them a living whether they work or not.

I believe that America was built on integrity, on faith in God, and on hard work. I do not believe that anyone has ever been successful in life without being willing to add that last ingredient—diligence or hard work. We now have second- and third-generation welfare recipients. Welfare is not always wrong. There are those who do need welfare, but we have reared a generation that understands neither the dignity nor the importance of work.

Every American who looks at the facts must share a deep concern and burden for our country. We are not unduly concerned when we say that there are some very dark clouds on America's horizon. I am not a pessimist, but it is indeed a time for truth. If Americans will face the truth, our nation can be turned around and can be saved from the evils and the destruction that have fallen upon every other nation that has turned its back on God.

There is no excuse for what is happening in our country. We must, from the highest office in the land right down to the shoe shine boy in the airport, have a return to biblical basics. If the Congress of our United States will take its stand on that which is right and wrong, and if our President, our judiciary system, and our state and local leaders will take their stand on holy living, we can turn this country around.

I personally feel that the home and the family are still held in reverence by the vast majority of the American public. I believe there is still a vast number of Americans who love their country, are patriotic, and are willing to sacrifice for her. I remember the time when it was positive to be patriotic, and as far as I am concerned, it still is. I remember as a boy, when the flag was raised, everyone stood proudly and put his hand upon his heart and pledged allegiance with gratitude. I remember when the band struck up "The Stars and Stripes Forever," we stood and goose pimples would run all over me. I remember when I was in elementary school during World War II, when every report from the other shores meant something to us. We were not out demonstrating against our boys who were dying in Europe and Asia. We were praying for them and thanking God for them and buying war bonds to help pay for the materials and artillery they needed to fight and win and come back.

I believe that Americans want to see this country come back to basics, back to values, back to biblical morality, back to sensibility, and back to patriotism. Americans are looking for leadership and guidance. It is fair to ask the question, "If 84 percent of the American people still believe in morality, why is America having such internal problems?" We must look for the answer to the highest places in every level of government. We have a lack of leadership in America. But Americans have been lax in voting in and out of office the right and the wrong people.

My responsibility as a preacher of the Gospel is one of influence, not of control, and that is the responsibility of each individual citizen. Through the ballot box Americans must provide for strong moral leadership at every level. If our country will get back on the track in sensibility and moral sanity, the crises that I have herein mentioned will work out in the course of time and with God's blessings.

It is now time to take a stand on certain moral issues, and we can only stand if we have leaders. We must stand against the Equal Rights Amendment, the feminist revolution, and the homosexual revolution. We must have a revival in this country.... As a preacher of the Gospel, I not only believe in prayer and preaching, I also believe in good citizenship. If a labor union in America has the right to organize and improve its working conditions, then I believe that the churches and the pastors, the priests, and the rabbis of America have a responsibility, not just the right, to see to it that the moral climate and conscience of Americans is such that this nation can be healed inwardly. If it is healed inwardly, then it will heal itself outwardly....

Americans have been silent much too long. We have stood by and watched as American power and influence have been systematically weakened in every sphere of the world.

We are not a perfect nation, but we are still a free nation because we have the blessing of God upon us. We must continue to follow in a path that will ensure that blessing....

Let us never forget that as our Constitution declares, we are endowed by our Creator with certain inalienable rights. It is only as we abide by those laws established by our Creator that He will continue to bless us with these rights. We are endowed our rights to freedom and liberty and the pursuit of happiness by the God who created man to be free and equal.

The hope of reversing the trends of decay in our republic now lies with the Christian public in America. We cannot expect help from the liberals. They certainly are not going to call our nation back to righteousness and neither are the pornographers, the smut peddlers, and those who are corrupting our youth. Moral Americans must be willing to put their reputations, their fortunes, and their very lives on the line for this great nation of ours. Would that we had the courage of our forefathers who knew the great responsibility that freedom carries with it....

Our Founding Fathers separated church and state in function, but never intended to establish a government void of God. As is evidenced by our Constitution, good people in America must exert an influence and provide a conscience and climate of morality in which it is difficult to go wrong, not difficult for people to go right in America.

I am positive in my belief regarding the Constitution that God led in the development of that document, and as a result, we here in America have enjoyed 204 years of unparalleled freedom. The most positive people in the world are people who believe the Bible to be the Word of God. The Bible contains a positive message. It is a message written by 40 men over a period of approximately 1,500 years under divine inspiration. It is God's message of love, redemption, and deliverance for a fallen race. What could be more positive than the message of redemption in the Bible? But God will force Himself upon no man. Each individual American must make His choice....

Americans must no longer linger in ignorance and apathy. We cannot be silent about the sins that are destroying this nation. The choice is ours. We must turn America around or prepare for inevitable destruction. I am listening to the sounds that threaten to take away our liberties in America. And I have listened to God's admonitions and His direction—the only hopes of saving America. Are you listening too?

Questions

1. What does Falwell see as the major threats to moral standards in 1970s America?

2. How does Falwell appear to understand the idea of freedom?

188. Phyllis Schlafly, "The Fraud of the Equal Rights Amendment" (1972)

Source: Phyllis Schlafly, "The Fraud of the Equal Rights Amendment," The Phyllis Schlafly Report, vol. 5, February 1972. Reprinted with permission of Phyllis Schlafly.

One of the first major conservative victories of the 1970s was the defeat of the Equal Rights Amendment (ERA), a proposed change in the Constitution that would have affirmed that "equality of rights under the law" could not be abridged because of sex. This seemingly uncontroversial measure passed Congress in 1972 with little opposition. It soon aroused unexpected protest from those who claimed it would discredit the role of wife and homemaker.

To its supporters, the amendment offered a guarantee of women's right to participate fully in public life. Its foes insisted that women should remain within the divinely appointed roles of wife and mother. They claimed it would subject women to the military draft and let men "off the hook" by denying their responsibility to provide for their wives and children. Phyllis Schlafly, a veteran of anticommunist politics of the 1950s, led the campaign against the ERA. Polls consistently showed that a majority of Americans, male and female, favored the measure. But thanks to the mobilization of conservative women, the amendment failed to achieve ratification by the required thirty-eight states.

———

In the last couple of years, a noisy movement has sprung up agitating for "women's rights." Suddenly, everywhere we are afflicted with aggressive females on television talk shows yapping about how mistreated American women are, suggesting that marriage has put us in some kind of "slavery," that housework is menial and degrading, and—perish the thought—that women are discriminated against. New "women's liberation" organizations are popping up, agitating and demonstrating, serving demands on public officials, getting wide press coverage always, and purporting to speak for some 100,000,000 American women.

It's time to set the record straight. The claim that American women are downtrodden and unfairly treated is the fraud of the century. The truth is that American women never had it so good. Why should we lower ourselves to "equal rights" when we already have the status of special privilege?

The proposed Equal Rights Amendment states: "Equality of rights under the law shall not be denied or abridged by the United States or by any state on account of sex." So what's wrong with that? Well, here are a few examples of what's wrong with it.

This Amendment will absolutely and positively make women subject to the draft. Why any woman would support such a ridiculous and un-American proposal as this is beyond comprehension. Why any Congressman who had any regard for his wife, sister, or daughter would support such a proposition is just as hard to understand. Foxholes are bad enough for men, but they certainly are *not* the place for women—and we should reject any proposal which would put them there in the name of "equal rights." ...

Another bad effect of the Equal Rights Amendment is that it will abolish a woman's right to child support and alimony, and substitute what the women's libbers think is a more "equal" policy, that "such decisions should be within the discretion of the Court and should be made on the economic situation and need of the parties in the case."

Under present American laws, the man is *always* required to support his wife and each child he caused to be brought into the world. Why should women abandon these good laws—by trading them for something so nebulous and uncertain as the "discretion of the Court"?

The law now requires a husband to support his wife as best as his financial situation permits, but a wife is not required to support her husband (unless he is about to become a public charge). A husband cannot demand that his wife go to work to help pay for family expenses. He has the duty of financial support under our laws and customs. Why should we abandon these mandatory wife-support and child-support laws so that a wife would have an "equal" obligation to take a job?

By law and custom in America, in case of divorce, the mother always is given custody of her children unless there is overwhelming evidence of mistreatment, neglect or bad character. This is our special privilege because of the high rank that is placed on motherhood in our society. Do women really want to give up this special privilege and lower themselves to "equal rights," so that the mother gets one child and the father gets the other? I think not....

What "Women's Lib" Really Means

Many women are under the mistaken impression that "women's lib" means more job employment opportunities for women, equal pay for equal work, appointments of women to high positions, admitting more women to medical schools, and other desirable objectives which all women favor. We all support these purposes, as well as any necessary legislation which would bring them about.

But all this is only a sweet syrup which covers the deadly poison masquerading as "women's lib." The women's libbers are radicals who are waging a total assault on the family, on marriage, and on children.

Questions

1. Why does Schlafly believe that the Equal Rights Amendment will actually harm women?

2. How does Schlafly's picture of the status of American women differ from that of the Equal Rights Amendment brochure?

189. James Watt, "Environmentalists: A Threat to the Ecology of the West" (1978)

Source: James G. Watt, "Environmentalists: A Threat to the Ecology of the West," Speech at the Conservation Foundation, May 8, 1978, American Heritage Center #7667. Reprinted by permission of the author.

The rapid growth of the environmentalist movement sparked a conservative reaction. New environmental regulations led to calls for less government intervention in the economy. These were most strident in the West, where measures to protect the environment threatened irrigation projects and private access to public lands. Using the language of freedom from government tyranny, western leaders denounced control of large areas of land by the Bureau of Land Management in Washington, D.C., and insisted that decision-making power over issues like grazing rights, mining development, and whether public lands should be closed to fishing and hunting be given to the states. Conservative westerners like James Watt, later secretary of the interior under President Reagan, insisted that environmentalism threatened to prevent the development of the West's energy resources and therefore would damage the national economy as a whole.

━━━━━━━━━

IN RECENT YEARS, the unique life style of the West has been challenged. The nation has demanded from our states additional supplies of coal, oil and gas, uranium, forest products, and food and fiber.

Because of good leadership and the rugged individualism of our citizens, the states of the West have accommodated the new pressures. We have struggled, and with but a few exceptions, have been able to protect our natural environment while the increased demands have been met. . . .

But now, all this is being threatened.

Today, there is a new political force in the land—a small group of extremists who don't concern themselves with a balanced perspective or a concern about improving the quality of life for mankind—they are called the environmentalists. Unlike the conservationists, they are single-minded and appear to be determined to accomplish their objectives at whatever cost to society....

The energy resources of the West are and will be the cornerstone of our future energy needs. There is no other major domestic energy resource base for the Nation.... These energy resources will be developed. The only question remaining is, when? Will it be orderly and phased-in over time with proper environmental safeguards? Or, will it be explosively developed, fired by a political-economic crisis...?

My thesis is that because of the actions being taken by extremists to delay or stop the orderly development of energy resources... the Nation is likely to suffer energy shortages and thus severe economic hardship.... When this happens, whether triggered by an Arab oil boycott, or slowly through time, the politicians in Washington will seize on the crisis and take whatever energy is necessary to extract energy from the Western states, in order to light and heat the East and to maintain jobs in the Midwest and on the East coast. The cost of taking our energy resources in a crisis atmosphere could be the ravaging of our land and the destruction of our natural resources....

I fear for our ecology in the West and for our lifestyle. When the economic pressures start strangling the Eastern states due to short supplies of energy, their political leadership will come after our resources. In the minds of the affected job holders, no price will be too great (including the destruction of the ecology of the West), to get the necessary energy resources to keep their homes heated and their employment secure....

What is the real motive of these extreme environmentalists? Is it to simply protect the environment? Is it to delay and deny energy development? Is it to weaken America?...

I am a concerned Westerner.... Today, the extremists—the environmentalists—are fighting this needed orderly development. I fear that our states may be ravaged as a result of the actions of the environmentalists—the greatest threat to the ecology of the West.

Questions

1. What does Watt see as the hidden motive of the environmentalist movement?

2. How does he argue that environmentalism actually threatens the natural environment in the West?

---

190. Ronald Reagan, Inaugural Address (1981)

Source: Inaugural Address, January 20, 1981, **Public Papers of the Presidents, Ronald Reagan, 1981** *(Washington, D.C., 1982), pp. 1–3.*

Riding a wave of dissatisfaction with the country's economic problems and apparently diminished strength in world affairs, Ronald Reagan was elected president in 1980. An excellent public speaker, Reagan reshaped the nation's agenda and political language more effectively than any other president since Franklin D. Roosevelt. He made conservatism seem progressive rather than an attempt to turn back the tide of progress. His inaugural address reflected how he made freedom the watchword of what came to be called the Reagan Revolution—an effort to scale back the scope of government, lower taxes, and reinvigorate the Cold War. He ended by invoking the time-honored idea that the United States has a mission to serve as a "beacon" of freedom for people throughout the world.

MR. PRESIDENT [speaking to former president Carter],... by your gracious cooperation in the transition process, you have shown a watching world that we are a united people pledged to maintaining a political system which guarantees individual liberty to a greater degree than any other, and I thank you and your people for all your help in maintaining the continuity which is the bulwark of our Republic.

The business of our nation goes forward. These United States are confronted with an economic affliction of great proportions. We suffer from the longest and one of the worst sustained inflations in our national history. It distorts our economic decisions, penalizes thrift, and crushes the struggling young and the fixed-income elderly alike. It threatens to shatter the lives of millions of our people.

In this present crisis, government is not the solution to our problem; government is the problem. From time to time we've been tempted to believe that society has become too complex to be managed by self-rule, that government by an elite group is superior to government for, by, and of the people. Well, if no one among us is capable of governing himself, then who among us has the capacity to govern someone else? All of us together, in and out of government, must bear the burden. The solutions we seek must be equitable, with no one group singled out to pay a higher price.

So, as we begin, let us take inventory. We are a nation that has a government—not the other way around. And this makes us special among the nations of the Earth. Our government has no power except that granted it by the people. It is time to check and reverse the growth of government, which shows signs of having grown beyond the consent of the governed.

It is my intention to curb the size and influence of the Federal establishment and to demand recognition of the distinction between the powers granted to the Federal Government and those reserved to the States or to the people. All of us need to be reminded that the Federal Government did not create the States; the States created the Federal Government.

Now, so there will be no misunderstanding, it's not my intention to do away with government. It is rather to make it work—work with us, not over us; to stand by our side, not ride on our back. Government can and must provide opportunity, not smother it; foster productivity, not stifle it.

If we look to the answer as to why for so many years we achieved so much, prospered as no other people on Earth, it was because here in this land we unleashed the energy and individual genius of man to a greater extent than has ever been done before. Freedom and the dignity of the individual have been more available and assured here than in any other place on Earth. The price for this freedom at times has been high, but we have never been unwilling to pay that price.

It is no coincidence that our present troubles parallel and are proportionate to the intervention and intrusion in our lives that result from unnecessary and excessive growth of government. It is time for us to realize that we're too great a nation to limit ourselves to small dreams. We're not, as some would have us believe, doomed to an inevitable decline. I do not believe in a fate that will fall on us no matter what we do. I do believe in a fate that will fall on us if we do nothing. So, with all the creative energy at our command, let us begin an era of national renewal. Let us renew our determination, our courage, and our strength. And let us renew our faith and our hope.

• • •

Well, I believe we, the Americans of today, are ready to act worthy of ourselves, ready to do what must be done to ensure happiness and liberty for ourselves, our children, and our children's children. And as we renew ourselves here in our own land, we will be seen as having greater strength throughout the world. We will again be the exemplar of freedom and a beacon of hope for those who do not now have freedom.

Questions

1. What is Reagan's definition of freedom?

2. What does Reagan mean when he says, "government is not the solution to our problem; government is the problem"?

CHAPTER 27

From Triumph to Tragedy, 1989–2004

191. Pat Buchanan, Speech to the Republican National Convention (1992)

Source: Patrick Buchanan, "The Culture Wars: Speech to the Republican National Convention, 1992," http://www.buchanan.org, by Patrick Buchanan. Reprinted with permission.

During the 1992 primaries, Pat Buchanan, a former special assistant to Richard Nixon who had emerged as a prominent conservative journalist and television host, campaigned for the Republican presidential nomination against President George H. W. Bush. Buchanan had little chance of depriving the president of renomination, but he used the campaign to spread his conservative ideas. At the Republican national convention in Houston, Buchanan delivered a fiery speech that condemned Democrats as responsible for moral decay in American society. The speech became one of the key artifacts of the "culture wars" of the 1990s; it rallied conservatives but offended many moderates and, according to some commentators, contributed to Bush's defeat by Bill Clinton.

THE PRESIDENCY IS America's bully pulpit, what Mr Truman called, "preeminently a place of moral leadership." George Bush is a defender of right-to-life, and lifelong champion of the Judeo-Christian values and beliefs upon which this nation was built.

Mr Clinton, however, has a different agenda.

At its top is unrestricted abortion on demand. When the Irish-Catholic governor of Pennsylvania, Robert Casey, asked to say a few words on behalf of the 25 million unborn children destroyed since Roe v Wade, he was told there was no place for him at the podium of Bill Clinton's convention, no room at the inn.

Yet a militant leader of the homosexual rights movement could rise at that convention and exult: "Bill Clinton and Al Gore represent the most pro-lesbian and pro-gay ticket in history." And so they do.

Bill Clinton supports school choice—but only for state-run schools. Parents who send their children to Christian schools, or Catholic schools, need not apply.

Elect me, and you get two for the price of one, Mr Clinton says of his lawyer-spouse. And what does Hillary believe? Well, Hillary believes that 12-year-olds should have a right to sue their parents, and she has compared marriage as an institution to slavery—and life on an Indian reservation.

Well, speak for yourself, Hillary.

Friends, this is radical feminism. The agenda Clinton & Clinton would impose on America—abortion on demand, a litmus test for the Supreme Court, homosexual rights, discrimination against religious schools, women in combat—that's change, all right. But it is not the kind of change America wants. It is not the kind of change America needs. And it is not the kind of change we can tolerate in a nation that we still call God's country. . . .

But tonight I want to talk to the 3 million Americans who voted for me. I will never forget you, nor the great honor you have done me. But I do believe, deep in my heart, that the right place for us to be now—in this presidential campaign—is right beside George Bush. The party is our home; this party is where we belong. And don't let anyone tell you any different.

Yes, we disagreed with President Bush, but we stand with him for freedom to choice religious schools, and we stand with him against the amoral idea that gay and lesbian couples should have the same standing in law as married men and women.

We stand with President Bush for right-to-life, and for voluntary prayer in the public schools, and against putting American women in combat. And we stand with President Bush in favor of the right of small towns and communities to control the raw sewage of pornography that pollutes our popular culture....

My friends, this election is about much more than who gets what. It is about who we are. It is about what we believe. It is about what we stand for as Americans. There is a religious war going on in our country for the soul of America. It is a cultural war, as critical to the kind of nation we will one day be as was the Cold War itself. And in that struggle for the soul of America, Clinton & Clinton are on the other side, and George Bush is on our side.

Questions

1. What elements of the cultural changes that began in the 1960s most seem to offend Buchanan?

2. Why does Buchanan believe that a "religious war" is underway in the United States?

---

192. Bill Clinton, Speech on Signing of NAFTA (1993)

Source: The White House.

Early in his first term as president, Bill Clinton signed the North American Free Trade Agreement (NAFTA). The fact that negotiations had begun under his predecessor, George H. W. Bush, illustrated that a consensus existed among political leaders of both parties on the virtues of free trade and economic globalization. NAFTA created a free-trade zone (an area

where goods can travel freely without paying import duties) including
Canada, the United States, and Mexico. In his speech promoting the agreement, Clinton asked Americans to accept economic globalization as an
inevitable form of progress and the path to future prosperity. Speaking as
the United States was emerging from a serious economic recession, he
promised, "There will be no job loss." In fact, NAFTA led many manufacturers to shift production to low-wage sites in Mexico.

———

As PRESIDENT, it is my duty to speak frankly to the American people about the world in which we now live. Fifty years ago, at the end
of World War II, an unchallenged America was protected by the
oceans and by our technological superiority and, very frankly, by
the economic devastation of the people who could otherwise have
been our competitors. We chose then to try to help rebuild our former enemies and to create a world of free trade supported by institutions which would facilitate it. . . . As a result, jobs were created, and
opportunity thrived all across the world.

But make no mistake about it: Our decision at the end of World
War II to create a system of global, expanded, freer trade and the
supporting institutions played a major role in creating the prosperity of the American middle class. Ours is now an era in which commerce is global and in which money, management, and technology
are highly mobile.

For the last 20 years, in all the wealthy countries of the world—
because of changes in the global environment, because of the
growth of technology, because of increasing competition—the middle class that was created and enlarged by the wise policies of
expanding trade at the end of World War II has been under severe
stress. Most Americans are working harder for less. They are vulner-
able to the fear tactics and the averseness to change that are behind
much of the opposition to NAFTA. But I want to say to my fellow
Americans: When you live in a time of change, the only way to
recover your security and to broaden your horizons is to adapt to

the change—to embrace, to move forward. . . . The only way we can recover the fortunes of the middle class in this country so that people who work harder and smarter can, at least, prosper more, the only way we can pass on the American dream of the last 40 years to our children and their children for the next 40, is to adapt to the changes which are occurring.

In a fundamental sense, this debate about NAFTA is a debate about whether we will embrace these changes and create the jobs of tomorrow or try to resist these changes, hoping we can preserve the economic structures of yesterday. . . . I believe that NAFTA will create 1 million jobs in the first 5 years of its impact. . . . NAFTA will generate these jobs by fostering an export boom to Mexico by tearing down tariff walls. . . . There will be no job loss.

Questions

1. Why does Clinton feel that free trade is necessary to American prosperity?

2. How does Clinton view the impact of globalization on the United States?

193. Declaration for Global Democracy (1999)

Source: Global Exchange, Declaration for Global Democracy, Seattle, 1999. Reprinted by permission of the Global Exchange.

During the 1990s, the country resounded with talk of a new era in human history, with a borderless economy and a "global civilization." The collapse of communism between 1989 and 1991 opened the entire world to the spread of market capitalism and the idea that government should interfere as little as possible with economic activity. Leaders of both parties spoke of an American mission to create a global free market as the path to greater worldwide freedom.

In December 1999, delegates gathered in Seattle for a meeting of the World Trade Organization, a 135-nation group that worked to reduce barriers to international commerce and settle trade disputes. To their astonishment, over 30,000 persons gathered to protest the meeting. A handful of self-proclaimed anarchists embarked on a window-breaking spree at local stores. Most demonstrators were peaceful. The Battle of Seattle placed on the national and international agendas a question that promises to be among the most pressing concerns of the twenty-first century—the relationship between globalization, economic justice, democracy, and freedom.

AS CITIZENS OF global society, recognizing that the World Trade Organization is unjustly dominated by corporate interests and run for the enrichment of the few at the expense of all others, we demand:

1. Representatives from all sectors of society must be included in all levels of trade policy formulations. All global citizens must be democratically represented in the formulation, implementation, and evaluation of all global social and economic policies.

2. The World Trade Organization must immediately halt all meetings and negotiations in order for a full, fair, and public assessment to be conducted of the impacts of the WTO's policies to date.

3. Global trade and investment must not be ends in themselves, but rather the instruments for achieving equitable and sustainable development including protection for workers and the environment.

4. Global trade agreements must not undermine the ability of each nation state or local community to meet its citizens' social, environmental, cultural or economic needs.

5. The World Trade Organization must be replaced by a democratic and transparent body accountable to citizens—not to corporations.

No globalization without representation!

Questions

1. What are the declaration's major complaints about the way globalization is being implemented?

2. How might decision making about globalization be made more democratic?

━━━━━━

194. The Beijing Declaration on Women (1995)

Source: United Nations, from "Report of the Fourth World Conference on Women (Beijing, 4–15 September 1995), © 1995 United Nations. Reprinted with permission of the United Nations.

The Fourth World Conference on Women, held in Beijing in 1995 under the auspices of the United Nations, illustrated the growing centrality of human rights in international discourse, and the growing importance of nongovernmental organizations (NGOs) in promoting human rights. Hillary Clinton, President Clinton's wife, attended and gave a widely quoted address pointing to the problems of adequate health care, access to education, and sexual abuse that afflicted women around the world. Nearly 200 countries sent official delegations, and thousands of representatives of various NGOs also attended. Of course, in so large and heterogeneous a gathering, controversy arose over whether the same rights applied in all societies. But the final declaration outlined an agenda for promoting women's freedom in the twenty-first century.

━━━━━━

1. WE, THE GOVERNMENTS participating in the Fourth World Conference on Women,

2. Gathered here in Beijing in September 1995, the year of the fiftieth anniversary of the founding of the United Nations,

3. Determined to advance the goals of equality, development and peace for all women everywhere in the interest of all humanity,

4. Acknowledging the voices of all women everywhere and taking note of the diversity of women and their roles and circumstances, honouring the women who paved the way and inspired by the hope present in the world's youth,

5. Recognize that the status of women has advanced in some important respects in the past decade but that progress has been uneven, inequalities between women and men have persisted and major obstacles remain, with serious consequences for the well-being of all people,

6. Also recognize that this situation is exacerbated by the increasing poverty that is affecting the lives of the majority of the world's people, in particular women and children, with origins in both the national and international domains,

7. Dedicate ourselves unreservedly to addressing these constraints and obstacles and thus enhancing further the advancement and empowerment of women all over the world, and agree that this requires urgent action in the spirit of determination, hope, cooperation and solidarity, now and to carry us forward into the next century.

We reaffirm our commitment to:

8. The equal rights and inherent human dignity of women and men and other purposes and principles enshrined in the Charter of the United Nations, to the Universal Declaration of Human Rights and other international human rights instruments, in particular the Convention on the Elimination of All Forms of Discrimination against Women and the Convention on the Rights of the Child, as well as the Declaration on the Elimination of Violence against Women and the Declaration on the Right to Development;

9. Ensure the full implementation of the human rights of women and of the girl child as an inalienable, integral and indivisible part of all human rights and fundamental freedoms;

• • •

We are convinced that:

13. Women's empowerment and their full participation on the basis of equality in all spheres of society, including participation in the decision-making process and access to power, are fundamental for the achievement of equality, development and peace;

14. Women's rights are human rights;

15. Equal rights, opportunities and access to resources, equal sharing of responsibilities for the family by men and women, and a harmonious partnership between them are critical to their well-being and that of their families as well as to the consolidation of democracy;

16. Eradication of poverty based on sustained economic growth, social development, environmental protection and social justice requires the involvement of women in economic and social development, equal opportunities and the full and equal participation of women and men as agents and beneficiaries of people-centred sustainable development;

17. The explicit recognition and reaffirmation of the right of all women to control all aspects of their health, in particular their own fertility, is basic to their empowerment;

18. Local, national, regional and global peace is attainable and is inextricably linked with the advancement of women, who are a fundamental force for leadership, conflict resolution and the promotion of lasting peace at all levels;

19. It is essential to design, implement and monitor, with the full participation of women, effective, efficient and mutually reinforcing gender-sensitive policies and programmes, including development policies and programmes, at all levels that will foster the empowerment and advancement of women;

20. The participation and contribution of all actors of civil society, particularly women's groups and networks and other non-governmental organizations and community-based organizations, with full respect for their autonomy, in cooperation with Governments, are important to the effective implementation and follow-up of the Platform for Action;

21. The implementation of the Platform for Action requires commitment from Governments and the international community. By making national and international commitments for action, including those made at the Conference, Governments and the international community recognize the need to take priority action for the empowerment and advancement of women.

We are determined to:

• • •

23. Ensure the full enjoyment by women and the girl child of all human rights and fundamental freedoms and take effective action against violations of these rights and freedoms;

24. Take all necessary measures to eliminate all forms of discrimination against women and the girl child and remove all obstacles to gender equality and the advancement and empowerment of women;

25. Encourage men to participate fully in all actions towards equality;

26. Promote women's economic independence, including employment, and eradicate the persistent and increasing burden of poverty on women by addressing the structural causes of poverty through changes in economic structures, ensuring equal access for all women, including those in rural areas, as vital development agents, to productive resources, opportunities and public services;

27. Promote people-centred sustainable development, including sustained economic growth, through the provision of basic education, life-long education, literacy and training, and primary health care for girls and women;

28. Take positive steps to ensure peace for the advancement of women and, recognizing the leading role that women have played in the peace movement, work actively towards general and complete disarmament under strict and effective international control, and support negotiations on the conclusion, without delay, of a universal and multilaterally and effectively verifiable comprehensive nuclear-test-ban treaty which contributes to nuclear disarmament and the prevention of the proliferation of nuclear weapons in all its aspects;

29. Prevent and eliminate all forms of violence against women and girls;

30. Ensure equal access to and equal treatment of women and men in education and health care and enhance women's sexual and reproductive health as well as education;

31. Promote and protect all human rights of women and girls;

32. Intensify efforts to ensure equal enjoyment of all human rights and fundamental freedoms for all women and girls who face multiple barriers to their empowerment and advancement because of such factors as their race, age, language, ethnicity, culture, religion, or disability, or because they are indigenous people;

33. Ensure respect for international law, including humanitarian law, in order to protect women and girls in particular;

34. Develop the fullest potential of girls and women of all ages, ensure their full and equal participation in building a better world for all and enhance their role in the development process.

We are determined to:

35. Ensure women's equal access to economic resources, including land, credit, science and technology, vocational training, information, communication and markets, as a means to further the advancement and empowerment of women and girls, including through the enhancement of their capacities to enjoy the benefits of equal access to these resources, inter alia, by means of international cooperation;

36. Ensure the success of the Platform for Action, which will require a strong commitment on the part of Governments, international organizations and institutions at all levels. We are deeply convinced that economic development, social development and environmental protection are interdependent and mutually reinforcing components of sustainable development, which is the framework for our efforts to achieve a higher quality of life for all people. Equitable social development that recognizes empowering the poor, particularly women living in poverty, to utilize environmental resources sustainably is a necessary foundation for sustainable development. We also recognize that broad-based and sustained economic growth in the context of sustainable development is necessary to sustain social development and social justice. The success of the Platform for Action will also require adequate mobilization of resources at the national and international levels as well as new and additional resources to the developing countries from all available funding mechanisms, including multilateral, bilateral and private sources for the advancement of women; financial resources to strengthen the capacity of national, subregional, regional and international institutions; a commitment to equal rights, equal responsibilities and equal opportunities and to the equal participation of women and men in all national, regional and international bodies and policy-making processes; and the establishment or strengthening of mechanisms at all levels for accountability to the world's women.

• • •

Questions

1. What kinds of rights for women does the declaration emphasize?

2. What changes on the part of men would be required to implement the recommendations of the declaration?

195. *Jaula de Oro* (Cage of Gold), by *Los Tigres del Norte* (Tigers of the North) (1984)

Source: Los Tigres del Norte. Jaula de Oro. Fonovisa, 1984. Lyrics by Enrique Franco. Translated by Alana Graffam. Reprinted with permission of TN Ediciones Musicales.

As the number of undocumented immigrants, mostly from Mexico, proliferated in the 1980s and 1990s, questions of belonging arose both for these newcomers and for American society at large. Could these immigrants become part of American life? Immigrants who had become naturalized citizens frequently returned to visit their countries of origin. But despite having sunk roots and established families in the United States, the undocumented were unable to visit Mexico for fear of not being able to return. Many suffered a crisis of identity. They felt trapped in a "cage of gold" and alienated from their Americanized children, who, if born in the United States, were automatically citizens, as mandated by the Fourteenth Amendment. The Mexican-American group Los Tigres del Norte developed these themes in a popular song.

I am established here
In the United States
Many years have passed
Since I crossed as a wetback
With no papers
I'm still an illegal

I have my wife and kids
That I brought so young
And they've already forgotten
My dear Mexico
Which I will never forget
And cannot return to

What use is money
If I'm like a prisoner
In this great nation
When I'm reminded, I cry
Although this cage is made of gold
It's still a prison

Listen son,
Would you like to go back and live in Mexico?
"Whatcha talkin' about dad?
I don't want to go back to Mexico.
No way, dad."

My kids don't talk to me
They have learned another language

And they've forgotten Spanish
They think like Americans
Deny that they're Mexicans
Even though they have my complexion

From my work to my home
I don't know what's wrong with me
Even though I'm man of the house
I barely go outside
Since I'm afraid that they'll catch me
And deport me

What use is money
If I'm like a prisoner
In this great nation
When I'm reminded, I cry
Although this cage is made of gold
It's still a prison

Questions

1. What elements of Mexican culture are disappearing in the United States according to the song?

2. How do you think the experience of the narrator compares with that of members of previous immigrant groups?

196. Robert Byrd on the War in Iraq (2003)

Source: Speech of Senator Robert Byrd, February 12, 2003, U.S. Senate.

The first implementation of the principles of the National Security Strategy came in 2003, when the United States invaded and occupied Iraq, overthrowing the dictatorial government of Saddam Hussein. The decision split the western alliance and inspired a massive antiwar movement throughout the world. In February 2003, between 10 and 15 million people across the globe demonstrated against the impending war.

With President Bush still widely popular, few elected officials were willing to criticize him as the country moved toward war. One who did so was Senator Robert Byrd of West Virginia. Byrd condemned his colleagues for refusing even to debate the question. He criticized the idea of an "unprovoked military attack" on another nation and the Bush administration's indifference to worldwide opposition to the impending war. Unable to obtain approval from the United Nations, the United States went to war anyway in March 2003. Within a month, American troops occupied Baghdad. But, as Byrd had warned, securing the peace proved to be extremely difficult.

———

TO CONTEMPLATE WAR is to think about the most horrible of human experiences. On this February day, as this nation stands at the brink of battle, every American on some level must be contemplating the horrors of war.

Yet, this Chamber is, for the most part, silent—ominously, dreadfully silent. There is no debate, no discussion, no attempt to lay out for the nation the pros and cons of this particular war. There is nothing.

We stand passively mute in the United States Senate, paralyzed by our own uncertainty, seemingly stunned by the sheer turmoil of events. Only on the editorial pages of our newspapers is there much substantive discussion of the prudence or imprudence of engaging in this particular war.

And this is no small conflagration we contemplate. This is no simple attempt to defang a villain. No. This coming battle, if it materializes, represents a turning point in U.S. foreign policy and possibly a turning point in the recent history of the world.

This nation is about to embark upon the first test of a revolutionary doctrine applied in an extraordinary way at an unfortunate time. The doctrine of preemption—the idea that the United States or any other nation can legitimately attack a nation that is not imminently threatening but may be threatening in the future—is a radical new twist on the traditional idea of self defense. It appears to be in contravention of international law and the UN Charter. And it is being tested at a time of world-wide terrorism, making many countries around the globe wonder if they will soon be on our—or some other nation's—hit list. High level Administration figures recently refused to take nuclear weapons off of the table when discussing a possible attack against Iraq. What could be more destabilizing and unwise than this type of uncertainty, particularly in a world where globalism has tied the vital economic and security interests of many nations so closely together? There are huge cracks emerging in our time-honored alliances, and U.S. intentions are suddenly subject to damaging worldwide speculation. Anti-Americanism based on mistrust, misinformation, suspicion, and alarming rhetoric from U.S. leaders is fracturing the once solid alliance against global terrorism which existed after September 11.

Here at home, people are warned of imminent terrorist attacks with little guidance as to when or where such attacks might occur. Family members are being called to active military duty, with no idea of the duration of their stay or what horrors they may face. Communities are being left with less than adequate police and fire protection. Other essential services are also short-staffed. The mood of the nation is grim. The economy is stumbling. Fuel prices are rising and may soon spike higher.

• • •

Calling heads of state pygmies, labeling whole countries as evil, denigrating powerful European allies as irrelevant—these types of crude insensitivities can do our great nation no good. We may have massive military might, but we cannot fight a global war on terrorism alone. We need the cooperation and friendship of our time-honored allies as well as the newer found friends whom we can attract with our wealth. Our awesome military machine will do us little good if we suffer another devastating attack on our homeland which severely damages our economy. Our military manpower is already stretched thin and we will need the augmenting support of those nations who can supply troop strength, not just sign letters cheering us on.

The war in Afghanistan has cost us $37 billion so far, yet there is evidence that terrorism may already be starting to regain its hold in that region. We have not found bin Laden, and unless we secure the peace in Afghanistan, the dark dens of terrorism may yet again flourish in that remote and devastated land.

Pakistan as well is at risk of destabilizing forces. This Administration has not finished the first war against terrorism and yet it is eager to embark on another conflict with perils much greater than those in Afghanistan. Is our attention span that short? Have we not learned that after winning the war one must always secure the peace?

And yet we hear little about the aftermath of war in Iraq. In the absence of plans, speculation abroad is rife. Will we seize Iraq's oil fields, becoming an occupying power which controls the price and supply of that nation's oil for the foreseeable future? To whom do we propose to hand the reins of power after Saddam Hussein?

Will our war inflame the Muslim world resulting in devastating attacks on Israel? Will Israel retaliate with its own nuclear arsenal? Will the Jordanian and Saudi Arabian governments be toppled by radicals, bolstered by Iran which has much closer ties to terrorism than Iraq?

Could a disruption of the world's oil supply lead to a world-wide recession? Has our senselessly bellicose language and our callous disregard of the interests and opinions of other nations increased the global race to join the nuclear club and made proliferation an even more lucrative practice for nations which need the income?

• • •

We are truly "sleepwalking through history." In my heart of hearts I pray that this great nation and its good and trusting citizens are not in for a rudest of awakenings.

To engage in war is always to pick a wild card. And war must always be a last resort, not a first choice. I truly must question the judgment of any President who can say that a massive unprovoked military attack on a nation which is over 50% children is "in the highest moral traditions of our country." This war is not necessary at this time. Pressure appears to be having a good result in Iraq. Our mistake was to put ourselves in a corner so quickly. Our challenge is to now find a graceful way out of a box of our own making. Perhaps there is still a way if we allow more time.

Questions

1. Why does Byrd consider the impending attack on Iraq as dangerous and unwarranted?

2. Why does he believe it essential for the United States to obtain the cooperation of other countries?

CHAPTER 28

A Divided Nation

197. Second Inaugural Address of George W. Bush (2005)

Source: The White House.

In his second inaugural address, in January 2005, Bush outlined a new American goal—"ending tyranny in the world." Striking a more conciliatory tone than during his first administration, he promised that the United States would not try to impose "our style of government" on others and that, in the future, it would seek the advice of allies. He said nothing specific about Iraq but tried to shore up falling support for the war by invoking the ideal of freedom: "the survival of liberty in our land increasingly depends on the success of liberty in other lands." In his first inaugural, in 2001, Bush had used the words "freedom," "free," and "liberty" seven times. In his second, they appeared forty-nine times. Again and again, Bush insisted that the United States stands for the worldwide triumph of freedom.

AT THIS SECOND gathering, our duties are defined not by the words I use, but by the history we have seen together. For a half century, America defended our own freedom by standing watch on distant borders. After the shipwreck of communism came years of relative quiet, years of repose, years of sabbatical—and then there came a day of fire.

We have seen our vulnerability—and we have seen its deepest source. For as long as whole regions of the world simmer in resentment and tyranny—prone to ideologies that feed hatred and excuse murder—violence will gather, and multiply in destructive power, and cross the most defended borders, and raise a mortal threat. There is only one force of history that can break the reign of hatred and resentment, and expose the pretensions of tyrants, and reward the hopes of the decent and tolerant, and that is the force of human freedom.

We are led, by events and common sense, to one conclusion: The survival of liberty in our land increasingly depends on the success of liberty in other lands. The best hope for peace in our world is the expansion of freedom in all the world.

America's vital interests and our deepest beliefs are now one. From the day of our Founding, we have proclaimed that every man and woman on this earth has rights, and dignity, and matchless value, because they bear the image of the Maker of Heaven and earth. Across the generations we have proclaimed the imperative of self-government, because no one is fit to be a master, and no one deserves to be a slave. Advancing these ideals is the mission that created our Nation. It is the honorable achievement of our fathers. Now it is the urgent requirement of our nation's security, and the calling of our time.

So it is the policy of the United States to seek and support the growth of democratic movements and institutions in every nation and culture, with the ultimate goal of ending tyranny in our world.

This is not primarily the task of arms, though we will defend ourselves and our friends by force of arms when necessary. Freedom, by its nature, must be chosen, and defended by citizens, and sustained by the rule of law and the protection of minorities. And when the soul of a nation finally speaks, the institutions that arise may reflect customs and traditions very different from our own. America will not impose our own style of government on the unwilling. Our goal instead is to help others find their own voice, attain their own freedom, and make their own way. . . .

We will persistently clarify the choice before every ruler and every nation: The moral choice between oppression, which is always wrong, and freedom, which is eternally right. America will not pretend that jailed dissidents prefer their chains, or that women welcome humiliation and servitude, or that any human being aspires to live at the mercy of bullies.

We will encourage reform in other governments by making clear that success in our relations will require the decent treatment of their own people. America's belief in human dignity will guide our policies, yet rights must be more than the grudging concessions of dictators; they are secured by free dissent and the participation of the governed. In the long run, there is no justice without freedom, and there can be no human rights without human liberty....

Today, America speaks anew to the peoples of the world:

All who live in tyranny and hopelessness can know: the United States will not ignore your oppression, or excuse your oppressors. When you stand for your liberty, we will stand with you.

Democratic reformers facing repression, prison, or exile can know: America sees you for who you are: the future leaders of your free country.

The rulers of outlaw regimes can know that we still believe as Abraham Lincoln did: "Those who deny freedom to others deserve it not for themselves; and, under the rule of a just God, cannot long retain it."

The leaders of governments with long habits of control need to know: To serve your people you must learn to trust them. Start on this journey of progress and justice, and America will walk at your side.

And all the allies of the United States can know: we honor your friendship, we rely on your counsel, and we depend on your help. Division among free nations is a primary goal of freedom's enemies. The concerted effort of free nations to promote democracy is a prelude to our enemies' defeat....

We go forward with complete confidence in the eventual triumph of freedom. Not because history runs on the wheels of inevitability; it is human choices that move events. Not because we consider ourselves a chosen nation; God moves and chooses as He wills. We have confidence because freedom is the permanent hope of mankind, the hunger in dark places, the longing of the soul. When our Founders declared a new order of the ages; when soldiers died in wave upon wave for a union based on liberty; when citizens marched in peaceful outrage under the banner "Freedom Now"—they were acting on an ancient hope that is meant to be fulfilled. History has an ebb and flow of justice, but history also has a visible direction, set by liberty and the Author of Liberty.

When the Declaration of Independence was first read in public and the Liberty Bell was sounded in celebration, a witness said, "It rang as if it meant something." In our time it means something still. America, in this young century, proclaims liberty throughout all the world, and to all the inhabitants thereof. Renewed in our strength—tested, but not weary—we are ready for the greatest achievements in the history of freedom.

May God bless you, and may He watch over the United States of America.

Questions

1. How convincing is Bush's description of a world divided into friends and enemies of freedom?

2. What traditional American ideals does Bush appeal to in this speech?

---

198. Archbishop Roger Mahoney, "Called by God to Help" (2006)

Source: Roger Mahoney, "Called by God to Help," The New York Times, March 22, 2006. Reprinted by permission of the author.

The influx of immigrants proceeded apace during the first years of the twenty-first century. Alongside legal immigrants, undocumented newcomers made their way to the United States, mostly from Mexico. At the end of 2005, it was estimated, there were 11 million "illegal aliens" in the United States. With many Americans convinced that the United States had lost control of its borders and that immigration was in part responsible for the stagnation of real wages, the House of Representatives approved a bill making it a felony to be in the country illegally and a crime to offer aid to undocumented immigrants. The response was utterly unexpected—a series of massive popular demonstrations by immigrants, legal and undocumented, and their supporters, demanding the right to remain in the country as citizens.

At the same time, church groups used to sheltering and feeding the destitute denounced the proposed bill as akin to the Fugitive Slave Law of 1850 for making it a crime to help a suffering human being and vowed to resist it. One eloquent statement of this position came from Roger Mahoney, the Roman Catholic archbishop of Los Angeles, a city with one of the highest proportions of immigrants, legal and undocumented, in the country. In 2006, Congress failed to agree on any immigration legislation, except for a law authorizing the construction of a fence along hundreds of miles of the border between the United States and Mexico.

I'VE RECEIVED A lot of criticism for stating last month that I would instruct the priests of my archdiocese to disobey a proposed law that would subject them, as well as other church and humanitarian workers, to criminal penalties. The proposed Border Protection, Antiterrorism and Illegal Immigration Control bill, which was approved by the House of Representatives in December and is expected to be taken up by the Senate next week, would among other things subject to five years in prison anyone who "assists" an undocumented immigrant "to remain in the United States."

Some supporters of the bill have even accused the church of encouraging illegal immigration and meddling in politics. But I stand by my statement. Part of the mission of the Roman Catholic Church is to help people in need. It is our Gospel mandate, in which Christ instructs us to clothe the naked, feed the poor and welcome the stranger. Indeed, the Catholic Church, through Catholic Charities agencies around the country, is one of the largest nonprofit providers of social services in the nation, serving both citizens and immigrants.

Providing humanitarian assistance to those in need should not be made a crime, as the House bill decrees. As written, the proposed law is so broad that it would criminalize even minor acts of mercy like offering a meal or administering first aid.

Current law does not require social service agencies to obtain evidence of legal status before rendering aid, nor should it. Denying aid to a fellow human being violates a law with a higher authority than Congress—the law of God.

That does not mean that the Catholic Church encourages or supports illegal immigration. Every day in our parishes, social service programs, hospitals and schools, we witness the baleful consequences of illegal immigration. Families are separated, workers are exploited and migrants are left by smugglers to die in the desert. Illegal immigration serves neither the migrant nor the common good.

What the church supports is an overhaul of the immigration system so that legal status and legal channels for migration replace illegal status and illegal immigration. Creating legal structures for migration protects not only those who migrate but also our nation, by giving the government the ability to better identify who is in the country as well as to control who enters it.

Only comprehensive reform of the immigration system, embodied in the principles of another proposal in Congress, the Secure America and Orderly Immigration bill, will help solve our current immigration crisis.

Enforcement-only proposals like the Border Protection act take the country in the opposite direction. Increasing penalties, building more detention centers and erecting walls along our border with Mexico, as the act provides, will not solve the problem.

The legislation will not deter migrants who are desperate to survive and support their families from seeking jobs in the United States. It will only drive them further into the shadows, encourage the creation of more elaborate smuggling networks and cause hardship and suffering. I hope that the Senate will not take the same enforcement-only road as the House.

The unspoken truth of the immigration debate is that at the same time our nation benefits economically from the presence of undocumented workers, we turn a blind eye when they are exploited by employers. They work in industries that are vital to our economy yet they have little legal protection and no opportunity to contribute fully to our nation.

While we gladly accept their taxes and sweat, we do not acknowledge or uphold their basic labor rights. At the same time, we scapegoat them for our social ills and label them as security threats and criminals to justify the passage of anti-immigrant bills.

This situation affects the dignity of millions of our fellow human beings and makes immigration, ultimately, a moral and ethical issue. That is why the church is compelled to take a stand against harmful legislation and to work toward positive change.

It is my hope that our elected officials will understand this and enact immigration reform that respects our common humanity and reflects the values—fairness, compassion and opportunity—upon which our nation, a nation of immigrants, was built.

Questions

1. Why does Archbishop Mahoney believe that he has a right to disobey the proposed law?

2. How does he believe the question of immigration should be addressed?

199. Justice Anthony Kennedy, Opinion of the Court in *Obergefell v. Hodges* (2015)

Source: James Obergefell, et al. v. Richard Hodges, *576 U.S. ___ (2015).*

One of the most remarkable changes in public sentiment in the first years of the twenty-first century concerned the rights of gay Americans. Long stigmatized as deviants of one kind or another, gay men and women, like other disadvantaged groups, had long sought to gain equal rights. But anti-gay feelings, fueled by religious conviction, a belief that gays somehow undermined the nation's resolve during the Cold War, and other prejudices, long held sway. In 2003, in the landmark case of *Lawrence v. Texas*, the Supreme Court declared unconstitutional a Texas law making homosexual acts a crime. The idea of liberty guaranteed in the Fourteenth Amendment, the majority held, extended into the most intimate areas of private life. In the years that followed, a number of states gave legal recognition to same-sex marriage, either through legislative acts or court rulings that followed the logic of *Lawrence*. Public opinion on this question evolved with remarkable rapidity, especially among younger Americans. In 2003, two-thirds of Americans opposed legalizing such marriages; by 2015, over 60 percent were in favor.

In 2015, in a 5–4 decision, the Supreme Court ruled that the Fourteenth Amendment establishes a constitutional right to marriage for gay Americans. Written by Justice Anthony Kennedy, who had also written the majority opinion in *Lawrence*, the Court's ruling included a brief history of marriage, a powerful exposition of the meaning of freedom in the early twenty-first century, and a reaffirmation of the liberal view of the Constitution as a living document whose protections expand as society changes.

━━━━━

FROM THEIR BEGINNING to their most recent page, annals of human history reveal the transcendent importance of marriage.... Marriage is sacred to those who live by their religions and offers unique fulfillment to those who find meaning in the secular realm. Its dynamic allows two people to find a life that could not be found alone, for a marriage becomes greater than just the two persons. Rising from the most basic human needs, marriage is essential to our most profound hopes and aspirations....

Since the dawn of history, marriage has transformed strangers into relatives, binding families and societies together.... The ancient origins of marriage confirm its centrality, but it has not stood in isolation from developments in law and society. The history of marriage is one of both continuity and change. That institution—even as confined to opposite-sex relations—has evolved over time. For example, marriage was once viewed as an arrangement by the couple's parents based on political, religious, and financial concerns; but by the time of the Nation's founding it was understood to be a voluntary contract between a man and a woman. As the role and status of women changed, the institution further evolved. Under the centuries-old doctrine of coverture, a married man and woman were treated by the State as a single, male-dominated legal entity. As women gained legal, political, and property rights, and as society began to understand that women have their own equal dignity, the law of coverture was abandoned. These and other developments in the institution of marriage over the past centuries were not mere superficial changes. Rather, they worked deep transformations in its structure, affecting aspects of marriage long viewed by many as essential.

These new insights have strengthened, not weakened, the institution of marriage. Indeed, changed understandings of marriage are characteristics of a Nation where new dimensions of freedom become apparent to new generations, often through perspectives that begin in pleas of protests and then are considered in the political sphere and the judicial process.

This dynamic can be seen in the Nation's experiences with the rights of gays and lesbians. Until the mid-20th century, same-sex intimacy long had been condemned as immoral by the state itself in most Western nations. For this reason, among others, many persons did not deem homosexuals to have dignity in their own distinct identity.... For much of the twentieth century, moreover, homosexuality was treated as an illness.... Only in recent years have psychiatrists and others recognized that sexual orientation is both a normal expression of human sexuality and immutable....

The identification and protection of fundamental rights is an enduring part of the judicial duty to interpret the Constitution.... It requires courts to exercise reasoned judgment in identifying interests of the person so fundamental that the State must accord them its respect.... History and tradition guide and discipline this inquiry but do not set its outer boundaries. That method respects our history and learns from it without allowing the past alone to rule the present.

The nature of injustice is that we may not always see it in our own times. The generations that wrote and ratified the Fourteenth Amendment did not presume to know the extent of freedom in all of its dimensions, and so they entrusted to future generations a charter protecting the right of all persons to enjoy liberty as we learn its meaning. When new insight reveals discord between the Constitution's central protections and a received legal structure, a claim to liberty must be addressed. . . .

The right to marry is fundamental as a matter of history and tradition, but rights come not from ancient sources alone. They rise, too, from a better informed understanding of how constitutional imperatives define a liberty that remains urgent in our own era. Many who see same-sex marriage to be wrong reach that conclusion based on decent and honorable religious or philosophical premises, and neither they nor their beliefs are disparaged here. But when that sincere, personal opposition becomes enacted law and public policy, the necessary consequence is to put the imprimatur of the State itself on an exclusion that soon demeans or stigmatizes those whose own liberty is then denied. Under the Constitution, same-sex couples seek in marriage the same legal treatment as opposite-sex couples, and it would disparage their choices and diminish their personhood to deny them this right.

The right to marry is a fundamental right inherent in the liberty of the person, and under the Due Process and Equal Protection Clauses of the Fourteenth Amendment couples of the same-sex may not be deprived of that right and that liberty.

Questions

1. How does Justice Kennedy believe we should understand the meaning of freedom?

2. Why does Kennedy distinguish between sincere personal beliefs of those who oppose gay marriage, and laws enacted by the government?

200. Security, Liberty, and the War on Terror (2008)

Source: Lakhdar Boumediene et al. v. George W. Bush,
553 U.S. 773 (2008).

In the aftermath of the attacks of 2001, the Bush administration claimed sweeping powers to fight the "war on terror," including the right to arrest and hold indefinitely without trial those declared by the president to be enemy combatants. The Supreme Court proved unreceptive to President Bush's claim of authority, backed in many instances by Congress, to suspend constitutional protections of individual liberties. In several widely publicized cases it reaffirmed the rule of law both for American citizens and for foreigners held prisoner under American jurisdiction.

In *Hamdi v. Rumsfeld* (2004), an 8–1 majority ruled that an American citizen who had moved to Saudi Arabia and been captured in Afghanistan and then imprisoned in a military jail in South Carolina had a right to a judicial hearing. Four years later, the Court considered the case of persons held at a detention camp the government had established at the American naval base at Guantánamo Bay, Cuba. Although not American citizens, the petitioners claimed the right of habeas corpus guaranteed by the U.S. Constitution—that is, the right for a detained person to demand that a charge be leveled against him and to have a judge determine if evidence warrants continued imprisonment. By 5–4, with Anthony Kennedy casting the deciding vote, the Court affirmed their claim. Kennedy began by exhaustively reviewing the history of habeas corpus, stretching back to Magna Carta of 1215. The idea of imprisoning a person without charge, Kennedy insisted, was a violation of basic principles of American freedom.

PETITIONERS ARE ALIENS designated as enemy combatants and detained at the United States Naval Station at Guantánamo Bay, Cuba. There are others detained there, also aliens, who are not parties to this suit. Petitioners present a question not resolved by our earlier cases relating to the detention of aliens at Guantanamo: whether they have the constitutional privilege of habeas corpus, a privilege not to be withdrawn except in conformance with the Suspension Clause [of the U. S. Constitution]. We hold these petitioners do have the habeas corpus privilege. Congress has enacted a statute, the Detainee Treatment Act of 2005 . . . that provides certain procedures for review of the detainees' status. We hold that those procedures are not an adequate and effective substitute for habeas corpus. Therefore . . . the Military Commissions Act of 2006 . . . operates as an unconstitutional suspension of the writ [of habeas corpus]. . . .

Our opinion does not undermine the Executive's powers as Commander in Chief. On the contrary, the exercise of those powers is vindicated, not eroded, when confirmed by the Judicial Branch. Within the Constitution's separation-of-powers structure, few exercises of judicial power are as legitimate or as necessary as the responsibility to hear challenges to the authority of the Executive to imprison a person. Some of these petitioners have been in custody for six years with no definitive judicial determination as to the legality of their detention. Their access to the writ is a necessity to determine the lawfulness of their status, even if, in the end, they do not obtain the relief they seek.

Because our Nation's past military conflicts have been of limited duration, it has been possible to leave the outer boundaries of war powers undefined. If, as some fear, terrorism continues to pose dangerous threats to us for years to come, the Court might not have this luxury. This result is not inevitable, however. The political branches, consistent with their independent obligations to interpret and uphold the Constitution, can engage in a genuine debate about how best to preserve constitutional values while protecting the Nation from terrorism. . . .

Officials charged with daily operational responsibility for our security may consider a judicial discourse on the history of the Habeas Corpus Act of 1679 and like matters to be far removed from the nation's present, urgent concerns. Established legal doctrine, however, must be consulted for its teaching. Remote in time it may be; irrelevant to the present it is not. Security depends upon a sophisticated intelligence apparatus and the ability of our Armed Forces to act and to interdict. There are further considerations, however. Security subsists, too, in fidelity to freedom's first principles. Chief among these are freedom from arbitrary and unlawful restraint and the personal liberty that is secured by adherence to the separation of powers. It is from these principles that the judicial authority to consider petitions for habeas corpus relief derives.

We hold that petitioners may invoke the fundamental procedural protections of habeas corpus. The laws and Constitution are designed to survive, and remain in force, in extraordinary times. Liberty and security can be reconciled; and in our system they are reconciled within the framework of the law. The Framers decided that habeas corpus, a right of first importance, must be a part of that framework, a part of that law.

Questions

1. How does Kennedy respond to the government's claim that a state of war allows it to ignore parts of the Constitution?

2. Why does Kennedy believe that devotion to freedom is as important a source of national strength as military might?

———

201. Barack Obama, Eulogy at Emanuel African Methodist Episcopal Church (2015)

Source: The White House.

In the summer of 2015, the nation was shocked by a spate of mass murders, but none created so much consternation and grief as the murder of nine black parishioners in a black church in Charleston by a white supremacist gunman who posted online a photograph of himself with the Confederate battle flag. President Obama traveled to the city to deliver a eulogy for one of the victims, Clementa Pinckney, the church's pastor and a member of the South Carolina Senate. His speech reflected on the history of race relations and the condition of black America fifty years after the height of the civil rights revolution. In the aftermath of the murders, the state of South Carolina removed the Confederate flag from the grounds of the state house in the capital, Columbia, and deposited it in a museum.

FRIENDS OF HIS remarked this week that when Clementa Pinckney entered a room, it was like the future arrived, that even from a young age, folks knew he was special, anointed. He was the progeny of a long line of the faithful, a family of preachers who spread God's words, a family of protesters who so changed to expand voting rights and desegregate the South.

As a senator, he represented a sprawling swathe of low country, a place that has long been one of the most neglected in America, a place still racked by poverty and inadequate schools, a place where children can still go hungry and the sick can go without treatment— a place that needed somebody like Clem.

Clem was often asked why he chose to be a pastor and a public servant. But the person who asked probably didn't know the history of AME Church. The church is and always has been the center of African American life ... a place to call our own in a too-often hostile world, a sanctuary from so many hardships. Over the course of centuries, black churches served as hush harbors, where slaves could worship in safety, praise houses, where their free descendants could gather and shout "Hallelujah" ... rest stops for the weary along the Underground Railroad, bunkers for the foot soldiers of the civil-rights movement.

There's no better example of this tradition than Mother Emanuel, ... a church built by blacks seeking liberty, burned to the ground because its founders sought to end slavery only to rise up again, a phoenix from these ashes. When there were laws banning all-black church gatherers, services happened here anyway in defiance of unjust laws. When there was a righteous movement to dismantle Jim Crow, Dr. Martin Luther King Jr. preached from its pulpit, and marches began from its steps.

A sacred place, this church, not just for blacks, not just for Christians but for every American who cares about the steady expansion... of human rights and human dignity in this country, a foundation stone for liberty and justice for all.

We do not know whether the killer of Reverend Pinckney and eight others knew all of this history, but he surely sensed the meaning of his violent act. It was an act that drew on a long history of bombs and arson and shots fired at churches, not random but as a means of control, a way to terrorize and oppress..., an act that he presumed would deepen divisions that trace back to our nation's original sin....

For too long, we were blind to the pain that the Confederate Flag stirred into many of our citizens. It's true a flag did not cause these murders. But... as we all have to acknowledge, the flag has always represented more than just ancestral pride. For many, black and white, that flag was a reminder of systemic oppression... and racial subjugation.

We see that now. Removing the flag from this state's capital would not be an act of political correctness. It would not be an insult to the valor of Confederate soldiers. It would simply be acknowledgment that the cause for which they fought, the cause of slavery, was wrong. The imposition of Jim Crow after the Civil War, the resistance to civil rights for all people was wrong. It would be one step in an honest accounting of America's history, a modest but meaningful balm for so many unhealed wounds....

For too long, we've been blind to the way past injustices continue to shape the present. Perhaps we see that now. Perhaps this tragedy causes us to ask some tough questions about how we can permit so many of our children to languish in poverty... or attend dilapidated schools or grow up without prospects for a job or for a career. Perhaps it causes us to examine what we're doing to cause some of our children to hate. Perhaps it softens hearts towards those lost young men, tens and tens of thousands caught up in the criminal-justice system and lead us to make sure that that system's not infected with bias....

Maybe we now realize the way a racial bias can infect us even when we don't realize it so that we're guarding against not just racial slurs but we're also guarding against the subtle impulse to call Johnny back for a job interview but not Jamal ... so that we search our hearts when we consider laws to make it harder for some of our fellow citizens to vote by recognizing our common humanity....

None of us can or should expect a transformation in race relations overnight.... Whatever solutions we find will necessarily be incomplete. But it would be a betrayal of everything Reverend Pinckney stood for, I believe, if we allow ourselves to slip into a comfortable silence again.... That's what we so often do to avoid uncomfortable truths about the prejudice that still infects our society.... What is true in the south is true for America. Clem understood that justice grows out of recognition of ourselves in each other; that my liberty depends on you being free, too.

Questions

1. Why does President Obama believe that the freedom of some Americans is interconnected with the freedom of others?

2. What does this document, along with the previous one, suggest about how much has changed in American life in the past half-century and how much has not changed?

202. Khizr Khan, Speech at the Democratic National Convention (2016)

During the 2016 presidential election campaign, Donald Trump's incessant attacks on Mexican immigrants as criminals, his association of Muslims with terrorism, and his promise to build a wall along the Mexico-U.S. border (with Mexico footing the bill) appealed to many Americans but alienated many others. In a powerful speech at the Democratic National Convention, with his wife, Ghazala, standing at his side, the Pakistani-American father of an American soldier killed during the Iraq War responded to Trump's nativist pronouncements. The Khans had moved to the United States in 1980; Khizr Khan graduated from Harvard Law School in 1986, the same year the couple became American citizens. The year after his speech, Khan published a memoir of his family's migration and struggles. The reviewer in the *Washington Post* wrote: "Khizr Khan is probably a better American than I am."

━━━━━━

FIRST, OUR THOUGHTS and prayers are with our veterans and those who serve today. Tonight, we are honored to stand here as the parents of Capt. Humayun Khan, and as patriotic American Muslims with undivided loyalty to our country.

Like many immigrants, we came to this country empty-handed. We believed in American democracy—that with hard work and the goodness of this country, we could share in and contribute to its blessings. We were blessed to raise our three sons in a nation where they were free to be themselves and follow their dreams. Our son, Humayun, had dreams of being a military lawyer. But he put those dreams aside the day he sacrificed his life to save his fellow soldiers. . . .

If it was up to Donald Trump, he never would have been in America. Donald Trump consistently smears the character of Muslims. He disrespects other minorities—women, judges, even his own party leadership. He vows to build walls and ban us from this country.

Donald Trump... let me ask you: Have you even read the U.S. Constitution? I will gladly lend you my copy. In this document, look for the words "liberty" and "equal protection of law." Have you ever been to Arlington Cemetery? Go look at the graves of the brave patriots who died defending America—you will see all faiths, genders, and ethnicities.

We can't solve our problems by building walls and sowing division. We are stronger together.

Questions

1. Why does Khan refer to the U.S. Constitution?

2. What evidence does he offer of the patriotism of immigrants?